PHOENIX CUISINE '96
Menus and Recipes from the Valley's Top Restaurants

Cover Chef's:

Pointe Hilton: Harry Esteep, John Watson, Gary Lohr, Roeger James, Warren Deveuve, Jessie Gonzales, Wade W. Simpson, Mike T. Shae; **Hops:** Alan Skversky, Teri Chinn; **OAXACA:** Travis Vivrthaler; **Backstage:** Mike Schook; **Mancuso's:** Steve Sierra, James Welshans; **Outback:** Gary Stewart; **Hyatt:** Manuel Ramos, Todd Berry, Anton Brunbaurer; **Biltmore:** Brian Tess; **6th Ave. Bistrot:** Francois Simorte; **Lo Cascio:** Giovanni; **Spageddies:** Greg Ponsford, Maria Domenico; **Molise Cucina:** Anthony De'Franco; **Impeccable Pig:** Tom Young; **Uncle Sal's:** Craig Robensteine; **Cafe Terra Cotta:** Chris White; **Avanti:** Mellino Benito, Angelo Livi; **Christopher's:** Christopher Gross; **Maria's When in Naples:** Maria Ranieri; **Timothy's:** Steven Munchbach; **Andres:** Todd Story; **Sushi on Shea:** Fred Yamada; **Greekfest:** Tony Makridis; **Vagara Bistro:** Peter Hoefler; **Rafaelle's:** Rafaelle Contasossi; **Los Olivos:** Juanita Recalde; **Franco's Trattoria:** Steve Martin; **Brunello:** Andres Quintana; **Phoenician:** Jeffery Gosselin, Steven Varga; **Baby Kay's:** Baby Kay, Rene Romero, Pierce Romero, Theresa Romero; **Il Forno:** Omar Matmati, Mario Perez

Chefs not appearing on the cover

Phoenician: Robert McGrath (picured below), Alessandro Stratta (pictured below); **La Fontanella:** Burt and Isabella (pictured below); **Ambrosino's:** Louis Ambrosino; **Goldie's:** Michael Goldman; **Franco's Trattoria:** Franco Fazzuoli; **Marche Gourmet:** Jean Marie Riggolete; **Marco Polo:** Scott Tompkins; **Pasta Segio's:** Tony Caputo; **Bamboo Club:** Benny Chan; **Black Rose:** Kevin McNeill; **Blue Burrito Grill:** Lenny Rosenburg; **Chianti:** Joe Carlucci; **Gianni:** Gianni Scovenna; **Pareesa:** Parviv Mognini; **Korean Garden:** C.H. Baie; **Nina L'Italiana:** Nina; **Pepin:** Raphaelle Souto; **Roxsand:** Roxsand Scocos; **Royal Barge:** Simon, Voltaire, Andramari; **Arizona Kitchen:** Azz Jazz Cafe; **Bagels & Bialy's;** **Carolina's Paradiso:** Coyote Springs; **Chances Are;** **Don & Charlie's;** **Jet Lag Lounge;** **Mirage Bar & Grill;** **Panama Rex;** **Pink Pepper;** **Pronto;** **Philly's;** **Steve Stone's.**

We would like to make special acknowledgments to:
Wide World of Maps

"This is fun!"
The Chefs

Our special thanks to those friends and associates who made this edition both interesting and exciting.

Publisher
Frank Aaron

Graphic design and art direction
the a®t department
Graham Walters
Pam Racich

Cover Photography
John Ormond

Support Staff
Deborah Aaron, Ashley Aaron, Cassie Aaron, Elanna Aaron and Jarett Aaron

Legal Council
David Dickerson

Published by Phoenix Cuisine Publishing
Marketed by Ryan Hart Marketing, Inc.
16605 East Palisades, Suite 124–271
FountainHills, AZ 85268

All Rights Reserved. No portion of this publication masy be reproduced without the the written consent of the publishers

©Copyright 1995 Ryan Hart Marketing, Inc

Welcome

Welcome to Phoenix Cuisine

We're pleased to present our fifth anniversary edition of Phoenix Cuisine, the Valley's best selling guide to the area's finest restaurants.

These restaurant's are locally owned and managed, and offer an outstanding selection of menu items that's simply not available at chain operations. The quality of their food, service and management—and the continued patronage of diners like you—are responsible for the continued popularity and success of the restaurants in our book.

We wish to thank the restaurant owners and chefs whose menus and recipes appear here, for their role in making the Phoenix area an exciting dining experience. Some of these restaurants have been with us for five years; others are new in our 1996 edition. But all of the people pictured on the cover of this book create gustatory pleasures, from the superb ethnic dishes to chef-created seasonings and sauces that surprise and satisfy your tastebuds.

Possibly the best service this book provides is the opportunity to review all or part of each restaurant's actual menu, so that you can discover and evaluate for yourself each restaurant's food, atmosphere and pricing, and find that place that fits the dining occasion—whether it's an intimate dinner for two or a big birthday bash.

As you look at the menus, maybe you'll find new places to try, new tastes to savor.

For your convenience, Phoenix Cuisine is indexed for cuisine served, and speciality dining. An area map helps you find the restaurants location. And a glossary of culinary and dining terms, as well as a recipe section, are provided for your enjoyment.

Although all of the information is current at the time of publication, the restaurants reserve the right to change menus and prices. Each restaurant's phone number is listed with its menu, so feel free to call ahead and confirm what you see in the book.

Here's wishing you many happy dining experiences in 1996!

Sincerely,

Frank Aaron
Publisher

Frank Aaron and his wife Debbie.

Contents

Introduction
Welcome to Phoenix Cuisine   2
Restaurants A–Z   6
Area Index   7
Styles   8
Speciality   9–11
Area Map   12–13
Culinary Events   14
Golf Course Guide   14

Restaurants   15-124
Menus from more than 80 of the top Phoenix and surrounding areas finest restaurants.

Recipes   125
Recipe Index   126
A gourmets pantry of delightful dishes from the kitchens of Phoenix's finest restaurants.

Glossary   149
A selection of culinary and dining terms.

Gourmet Pastries

"Best of Phoenix, 1993"

For those who appreciate quality baked goods you will find it at Gourmet Pastries

Satisfied Gourmet Pastries customers:

Wilt Chamberlin • Richard Nixon • Ben Vereen • Dennis Farina

Gourmet Pastries
New York German Bakery

Fax & Phone
(602) 391-0751

9393 North 90th St., Suite 115
Scottsdale, AZ 85258

INDEXES

Alphabetical Index

A

Ambrosino's	16-17
Andramari	18
Andre's	19
Radisson	
Arizona Cafe & Grill	20-21
Arizona Kitchen	22
Wigwam Resort	
Aunt Chilada's	23
Avanti of Phoenix	26
Azz Jazz	24-25

B

Baby Kay's	28-29
Backstage	27
Bagels & Bialys	34
Bamboo Club	30-31
Black Rose	32-33
Blue Burrito Grille	35
Brunello	36

C

Cafe Terra Cotta	38-39
Cafestia	41
Carolinas Paradiso	37
Chances Are	42-43
Chianti	44-45
Christopher's	46-47
Christopher's Bistro	48-49
Coyote Springs	40

D

Different Pointe of View	50
Pointe	
Don & Charlie's	51

E

El Choro Lodge	52

F

Franco's Trattoria	53

G

Gianni	55
Golden Swan	58
Hyatt	
Goldies	56-57
Greekfest	54
Guido's	59

H

Hole in the Wall	62
Pointe	
Hops	60-61

I

Il Forno	64-65
Impeccable Pig	63

J

Jet Lag Lounge	66

K

Korean Garden	67

L

La Fontanella	68-69
Lo Cascio	72
Los Olivos	70-71

M

Mancusso's	73
Marches Gourmet	74-75
Marco Polo Italian Oriental Cafe	80
Maria's When in Naples	76-77
Mary Elaines	81
Phoenician	
Mirage Bar & Grille	78-79
Molise Cucina Italiana	82

N

Nina L'Italiana	84-85

O

Oaxaca at Pinnacle Peak	83
Outback Steak House	86-87

P

Palm Court	88
Scottsdale Conference Resort	
Panama Rex	89
Pareesa	92
Pasta Segio's	90-91
Peppin	93
Philly's Sports Bar	98
Pink Pepper	94-95
Pronto	96-97

R

Raffaele's	99
Riazzi's	100-101
Roxsands	102
Royal Barge	104-105
Rustler's Roost	103
Pointe	

S

Sandolo's	106
Hyatt	
Sixth Avenue Bistrot	108-109
Spagheddi's	107
Steve Stones	112
Sushi on Shea	110-111

T

The Terrace Dining Room	114
Phoenician	
The Terrace	113
Wigwam Resort	
Timothy's	116
Timothy's	117
Tucchetti's	115

U

Uncle Sal's	118

V

Vagara Bistro	119
Ventura Grill	120-121
Voltaire	122

W

Windows on the Green	123
Phoenician	
Wrights	124
Biltmore	

Area Index

Tempe

Korean Garden	67
Lo Cascio	72
Outback Steak House	86-87
Riazzi's	100-101

Fountain Hills

Mirage Bar & Grille	78-79

Litchfield Park

Arizona Kitchen	22
Wigwam Resort	
The Terrace	113
Wigwam Resort	

Mesa

Brunello	36
Outback Steak House	86-87
Pink Pepper	94-95
Steve Stones	112
Raffaele's	99

North Scottsdale

Ambrosino's	16-17
Arizona Cafe & Grill	20-21
Hops	60-61

Phoenix

Aunt Chilada's	23
Avanti of Phoenix	26
Azz Jazz	24-25
Baby Kay's	28
Bamboo Club	30-31
Blue Burrito Grille	35
Cafestia	41
Chianti	44-45
Christopher's	46-47
Christopher's Bistro	48-49
Coyote Springs	40
Different Pointe of View	50
Pointe	
Greekfest	54
Pointe	
Hole in the Wall	62
Hops	60-61
Il Forno	64-65
La Fontanella	68-69
Nina L'Italiana	84-85
Pareesa	92
Pasta Segio's	90-91
Pronto	96-97
Pink Pepper	94-95
Roxsands	102
Rustler's Roost	103
Pointe	
Timothy's	116-117
Tucchetti's	115
Wrights	124
Biltmore	
Raffaele's	99
Spageddi's	107

Scottsdale

Avanti of Phoenix	26
Spageddi's	107
Pink Pepper	94-95
Hops	60-61
Andramari	18
Andre's	19
Radisson	
Baby Kay's	28-29
Backstage	27
Bagels & Bialys	34
Black Rose	32-33
Cafe Terra Cotta	38-39
Carolinas Paradiso	37
Chances Are	42-43
Don & Charlie's	51
El Choro Lodge	52
Franco's Trattoria	53
Gianni	55
Golden Swan	58
Hyatt	
Goldies	56-57
Guido's	59
Impeccable Pig	63
Jet Lag Lounge	66
Los Olivos	70-71
Mancusso's	73
Marches Gourmet	74-75
Marco Polo	80
Italian Oriental Cafe	
Maria's When in Naples	76-77
Mary Elaines	81
Phoenician	
Molise Cucina Italiana	82
Oaxaca at Pinnacle Peak	83
Palm Court	88
Scottsdale Conference Resort	
Panama Rex	89
Peppin	93
Philly's Sports Bar	98
Royal Barge	104-105
Sandolo's	106
Hyatt	
Sixth Avenue Bistrot	108-109
Sushi on Shea	110-111
The Terrace Dining Room	114
Phoenician	
Uncle Sal's	118
Vagara Bistro	119
Ventura Grill	120-121
Voltaire	122
Windows on the Green	123
Phoenician	

Food Style

American

Andre's	19
Radisson	
Christopher's Bistro	48-49
Don & Charlie's	51
Golden Swan	58
Hyatt	
Impeccable Pig	63
Jet Lag Lounge	66
Oaxaca at Pinnacle Peak	83
Philly's Sports Bar	98
Roxsands	102
Steve Stones	112
The Terrace	113
Wigwam Resort	
Ventura Grill	121
Wrights	124
Biltmore	

Cajun

Baby Kay's	28-29
Timothy's	116-117

Contemporary

Mary Elaines	81
Phoenician	

Continental

Mirage Bar & Grille	78-79
Chances Are	42-43
Cross Cultural	
Vagara Bistro	119
Ventura Grill	120

Deli

Bagels & Bialys	34
Guido's	59
Eclectic American	
Azz Jazz	24-25
Backstage	27

French

Christopher's	46-47
Marches Gourmet	74-75
Palm Court	88
Scottsdale Conf Resort	
Sixth Avenue Bistrot	108-109
Voltaire	122

Greek

Cafestia	41
Greekfest	54
Phillies	98

Irish American

Black Rose	32-33

Italian

Ambrosino's	16-17
Avanti of Phoenix	26
Brunello	36
Carolinas Paradiso	37
Chianti	44-45
Franco's Trattoria	53
Gianni	55
Il Forno	64-65
La Fontanella	68-69
Lo Cascio	72
Mancusso's	73
Marco Polo	80
Italian Oriental Cafe	
Maria's When in Naples	76-77
Molise Cucina Italiana	82
Nina L'Italiana	84-85
Pareesa	92
Pasta Segio's	90-91
Pronto	96-97
Raffaele's	99
Riazzi's	100-101
Sandolo's	106
Hyatt	
Spageddi's	107
The Terrace Dining Room	114
Phoenician	
Tucchetti's	115
Uncle Sal's	118

Japanese

Sushi on Shea	110-111

Korean

Korean Garden	67

Mexican

Aunt Chilada's	23
Blue Burrito Grille	35
El Choro Lodge	52
Los Olivos	70-71
Panama Rex	89

Microbrewery

Coyote Springs	40
Hops	60-61

Pacific Rim

Bamboo Club	30-31

Southwestern

Arizona Kitchen	22
Wigwam Resort	
Arizona Cafe & Grill	20-21
Cafe Terra Cotta	38-39
Windows on the Green	123
Phoenician	
Coyote Springs	40

Spanish

Andramari	18
Peppin	93

Sports Bar

Goldies Sports Bar	56-57
Philly's	98

Steak House

Don & Charlie's	51
Outback Steak House	87

Thai

Pink Pepper	94-95
Royal Barge	104-105

Western

Hole in the Wall	62
Pointe	
Rustler's Roost	103
Pointe	

Speciality Index

After theater

Aunt Chilada's	23
Baby Kay's	28-29
Backstage	27
Black Rose	32-33
Blue Burrito Grille	35
Brunello	36
Chances Are	42-43
Coyote Springs	40
Gianni	55
Hops	60-61
Jet Lag Lounge	66
Lo Cascio	72
Los Olivos	70-71
Pareesa	92
Pasta Segio's	90-91

Terrace/Patio

Andramari	18
Arizona Cafe & Grill	20-21
Aunt Chilada's	23
Azz Jazz	25-24
Baby Kay's	28-29
Backstage	27
Bagels & Bialys	34
Bamboo Club	30-31
Black Rose	32-33
Blue Burrito Grille	35
Brunello	36
Cafe Terra Cotta	38-39
Carolinas Paradiso	37
Christopher's Bistro	48-49
Coyote Springs	40
Different Pointe of View	50
Pointe	
El Choro Lodge	52
Golden Swan	58
Hyatt	
Guido's	59
Hole in the Wall	62
Pointe	
Il Forno	64-65
Los Olivos	70-71
Marches Gourmet	74-75
Marco Polo	80
Italian Oriental Cafe	
Maria's When in Naples	76-77
Mirage Bar & Grille	79-78
Nina L'Italiana	84-85
Oaxaca at Pinnacle Peak	83
Palm Court	88
Scottsdale Conference Resort	
Panama Rex	89
Pareesa	92
Pasta Segio's	90-91
Philly's Sports Bar	98
Raffaele's	99
Roxsands	102
Rustler's Roost	103
Pointe	
Sandolo's	106
Hyatt	
Steve Stones	112
The Terrace Dining Room	114
Phoenician	
The Terrace	113
Wigwam Resort	
Timothy's	116-117
Tucchetti's	115
Vagara Bistro	119
Ventura Grill	120
Windows on the Green	123
Phoenician	
Wrights	124
Biltmore	

Bar/Lounge

Ambrosino's	16-17
Andre's	19
Radisson	
Aunt Chilada's	23
Avanti of Phoenix	26
Azz Jazz	25-24
Backstage	27
Bamboo Club	30-31
Black Rose	32-33
Blue Burrito Grille	35
Brunello	36
Cafe Terra Cotta	38
Chances Are	42-43
Coyote Springs	40
Different Pointe of View	50
Pointe	
Don & Charlie's	51
El Choro Lodge	52
Gianni	55
Goldies	56-57
Hole in the Wall	62
Pointe	
Hops	60-61
Jet Lag Lounge	66
Mancusso's	73
Marco Polo	80
Italian Oriental Cafe	
Mary Elaines	81
Phoenician	
Mirage Bar & Grille	79-78
Nina L'Italiana	84-85
Oaxaca at Pinnacle Peak	83
Outback Steak House	87-86
Panama Rex	89
Pasta Segio's	90-91
Peppin	93
Philly's Sports Bar	98
Pink Pepper	94-95
Raffaele's	99
Roxsands	102
Rustler's Roost	103
Pointe	
Steve Stones	112
The Terrace Dining Room	114
Phoenician	
Tucchetti's	115
Uncle Sal's	118
Ventura Grill	120
Windows on the Green	123
Phoenician	
Wrights	124
Biltmore	

Entertainment

Arizona Kitchen	22
Wigwam Resort	
Aunt Chilada's	23
Azz Jazz	25-24
Baby Kay's	28-29
Backstage	27
Black Rose	32-33
Carolinas Paradiso	37
Chances Are	42-43
Different Pointe of View	50
Pointe	
Hole in the Wall	62
Pointe	
Jet Lag Lounge	66
Los Olivos	70-71
Mancusso's	73
Marco Polo	80
Italian Oriental Cafe	
Mary Elaines	81

Speciality Index

Phoenician
Nina L'Italiana ... 84-85
Peppin ... 93
Rustler's Roost ... 103
Pointe
Sandolo's ... 106
Hyatt
The Terrace ... 113
Wigwam Resort
Timothy's ... 116-117

Brunch

Andre's ... 19
Radisson
Aunt Chilada's ... 23
Different Pointe of View ... 50
Pointe
Golden Swan ... 58
Hyatt
Impeccable Pig ... 63
Marches Gourmet ... 74-75
Mirage Bar & Grille ... 79
Palm Court ... 88
Scottsdale Conference Resort
The Terrace Dining Room ... 114
Phoenician
The Terrace ... 113
Wigwam Resort
Windows on the Green ... 123
Phoenician
Wrights ... 124
Biltmore

Banquets

Ambrosino's ... 16-17
Avanti of Phoenix ... 26
Azz Jazz ... 25
Carolinas Paradiso ... 37
Chances Are ... 42-43
Coyote Springs ... 40
Don & Charlie's ... 51
El Choro Lodge ... 52
Golden Swan ... 58
Hyatt
Mirage Bar & Grille ... 79
Oaxaca at Pinnacle Peak ... 83
Palm Court ... 88
Scottsdale Conference Resort
Pasta Segio's ... 90-91
Peppin ... 93
Riazzi's ... 100-101

Roxsands ... 102
Rustler's Roost ... 103
Pointe
Tucchetti's ... 115

Catering

Ambrosino's ... 16-17
Andramari ... 18
Arizona Cafe & Grill ... 20-21
Avanti of Phoenix ... 26
Azz Jazz ... 25
Bagels & Bialys ... 34
Blue Burrito Grille ... 35
Carolinas Paradiso ... 37
Chances Are ... 42-43
Christopher's ... 46-47
Christopher's Bistro ... 48-49
Coyote Springs ... 40
Don & Charlie's ... 51
El Choro Lodge ... 52
Franco's Trattoria ... 53
Greekfest ... 54
Hole in the Wall ... 62
Pointe
Marches Gourmet ... 74-75
Mirage Bar & Grille ... 79
Molise Cucina Italiana ... 82
Nina L'Italiana ... 84-85
Pareesa ... 92
Pasta Segio's ... 90-91
Peppin ... 93
Roxsands ... 102
Rustler's Roost ... 103
Pointe
Sixth Avenue Bistrot ... 108

Vegetarian Meals

Andre's ... 19
Radisson
Arizona Cafe & Grill ... 20-21
Aunt Chilada's ... 23
Azz Jazz ... 25-24
Backstage ... 27
Bagels & Bialys ... 34
Bamboo Club ... 30-31
Blue Burrito Grille ... 35
Brunello ... 36
Carolinas Paradiso ... 37
Chances Are ... 42-43
Chianti ... 44-45
Christopher's ... 46-47
Christopher's Bistro ... 48-49

Coyote Springs ... 40
Different Pointe of View ... 50
Pointe
El Choro Lodge ... 52
Franco's Trattoria ... 53
Gianni ... 55
Golden Swan ... 58
Hyatt
Goldies ... 56-57
Greekfest ... 54
Guido's ... 59
Hole in the Wall ... 62
Pointe
Hops ... 60-61
Il Forno ... 64-65
Korean Garden ... 67
La Fontanella ... 68-69
Lo Cascio ... 72
Los Olivos ... 70
Maria's When in Naples ... 76-77
Mirage Bar & Grille ... 79
Molise Cucina Italiana ... 82
Nina L'Italiana ... 84-85
Outback Steak House ... 87-86
Panama Rex ... 89
Pasta Segio's ... 90-91
Peppin ... 93
Philly's Sports Bar ... 98
Pink Pepper ... 94-95
Raffaele's ... 99
Riazzi's ... 100-101
Roxsands ... 102
Royal Barge ... 104-105
Rustler's Roost ... 103
Pointe
Sandolo's ... 106
Hyatt
Sushi on Shea ... 110-111
Timothy's ... 116-117
Tucchetti's ... 115
Uncle Sal's ... 118

Dancing

Aunt Chilada's ... 23
Avanti of Phoenix ... 26
Chances Are ... 42-43
Different Pointe of View ... 50
Pointe
Jet Lag Lounge ... 66
Marco Polo ... 80
Italian Oriental Cafe

Speciality Index

Peppin 93
Rustler's Roost 103
Pointe

Meeting Facilities

Azz Jazz 25
Carolinas Paradiso 37
Coyote Springs 40
Guido's 59
Mirage Bar & Grille 79
Pasta Segio's 90-91
Tucchetti's 115

Lodging

Andre's 19
Radisson
Golden Swan 58
Hyatt
Mary Elaines 81
Phoenician
Palm Court 88
Scottsdale Conference Resort
Rustler's Roost 103
Pointe
Sandolo's 106
Hyatt
The Terrace Dining Room 114
Phoenician
The Terrace 113
Wigwam Resort
Windows on the Green 123
Phoenician
Wrights 124
Biltmore

Other

Early Bird Diners
La Fontanella 68-69
Early Evening Menu
Don & Charlie's 51
Late Night Menu
Hops 61
Private Rooms
Avanti of Phoenix 26
Pareesa 92
The Terrace Dining Room 114
Phoenician
Valet Parking
Christopher's 46-47
Christopher's Bistro 48-49

Map

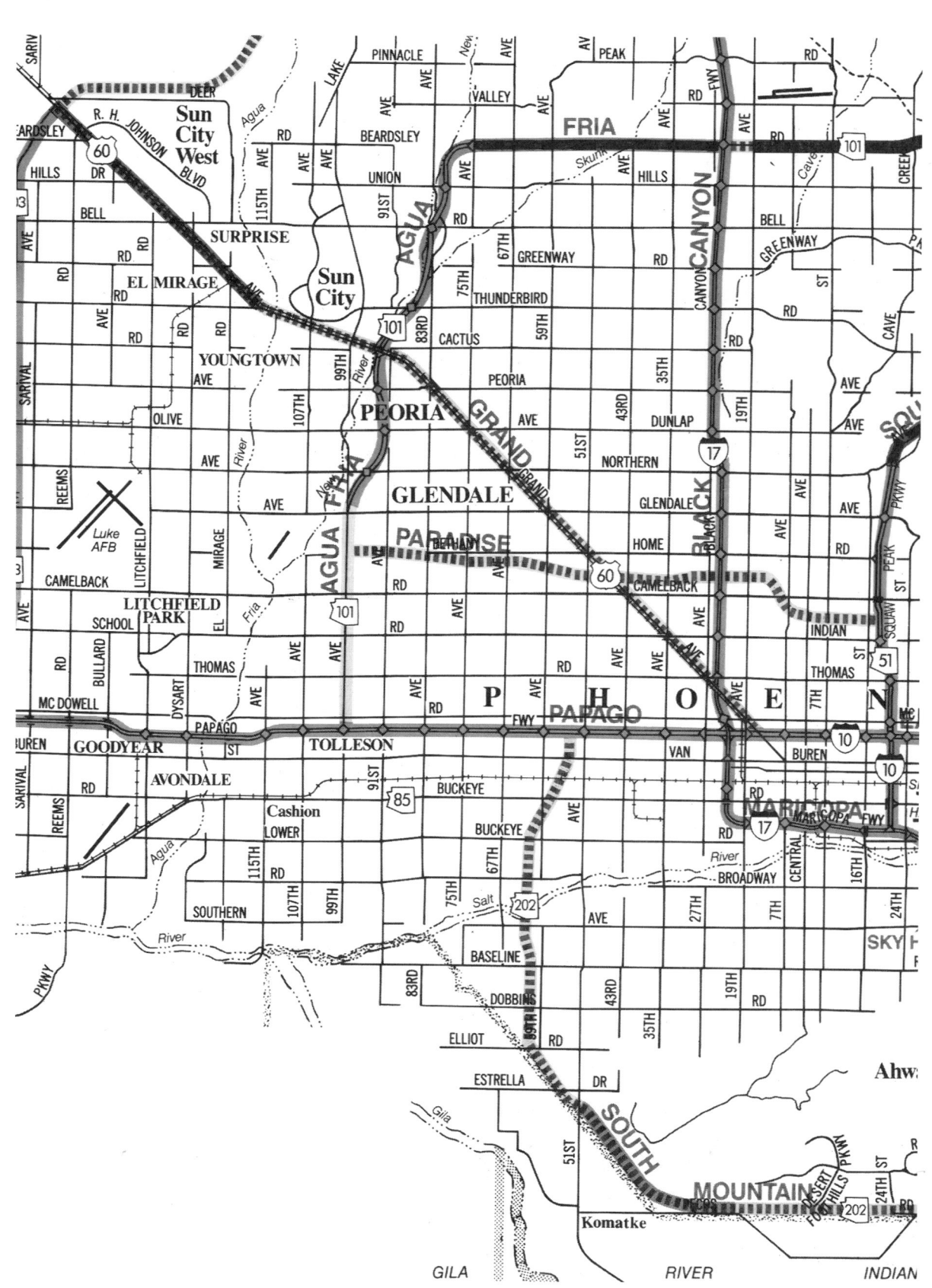

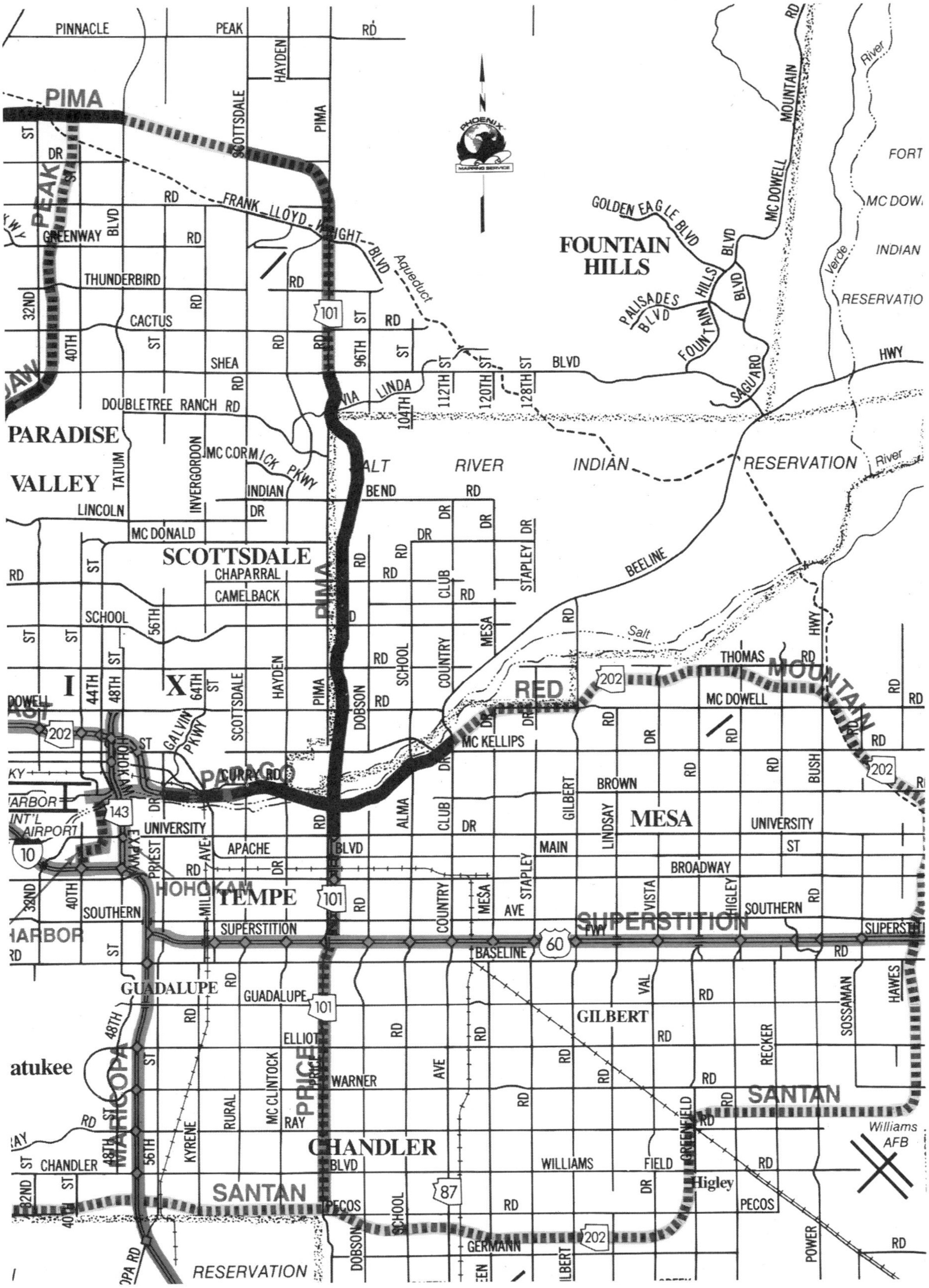
PINNACLE
PEAK
RD
PIMA
HAYDEN
SCOTTSDALE
PEAK
GREENWAY
THUNDERBIRD
CACTUS
SHEA
DOUBLETREE RANCH RD
FRANK LLOYD WRIGHT BLVD
Aqueduct
VIA LINDA
96TH
104TH
112TH
120TH
128TH
BLVD
PHOENIX MAPPING SERVICE
GOLDEN EAGLE BLVD
FOUNTAIN HILLS
PALISADES BLVD
FOUNTAIN HILLS BLVD
SAGUARO BLVD
MC DOWELL
MOUNTAIN RD
River
FORT
MC DOW
INDIAN
Verde
RESERVATIO
HWY
PARADISE VALLEY
TATUM
INVERGORDON
MC CORMICK PKWY
INDIAN BEND RD
SALT RIVER INDIAN RESERVATION
LINCOLN
MC DONALD
SCOTTSDALE
CHAPARRAL
CAMELBACK
SCHOOL
STAPLEY DR
BEELINE
Salt
CLUB
MESA
COUNTRY
DOBSON
ALMA
THOMAS
RED MOUNTAIN
202
MC DOWELL
MC KELLIPS
GALVIN PKWY
PAPAGO
CURRY RD
HOHOKAM
143
10
UNIVERSITY
INT'L AIRPORT
HARBOR
APACHE BLVD
PRIEST
MILL AVE
BROWN
GILBERT
LINDSAY
MESA
UNIVERSITY
MAIN
BROADWAY
BUSH HWY
TEMPE
101
SOUTHERN
SUPERSTITION
60
BASELINE
VISTA
HIGLEY
GUADALUPE
VAL VISTA
GILBERT
SOSSAMAN
HAWES
RECKER
ELLIOT
WARNER
ahwatukee
MARICOPA
KYRENE
RURAL
MC CLINTOCK
RAY
PRICE
SANTAN
CHANDLER
CHANDLER BLVD
WILLIAMS FIELD
GREENFIELD
Higley
Williams AFB
PECOS
87
GERMANN
POWER
RESERVATION

Culinary Events

October 28–April	**The Market at Vincent's**, 9:00 am–1:00 pm, Saturdays	224-0225
November	**Beers and Waters of the World Tasting Festival**, 6:00 pm–9:00 pm	231-0500
November 4-5	**New York Festival**, 9:00 am–4:00 pm, Paradise Market at Turf Paradise	588-2000
November 18-19	**Jewish Festival**, 9:00 am–4:00 pm, Paradise Market at Turf Paradise	588-2000
November 24-25	**Buttestock Music, Food & Wine Festival**, The Buttes Resort	225-9000
January 12-14	**Indian Festival**, Gila River Indian Community	945-0771
Jan 20	**Beers of Winter**, 5:00 pm–8:00 pm, Woodlands Hotel Flagstaff	231-0500
February	**International Food Festival**, St. George's Church, Scottsdale	953-1921
March 30-31	**The Great Arizona Beer Festival**, 5:00 pm, Arizona Center	231-0500
April 28	**Taste of the Nation**, Sheraton Cresent Hotel	242-3663
April 10-14	**Scottsdale Culinary Festival**, Scottsdale Civic Center	945-7193

Golf Courses

		Number of Holes	Par	Summer peak rate $	Driving Range	Practice green	Restaurant
Phoenix Area							
Ahwatukee Country Club • 12432 S. 48th St.	893-1161	18	72	20	•	•	
Ahwatukee Lakes Golf Courses • 13431 S. 44th St.	893-3004	18	60	10	•	•	
Arrowhead Country Club • 19888 N. 73rd. Ave.	561-9625	18	72	38	•	•	•
Arizona Biltrnore Country Club • 24th St. & Missouri	955-9655	36	72	30	•	•	•
Cave Creek Golf Course • 15202 N. 19th Ave.	866-8076	18	72	12	•	•	•
Encanto Golf Course • 2705 N. 15th Ave	253-3963	18	70	7	•	•	•
500 Club, the • 4707 W. Pinacle Peak Rd.	492-9500	18	72	25	•	•	
Legend Golf Club, The • 21025 N. 67th Ave.	561-9778	18	72	30	•	•	•
Maryvale Golf Course • 5902 W. Indian School Rd.	846-4022	18	72	12	•	•	•
Papago Golf Club • 5595 E. Moreland	275-8428	18	72	12	•	•	•
Pointe-Lookout Mountain • 11111 N. 7th St.	866-9816	18	72	37	•	•	•
Pointe-South Mountain • 7777 S. Pointe Pkwy.	438-1413	18	70	32		•	•
Tatum Ranch Golf Club • 4410 E. Disiletta Dr.	252-1230	18	72	32	•	•	•
Thunderbird Country Club • 701 E. Thunderbird Trail	243-1262	18	72	13	•	•	•
Tom Weiskopf's Foothills • 2201 E. Clubhouse Dr.	460-8337	18	72	65	•	•	•
Villa de Paz Golf Course • 4220 N. 103rd Ave.	877-1171	18	72	16	•	•	•
Westbrook Village • 19260 N. Westbrood Pkwy.	933-0174	18	71	25	•		•
Scottsdale / Paradise Valley							
Camelback Golf Club • 7847 N. Mockingbird Ln.	948-6770	36	72	35	•	•	•
Continental Golf Course • 7920 E. Osborn Rd.	941-1585	18	60	20	•	•	•
Coronado Golf Club • 2829 N. Miller Rd.	947-8364	9	31	6	•	•	
Cypress Golf Course • 10801 E. McDowell Rd.	946-5155	18	38	7	•	•	
Gainey Ranch Golf Club • 7600 E. Gainey Club Dr.	951-2227	72	56	21	•	•	•
McCormick Ranch Golf Course • 7505 E.McCorrrick Pkwy	948-0260	36	72	36	•	•	•
Mountain Shadows Golf Club • 5641 E. Lincoln Dr.	991-6656	18	56	21	•	•	•
Orange Tree Golf Resort • 10601 N. 56th St.	948-6100	18	72	35	•	•	•
Phoenician Golf Club • 6000 E. Camelback Rd.	423-2449	18	71	55	•	•	•
Pima Golf Resort • 7331 N. Pima Rd.	948-3370	18	72	20	•	•	•
Scottsdale Country Club • 7702 E. Shea Blvd.	948-6911	27	71	29		•	•
Stonecreek, The Golf Club • 4435 E. Paradise Village	953-9110	18	71	32	•	•	•
TPC Scottsdale • 17020 N. Hayden Rd.	585-3939	36	71	40	•	•	•
Troon North • 10320 Dynamite Blvd.	585-5300	18	72	45	•		•
Villa Monterey Golf Course • 8100 E. Camelback Rd.	990-7100	9	31	11			

MENUS

Ambrosino's

Cucina Amore

"Classe" is the Italian word for class. In Scottsdale, the translation reads "Ambrosino's." For the past 20 years, Ambrosino's has been one of the standard bearers for Italian cuisine in the Valley of the Sun. From it's Roman fountain in the front, to its statuettes in the dining room, Ambrosino's says "that's Italian".

"We serve both northern and southern Italian food," says Louis Ambrosino. " We make homemade ravioli that are like little king sized pillows, fresh mozzarella cheese and homemade deserts." All our dishes are homemade, everything is made from scratch, from appetizers to desserts.

Antipasti

Napolitan

Garlic bread (family recipe from Naples)	$1.95
Tomato bread (based with fresh, sliced tomatoes and cheese)	$2.95
Zucchini (lightly breaded and sauteed)	$2.95
Stuffed Mushrooms (with homemade Italian sausage)	$3.95

Frutti di Mar Vongole (Clams)

Casino-style	$5.95
Steamed in the half-shell	$4.95
Homemade Buffalo Mozzarella (plum tomatoes, fresh basil with olive oil)	$5.95

Gourmet Pastas

Fettucini Alfredo a la Ambrosino — $9.95
Delicate sauce is prepared with an array of cheese, heavy cream, and rich, creamy butter.

with Broccoli — $10.95

Pesto (Choice of Pasta) — $10.95
Fresh sweet basil, Italian parsley garlic in olive oil, and other selected spices make up this very special sauce, with pignoli nuts.

Lasagne — $8.95
Egg noodles Ricotta, Mozzarella, parsley, eggs and topped with our particular sauce.

Manicotti — $9.95
Delicately prepared with unique crepe dough, including Italian parsley and baked to perfection with Lou's renowned sauce.

Cannelloni — $9.95
Homemade crepe delicacy stuffed with veal, chicken, spinach and some very unique seasonings, Alfredo style.

Pasta Primavera — $9.95
Linguini with mixed vegetables, sauteed in butter and garlic, white wine and special herbs.

Veal Cutlet Pasta Primavera — $16.95
Baby veal cutlets with pasta & mixed vegetables, sauteed in butter and garlic, white wine and special herbs.

Ravioli — $9.95
Delicately prepared with unique crepe dough, including Italian Ricotta cheese, eggs, parsley and baked to perfection with Lou's renowned sauce.

Paucetta — $12.95
Imported Italian bacon, ham, peas, pinenuts and Alfredo sauce. Served with fettuccini.

Portofino — $12.95
Veal tortellini in Alfredo sauce with walnuts and fresh mushrooms.

Tortellini a la Romano — $12.95
In Alfredo sauce with peas and carrots.

Trenette Con Broccoli & Pesto — $11.95
Fresh Angel Hair with Pesto sauce and broccoli.

Pollame

Scallopini — $11.95
Boneless breast of chicken sauteed with Peppers, mushrooms, and tomatoes marinara with spaghettini.

Cacciatore — $11.95
Halved spring chicken cut in small pieces, sauteed with red wine peppers mushrooms onions and tomatoes marinated, served with spaghettini.

Piccante — $10.95
Boneless breast of chicken sauteed in lemon butter & sherry wine with broccoli.

Vesuvio — $11.95
Recipe from Salerno near Mt Vesuvius—halved spring chicken cut in small pieces with quartered potatoes sauteed in oil, garlic & oregano.

Genovesa — $12.95
Boneless breast of chicken with eggplant over creamed spinach (Florentina).

Rollatini — $12.95
Boneless breast of chicken stuffed with creamed Ricotta, Mozzarella, Italian ham (with Fettucini verde and fresh broccoli).

Babino Vitello

Piccante — $14.95
Scallopini of veal sauteed with sherry wine & lemon with fresh broccoli.

Marsala — $14.95
Scallopini of veal sauteed in Marsala wine with fresh mushrooms and side of spaghetti.

Francaise — $14.95
Scallopini of veal with light egg batter sauteed in Mareda wine with Amaretto, served with broccoli.

Scallopini — $14.95
Veal with peppers mushrooms and tomatoes, sauteed in wine marinara with side of spaghetti.

San Remo — $14.95
Veal baked with eggplant and prosciutto, topped with Alfredo sauce.

Osso Buco ala Ambrosino — $16.95
Braised veal shanks topped with julienne vegetables.

Saltimbocca — $15.95
Francaise-style veal with prosciutto over bed of creamed spinach florentine.

Voldastana — $15.95
Sauteed veal cutlet rolled and stuffed with Italian ham with cheese a la Bordelaise with Fettucini and broccoli.

Pesce (Fish)

Orange Roughy Italian Style — $11.95
Plum tomatoes, Italian wine and Italian olives.

Orange Roughy Almondine — $11.95
Served with fresh broccoli.

Scallops La Soin — $13.95
Sauteed in white wine, garlic and butter served with linguini.

Scallops Milanese — $13.95
Sauteed in a red wine sauce. Served with linguini.

Frutti De Mare (Shellfish)

Baby Clams & Sauce — $9.95
Over Linguini, red or white.

New Zealand Mussels — $13.95
Over Linguini, red or white.

Chicago Style Open Shelled Steamed Clams — $13.95
Red or white.

Calamari (Squid) — $13.95
Over Linguini, red or white.

Jumbo Shrimp

Piccante — $15.95
Lemon butter and sherry wine served over linguini.

Shrimp Scallopini — $15.95
With peppers and mushrooms over linguini.

Shrimp Alfredo — $16.95
Over linguini.

Carne (Beef)

New York Strip Steak — $15.95
Served with seasoned Roman potatoes and broccoli.

Pepper Steak Chicago Style — $15.95
Medallions of tenderloin beef, green peppers, fresh mushrooms and fresh tomatoes. Served seasoned Roman potatoes.

Angello (Lamb)

Prime Loin Lamb Chops — $17.95
Char-broiled served with veal tortellini a la Romano, seasoned Roman potatoes and vegetable of the day.

Angello al Forno (dinner for two) — $36.95
New Zealand full baby rack of lamb. Served with Tortellini a la Romano, seasoned Roman potatoes, and vegetables of the day. (Available for one.)

Ambrosinos

PHONE
994-8404

HOURS
Tuesday–Sunday
5:00 pm–10:00 pm
Saturday & Sunday
5:00 pm–11:00 pm
Closed Monday

LOCATION
2122 N.
Scottsdale Road
Scottsdale, AZ 85257

CUISINE
Italian

ATTIRE
Casual

FULL BAR

BANQUET FACILITIES
Up to 150

CATERING

RESERVATIONS
4 or more

CREDIT CARDS
MasterCard, Visa, American Express

CHECKS ACCEPTED
With Guarantee carde

SMOKING
Section Available

HANDICAP FACILITIES

Andramari

PHONE
661-6499

HOURS
Lunch
Monday–Saturday
11:00 am–2:00 pm

Dinner
Monday–Sunday
5:00 pm–10:00 pm

LOCATION
9393 North
90th Street
Scottsdale, AZ 85258

CUISINE
Spanish Basque Country

ATTIRE
Casual

TERRACE DINING
FULL SERVICE CATERING

RESERVATIONS
Requested

CREDIT CARDS
MasterCard, Visa, American Express

SMOKING
Section Available

The Basque Country Kitchen

Bordered by France and the Cantabrico Sea, Basque country is the rich gastronomic region of Spain. Its bounty ranges from plump Cantabrico sea prawns and spiny lobsters to dozens of types of wild mushrooms, succulent fruits and vegetables and all sorts of wild game and poultry.

One of Europe's best kept culinary secrets, the remarkable cuisine of Basque country is based on thousands of years cooking and reflects the heritage of Provence.

Each of these regional treats from tapas, paellas and seafood stews to elegant poultry and game dishes and tantalizing desserts, is introduced by personal anecdotes that recreate the ambiance of village life and the historic culture of Basque Country.

Food From Spain

ANDRAMARI
Restaurant ✶ Tapas Bar

Tapas-Appetizers

TIGRES EN SALSA ROJA	$5.95
Mussels spicy hot sauce.	
MEJILLONES MARINERA	$5.95
Mussels sauted in brandy sauce.	
ALCACHOFAS ROMANA	$5.95
Fried artichoke with allioli.	
GAMBAS AL AJILLO	$6.95
Fried shrimp with garlic and olive oil.	
TXITORRA FRITAS	$6.95
Fried Spanish sausage.	
TORTILLA ESPANOLA	$4.95
With roasted peppers and potato.	
LANGOSTINOS AL PIL PIL	$6.95
Fried shrimp sauted in olive oil with guindillas.	
PINCHITOS MORUNOS	$6.95
Brochette of lamb with fresh herbs.	

Soups

GASPACHO ANDALUZ	$4.75
Chilled vegetable soup.	
SOPA DE PESCADO	$5.25
Combination of shell fish.	

Ensaladas-Salads

MEDITERRANEAN	$5.95
Fresh romaine lettuce, orange and onions with garlic & basil olive sauce.	
ENSALADA VASCA	$6.95
Marinated tomatoes with olive oil and bonita.	

Favorites of Spain

PAELLA VALENCIANA	$16.95
Masterpiece of rice, zafron and seafood.	
PAELLA DE POLLOS	$12.95
Masterpiece of rice, zafron and chicken.	
PAELLA VEGETAL	$11.95
Masterpiece of rice, zafron and fresh vegetables.	

Pollos-Chicken

POLLO AL CHILINDRON	$12.95
Chicken breast with capers, sweet peppers and hot tomato.	
POLLO FLORENTINA	$12.95
Breast of chicken sauted in butter, spinach and mozarella cheese.	
POLLO ALA RIOJA	$12.95
Breast of chicken with red wine sauce.	

Mariscos-Fish

ZORTZIKO DE PESCADO	$16.95
Casserole of fresh fish with shrimp, mussels and clams with American sauce.	
BERMEO COSTA	$17.95
Medallion of fresh fish with scallops and shrimp in Spanish brandy.	
BACALO CLUB RANERO	$15.95
Cod fish with fresh vegetables and white wine.	
MARISCOS CON ESPINACAS	$16.95
Shrimp sauteed in garlic with spinach, spices and white wine.	

Carnes-Meats

SOLOMILLO ALA RIOJA	$16.95
Medallion of beef with red wine sauce and roasted red peppers and capers, with shrimp.	
PATA DE CORDERO	$16.95
Roasted lamb with fresh herbs.	
CONEJO AL AZAFRAN	$16.95
Tender rabbit with zafron.	

Postres-Desserts

FLAN	$4.50
A delicious caramelled custard.	
PASTEL DE PAN	$4.50
Bread pudding.	
TIRAMISU	$4.50
A famous coffee flavored dessert.	

Andre's

As the main dining room of the resort, Andre's is open daily, serving breakfast lunch and dinner. American Regional Cuisine is the primary foundation in both the lunch and dinner menu selections.

Overlooking the lush gardens and Olympic size pool at the Radisson Resort Scottsdale, Andre's has a feeling of warmth and distinction, as if it were a free standing dining establishment.

As the main dining room of the resort, Andre's is open daily, serving breakfast, lunch and dinner. American Regional Cuisine is the primary foundation in both the lunch and dinner menu selections.

Andre's is highly noted for its "Special Meals for Special Friends" promotion, which consists of an elaborate salad bar, choice of entree, pastry table and coffee starting at $14.50 per person. It is known as one of the best kept secrets of Scottsdale.

In addition, Andre's hosts a different type of brunch...Sundays from 11:30–2:30 pm. Enjoy delectable hot entrees prepared to order and served tableside...accompanied by an elaborate multi-course cold buffet featuring sumptuous salads, exotic fruits and cheeses and award winning pastries. Harp music and champagne are included.

Andre's—discover it today!

Andre's at the Radisson

PHONE
991–3800

HOURS
Daily
6:30 am–10:00 pm

LOCATION
At the
Radisson Resort
7171 North
Scottsdale Road
Scottsdale, AZ 85253

CUISINE
American Regional

ATTIRE
Casual

LOUNGE
5:30–Closing

AL FRESCO DINING

SUNDAY BRUNCH

VEGETARIAN MEALS

RESERVATIONS
Recommended

CREDIT CARDS
MasterCard, Visa,
American Express,
Diners Club, Discover

SMOKING
Section Available

HANDICAP FACILITIES

Arizona Cafe & Grill is a casual cowboy bistro featuring food with flavors as vast as the Arizona desert. Mouth watering starters, crisp salads, sensational grilled steaks, oven roasted pizzas and fabulous fresh fish along with Arizona inspired interpretations of American dessert favorites. ACG features a marvelous wine list which is sure to include some of your favorites and a unique collection of beers, imported and domestic, which are paired with menu selections. Try ACG's patio for food with Arizona style and the best view in Phoenix. ACG's menu selection will tempt diners of all ages and is designed with a casual family dining experience in mind.

STARTERS & SALADS

FRIJOLES SOUP WITH CILANTRO PESTO — $3.95
Celis White $ 5.25/Flora Springs, Sauvignon Blanc $ 4.25

YELLOW BELL PEPPER SOUP WITH SOUR CREAM — $3.95
Chimay Premier Red Cap $5.50
Roederer Estate, Champagne $6.50

BAVOSOS ACG — $8.95
(As the French would say escargots or just plain snails, with cilantro garlic butter)
Guiness Extra Stout Ale $4.00/Saintsbury Garnet, Pinot Noir $4.75

ACG BROCHETTES OF DUCK — $7.95
Smoked Breast of Duck served on Skewers with ACG Hot Sauce
Chili Beer $3.25/Clos de Gilroy, Grenache $4.00

ACG SHRIMP COCKTAIL — $8.95
with a Splash of Absolut Peppar Vodka
Black Hawk Ale $7.00/Mumm Cuvée Napa Brut $5.50

Arizona Cafe & Grill

ACG CAESAR SALAD — $5.95
A zesty remake of a classical favorite with Parmesan Tuile
Ayinger Brau Weisse Ale $4.50/Pacific Rim Riesling $4.25

SATAY GRILLED SESAME CHICKEN SALAD — $8.50
Celis White Ale $3.25
Murphy Goode, Sauvignon Blanc $4.75

SALAD FRESCA — $5.95
Tomatoes, Onions, Iceberg and fresh Mexican Cheese with Cilantro Vinaigrette
Harp $2.50/Morgan, Sauvignon Blanc $4.50

SALAD OF FIELD GREENS — $4.25
with ACG Vinaigrette
Lindemans Framboise $7.30/Chapellet Chenin Blanc $4.00

PIZZAS

MESQUITE SMOKED CHICKEN PIZZA — $7.95
Bass Ale $3.50/Chateau Woitner "Howell Mt.", Chardonnay $4.50

CHORIZO WITH MEXICAN CHEESE — $7.95
Dos Equis Amber Ale $3.25/ Cline Zinfandel $4.25

ROASTED PEPPERS WITH ASSORTED GRILLED VEGETABLES — $8.95
Moosehead $2.50/David Bruce Pinot Noir $5.75

TOMATO CHEESE WITH FRESH BASIL — $6.95
Newcastle Brown Ale $4.00/ Saintsbury Garnet, Pinot Noir $4.75

GARDEN GREENS PIZZA WITH SPINACH AND ARUGULA — $8.95
Pilsner Urquell $4.00/Calera, Chardonnay $6.75

MAIN COURSES
ALL MEAT AND FISH PREPARED MEDIUM RARE UNLESS OTHERWISE REQUESTED

PESTO PASTA — $8.75
Pete's Wicked Summer Brew $3.25/Grgich Hills, Sauvignon Blanc $6.00

SEAFOOD PASTA — $14.95
Penne Pasta tossed with fresh Salmon, Shrimp, Tuna, Tomatoes and Herbs
Pilsner Urquell $4.00/Morgan, Sauvignon Blanc $4.50

CHICKEN ROASTED OVER A WOOD FIRE — 1/2 or whole $8.75/$14.95
Pete's Wicked Ale Red $3.50/Trefethen, Chardonnay $6.00

**BARBECUE RIBS WITH ACG SAUCE — 1/2 slab or full slab $9.95/$16.95
Anchor Steam Lager $4.25/Atlas Peak, Sangiovese $6.00

**OVEN ROASTED PRIME RIB–8 OUNCE OR 14 OUNCE — $12.95/$15.95 (Served after 4:00 pm.)
Ayinger Dunkel (Dark) Lager $4.50/Sterling Diamond Mountain Ranch, Cabernet Sauvignon $6.75

*GRILLED FILET 5 OR 8 OUNCE — $11.95/15.95
Blue Heron Ale $6.50/Freemark Abbey, Merlot $6.25

*GRILLED NEW YORK CUT 12 OUNCE — $16.25
Samuel Smith Brown Nut Ale $4.50/Terra Rossa, Cabernet Sauvignon $5.75

*GRILLED ACG T-BONE — $19.95
Sealed with Chili Herb Oil—20 OUNCE
Pete's Wicked Ale Red $3.50/Santa Rita Medalla Real, Cabernet Sauvignon $4.75

ACG BURGER — $6.95
with Fries. With Cheese add $1.00
Brasseurs Lager $7.00/Ferrari-Carano, Merlot $6.75

FISH OF THE GRILL — MARKET PRICE
Orval Trappist Ale $6.00/ Sonoma Cutrer, Chardonnay $6.25

GRILLED SALMON WITH PEARL BARLEY RISOTTO — $15.95
Red Tail Ale $3.50/Sanford "Central Coast," Chardonnay $6.75

GRILLED HALIBUT WITH OVEN ROASTED VEGETABLES — $13.95
Bass Ale $3.50/Chateau Woltner "Mt. Howell," Chardonnay $4.50

Main courses are subject to a $1.00 split plate charge.

* Served with ACG sauces on the side, Red Pepper Béarnaise, Grain Mustard and Whiskey Peppercorn and your **choice of French Fries, Gratin, Pureed or Baked Potato (available after 4 pm.)

SIDES

Pureed Potatoes	$1.75
Baked Carrots with Cumin	$1.75
Baked Potato	$1.95
Steamed Broccoli	$1.95
French Fries	$1.75
Black Beans	$1.95
Gratin Potatoes	$2.25

Enjoy your menu selection with a glass of wine or beer expertly matched by ACG Beverage Director, Paola Gross

---

Arizona Cafe & Grill

PHONE
957–0777

HOURS
Daily
Lunch
11:00 am–5:00 pm
Dinner
5:00 pm–10:00 pm

LOCATION
3113 East
Lincoln Drive
Phoenix, AZ 85016

CUISINE
American with a Southern Flair

ATTIRE
Casual

PATIO DINING

FULL SERVICE CATERING

TAKE OUT

VEGETARIAN MEALS

RESERVATIONS
Accepted

CREDIT CARDS
MasterCard, Visa, American Express, Diners Club, Discover

HANDICAP FACILITIES

The Arizona Kitchen

PHONE
935-3811

HOURS
Monday–Saturday
6:00 pm–10:30 pm

LOCATION
The Wigwam Resort
Litchfield Park
AZ 85340

CUISINE
Southwestern

ATTIRE
Resort Casual

ENTERTAINMENT
Guitarist Bryun Kayler

AFTER THEATRE DINING

VEGETARIAN MEALS

RESERVATIONS
Suggested

CREDIT CARDS
MasterCard, Visa,
American Express,
Discover

SMOKING
Section Available

HANDICAP FACILITIES

The Arizona Kitchen offers delightful Authentic Arizona Cuisine prepared in an exhibition kitchen amidst brick floors, timbered ceilings and adobe fireplaces. A "Best of Phoenix" award winner for Southwestern restaurants for '95.

Delectable Southwestern choices such as:

- Smoked Shrimp Quesadilla with Grilled Mango Jicama Salsa
- Hearth Oven Pizza with Jalapeno and Frybread Crust
- Grilled Medallions of Venison with Blackberry Zinfandel Cocoa Sauce
- Turkey Medallions with Sundried Cranberry Ancho Chile Sauce

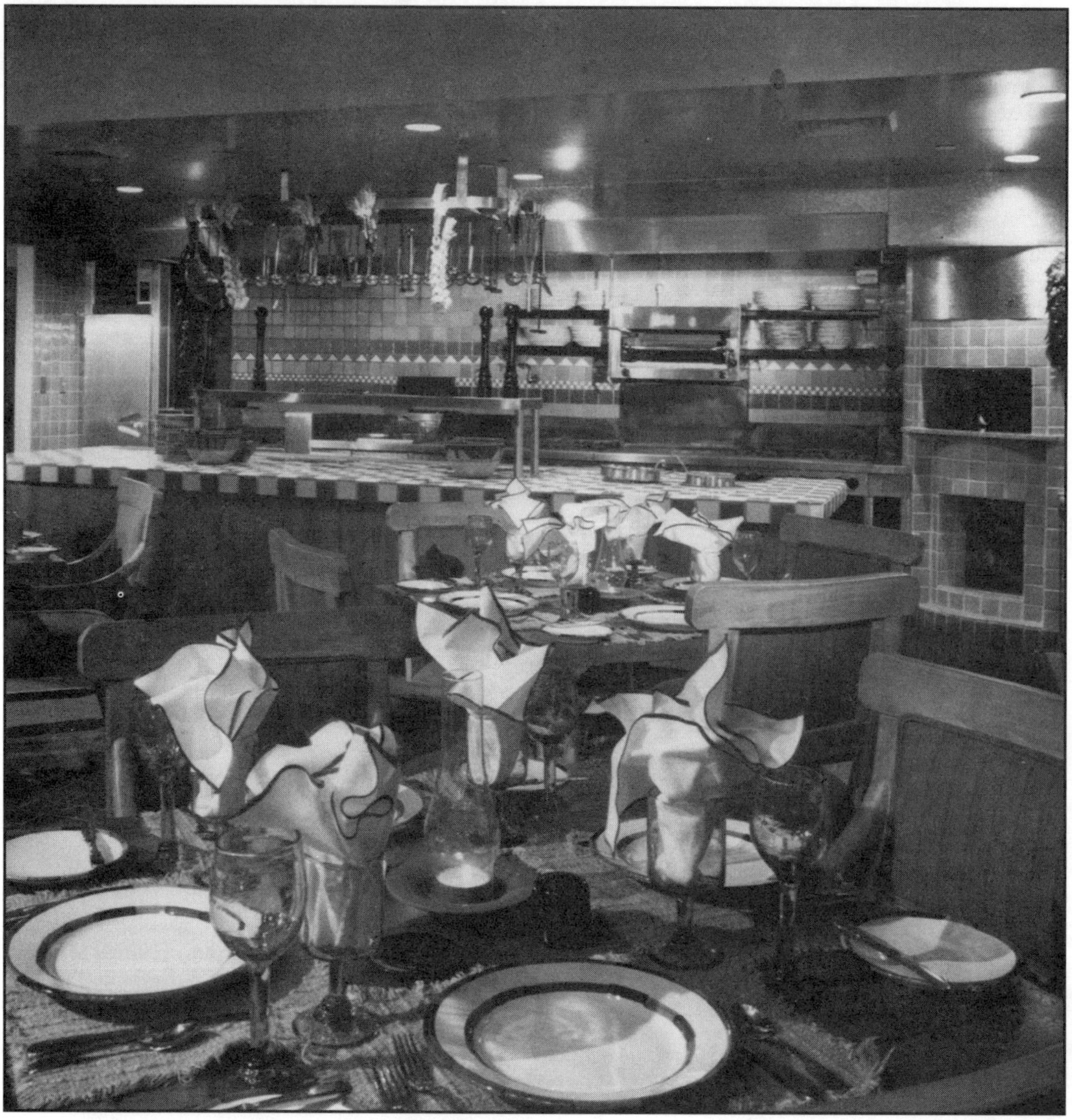

"A Beanery Refried"

Step back in time when gunpowder was blasting from the guns of Geronimo and Pancho Villa. Aunt Chilada's north room was the foundation of a general store that served miners camped where Pointe Hilton Resort at Squaw Peak is located today. These dusty miners worked the old Rico Mercury Mine, and after a long day of working and inhaling mercury fumes, walked back with dreamy looks on their faces, giving the area the name, "Dreamy Draw."

Later the store soon became "The Peek Steak House". Many guests from The Camelback Inn & The Biltmore rode over on horseback to slake their thirst with a cool libation, a good steak and an enchilada. The restaurant took its name, not from nearby Squaw Peak, but rather from a Plexiglas window set in the ceiling of the bar (now the Mercado area). Scantily clad dancers climbed into the attic to do the hoochie-cootchie on their stomachs while patrons "peeked" up at the window.

"George's Ole!" George Cocherham, captain with the Phoenix Fire Department, added to the structure (hiring off-duty firefighters), using old railroad ties and heavy stones. A most impressive addition was the antique meat smoker on the back patio.

After becoming a part of the Pointe Resorts this hide-away became famous for good food and good times. Ken Nagel, working with Gosnell from the beginning, designing the food and beverage operation for the resorts, always dreamed of owning Aunt Chilada's himself someday. And in January 1995, his dream came true.

The years have only enhanced the beautiful and spacious patios and banquet facilities. The locals gather not only for dinner but to have fiestas, wedding receptions, anniversaries, meetings and other gatherings to create more memories. Aunt Chilada's hosts the largest Cinco de Mayo in the Southwest and the infamous Xerox Southwest Salsa Challenge. Aunt Chilada's specializes in traditional Mexican food and fabulous grill and smokehouse specials.

ESPECIALES DE LA CASA
Served with fideo and Four Bean Casserole

FAJITAS **$9.95**
Your choice of grilled chicken, smoked steak, smoked pork or vegetables. Or a combination of any two. Served sizzling at tableside with gorditas, guacamole, fresh pico de gallo and sour cream.

SHRIMP FAJITAS **$13.50**

SMOKED RED CHILE CON CARNE BURRO **$6.95**

MESQUITE-GRILLED CHICKEN PECHUGAS **$8.95**
Grilled chicken, wrapped in a flour tortilla and smothered in spicy Mexican cheese sauce.

SMOKEHOUSE SPECIALS
All Smokehouse Specials are served with Nacho Papas and Mexican Corn Relish. Available after 5pm.

SLICED NEW YORK STEAK **$11.95**
With roasted corn chili sauce.

RED CHILI BARBEQUED PORK RIBS **$9.95**
Cut and ready to eat.

SLOW SMOKED PORK LOIN **$10.95**

SMOKED AND SLOW ROASTED DOUBLE BREAST OF CHICKEN **$7.95**
With green sauce.

SMOKED VEGETABLE PLATE **$6.95**
With salsa fresca.

Aunt Chiladas at Squaw Peak

PHONE
944-1286

FAX
943-8792

HOURS
Sunday–Thursday
11:00 am–10:00 pm
Friday & Saturday
11:00 am–11:00 pm

LOCATION
7330 North
Dreamy Draw Drive
Phoenix, AZ

CUISINE
Mexican/Southwestern

ATTIRE
Casual

LOUNGE
Monday–Friday
11:00–Closing
Saturday & Sunday
9:00 pm–11:00 pm

ENTERTAINMENT
Friday
Live Band & Dancing

PATIO DINING

BANQUET FACILITIES

MEETING FACILITIES

AFTER THEATRE DINING

FULL SERVICE CATERING

TAKE OUT

VEGETARIAN MEALS

RESERVATIONS
Suggested

CREDIT CARDS
MasterCard, Visa,
American Express,
Diners Club, Discover

SMOKING
Section Available

HANDICAP FACILITIES

The "In" Place for Jazz!

APPETIZERS

CHILLIN SHRIMP
Large firm & fresh shrimp served in a chilled glass bowl with a zesty cocktail sauce & lemon.

"CAN YOU DIG IT"
1/2 Pound of shrimp, with zesty cocktail sauce & lemon, that you peel & eat all by yourself.

N'AWLINS SHRIMP
Large shrimp sauteed in butter with our secret cajun beer sauce. Made for the old moonshiners.

"S CAR GO"
Sauteed in garlic butter, green onions, fresh herbs & spices, in a light white wine sauce.

JAMMIN SALMON MOUSSE
Canadian pink salmon blended with dill, cream and sherry served with corn tortilla chips.

ARTIE DON'T CHOKE DIP
Blended artichoke & parmasan cheese, mayo, garlic, fire roasted chilis. fresh herbs & spices served warm with corn chips.

MO BETTER MUSSEL.
That's right! More. A whole pound of New Zealand green lip mussels. Cooked in a spicy red wine tomato sauce or a garlic white wine sauce.

CRABBY MUSHROOM CAPS
Mushrooms stuffed with crab, cheeses, fresh herbs & spices baked to a golden brown glaze.

SWINGING LIVER PATE
Chicken liver pate baked with bacon, served with corn tortilla chips.

AZZ JAZZ COMBO PLATTER
Peel & eat shrimp, salmon mousse and artichoke dip, served with corn tortilla chips.

CHORIZOS SAUSAGES
A mixture of beef and pork served with chimichurri sauce.

EMPANADAS
Delicate pastry stuffed with meat, raisins and spices.

SALADS

CAESAR SALAD
Grilled chicken breast atop a crisp bed of romaine lettuce and the tastiest zesty dressing.

HEARTS OF PALM, ARTICHOKE & MUSHROOMS
Marinated in fresh herbs & spices in a red wine vinaigrette.

SPINACH SALAD
Tender leaves of spinach, red bermuda onions in a hot bacon dressing.

SHRIMP & CRAB SALAD
Shrimp & crab on a bed of greens, tomatoes, artichoke hearts, baby corn, olives in a rose wine vinaigrette.

PASTA

JAZZ MEDLEY
Medley of sauteed vegetables tossed in rigatoni pasta smothered with loads of garlic, fresh basil & white wine.

HOW SWEET IT IS!!
Fresh tomato pommodores in a creamy sweet tomato basil sauce with penne noodles. That'll make you get up and dance.

ENTREES

BEEF SELECTION
PRIME RIB-USDA
8oz & 12 oz
Blow your horn to our aged beef, slow roasted to your perfection served au jus or cajun style.

FILET MIGNON FLAMBE
Centercut tenderloin of beef sauteed in a rich dry cream sherry sauce with mushrooms and brandy. Talk about funky, this is it.

PORK SELECTION
MEDALLIONS OF PORK D' ANGELO
Sauteed with delicious apples, onions, raisins & walnuts in a Remy Martin cognac sauce. Charlotte, would even stop weaving her web for this one.

CHICKEN SELECTION
TOURNEDOS OF CHICKEN BOURSIN
Medallions of tender chicken breast set afire in a brandy cream sauce with mushrooms, served over large homemade croutons, artichoke & mushroom caps.

BLUENOTE CHICKEN
Tender chicken breast sauteed and topped with smoked ham, cheese and tomato slices laced in a hollandaise sauce.

LEMON BYRD
Tender breast of chicken lightly seasoned with lemon, fresh basil and grated Romano cheese served on a bed of jazzed-up rice.

SEAFOOD SELECTION
LADY & THE SCAMPI
Large shrimp seasoned with fresh herbs, spices sauteed in a white wine and lemon garlic sauce, served with rice. This one's the cats meow.

TROUT BASIE
Rainbow trout lightly seasoned topped with shrimp, mushrooms, scallions and white wine. For you cool cats.

SMOKIN SEAFOOD NEWBERG
Tender morsels of shrimp, scallops and crab boogie woogied with mushrooms in a creamy garlic cheese sauce served on a bed of jazzed rice.

SWORD FISH
Sauteed in a tomato basil wine sauce. For the steak lovers in all of us.

CAT FISH "MAN DOO"
Cat Fish filet pan fried, served cajun style with rice. Don't let the bears catch you with this one they'll eat it for you.

DESSERT
Your server will be more than happy to describe our assortment of delectable desserts.

The Azz Jazz Cafe

PHONE
263-8482

HOURS
Monday–Saturday
5:30 pm–10:00

LOCATION
1906 East
Camelback Road
Phoenix, AZ 85016

CUISINE
Eclectic American

ENTERTAINMENT
Jazz every night
5:00 until closing

TERRACE DINING

SUNDAY BRUNCH

BANQUET FACILITIES

AFTER THEATRE DINING

ART WALK EVERY THURSDAY

FULL SERVICE CATERING

TAKE OUT

VEGETARIAN MEALS

RESERVATIONS
Suggested

CREDIT CARDS
MasterCard, Visa, Diners Club, American Express

SMOKING
Section Available

HANDICAP FACILITIES

Avanti

PHOENIX
PHONE
956-0900

HOURS
Lunch
Monday–Friday
11:00 am–2:00 pm

Dinner
Monday–Sunday
5:00 pm–10:00 pm

LOCATION
2728 East
Thomas Road
Phoenix, AZ 85016

SCOTTSDALE
PHONE
949-8333

HOURS
Monday–Sunday
5:00 pm–10:30 pm

LOCATION
3102 North
Scottsdale Road
Scottsdale, AZ 85251

CUISINE
Italian/Continental

ATTIRE
Casual

LOUNGE
Piano Bar/Dancing
Wednesday-Saturday
7:00 pm– Closing

BANQUET FACILITIES

PRIVATE DINNING ROOMS

FULL SERVICE CATERING

CREDIT CARDS
MasterCard, Visa,
American Express,
Diners Club, Discover

SMOKING
Section Available

HANDICAP FACILITIES

The interior of Avanti is dramatic black and white with an art-deco influence and passionate contemporary artwork. Suspended votive candles create soft lighting and a romantic ambiance perfect for intimate conversation. The service staff is professional and accommodating without being pretentious.

Owners, **Angelo Livi** and **Benito Mellino** take great pride in greeting their guest each evening and offering the best in classically prepared dishes from around the globe.

After dinner entertainment is offered at both locations featuring a piano-bar type atmosphere where dancing and singing can go on till late.

Avanti also provides excellent personalized catering facilities off-premise or in-house and is the preferred caterer to dignitaries, entertainment music groups, television, stage and theater actors.

A Valley Tradition Since 1974...

The Beginning...

Marinated Grilled Vegetables	$7.95
topped with goat cheese, balsamic vinegar and olives	
Escargots 'De Bourgogne	$7.95
garlic butter & Meursault wine	
Octopus Salad	$8.95
Calamari Fritti	$7.50
deep fried squid served with marinara sauce	
Mozzarella Fritta	$7.50
served with marinara sauce	
Jumbo Shrimp Cocktail	$9.95
Beluga Caviar	30g. $68.00
frozen Stolichnaya is on us!	
Fresh Mussels	$8.95
in a marinara sauce (red) or mariniere (shallots, white wine, cream)	
Oyster's Rockefeller	$8.95
baked with spinach and topped with cheese	
Oysters in Half Shell	$8.95

And Next

Soup of the Day	$3.50
Tortellini in Brodo	$4.50

The Greens

Benito Salad	$7.50
mixed lettuce, hearts of palm, tomatoes, octopus, avocado with garlic basil dressing	
Avanti Salad	$7.50
bibb lettuce, watercress, hearts of palm, artichokes, avocado and asparagus topped with our famous dressing	
"Chop Chop" Salad	$7.50
finely chopped mix of lettuces, tomatoes, celery, carrots, with vinaigrette dressing topped with peanuts and feta cheese	
Angelo Salad	$7.50
tomatoes, mushrooms, onions, peppers, watercress and basil	
Caesar Salad for One	$6.50
Mozzarella Caprese	$7.50
fresh mozzarella, tomatoes, basil, red onion balsamic vinaigrette	

Pasta as we like it in Italy!

Fettuccini Salsa Cruda	$13.95
sauteed garlic, escarole, white beans, sun dried tomatoes	
Linguine Primavera	$13.95
mix of fresh vegetables, basil, garlic, in tomato sauce	
Homemade Lasagna	$13.95
in a classic meat sauce	
Rigatoni Bolognese	$13.95
tubular pasta with rich meat sauce	
Tortellini Portofino	$13.95
round pasta filled with meat in a cream, parmesan cheese sauce topped with walnuts and mushrooms	
Penne Alla Vodka	$13.95
small tubular pasta with prosciutto in a vodka cardinal sauce	
Spaghetti Alla Carbonara	$13.95
prosciutto, peas, in a light parmesan cream sauce	
Cannelloni Fiorentina	$13.95
pasta filled with chicken, veal, spinach, with bechamel sauce	
Linguine with Clam Sauce	$13.95
your choice, white or red sauce	
Risotto of the Day	market price

Avanti Artwork

all entrees are served with soup du jour or salad maison and fresh vegetables

Chef's Seafood Catch	market Price
please ask you server	
Fresh Grilled Salmon	$19.95
Scallops or Scampi Avanti	$22.95
sauteed in garlic, butter, brandy and white wine	
Scampi and Scallops Fradiavolo	$22.95
served on a bed of pasta	
Paella	$25.95
a combination of mixed seafood, meat and saffron rice	
Cioppino Mediterraneo	$24.95
Ossobuco Milanese	$24.95
braised veal shank with fresh vegetables served with rice	
Avanti Veal Chop	$26.95
Veal Piccata	$19.95
sauteed with butter, lemon, white wine and capers	
Veal Saltimbocca Fiorentina	$19.95
spinach, prosciutto, mushrooms in a Marsala wine sauce	
Veal Parmigiana	$19.95
Chicken Rollatini	$16.50
chicken roll stuffed with ham & mozzarella cheese. served with a cream brandy sauce peas and mushrooms	
Chicken Breast Francese	$16.50
lemon sauce with capers and artichoke hearts	
Grilled Breast of Chicken Angelo	$16.50
marinated in virgin olive oil, rosemary & garlic served on a bed of mixed greens	
Long Island Roast Duckling	$20.95
orange or green peppercorn sauce	
Lamb Chops	$24.95
marinated in herbs & garlic	
Filet Mignon Alla Benito	$22.95
wild porcini mushrooms in a barolo wine sauce	
Medallion of Beef	$22.95
filet mignon served with a delicious cream brandy, green peppercorn sauce	
Bistecca Alla Fiorentina	$21.50
broiled T-bone steak marinated in garlic & herbs. Served with sauteed Florentine style beans	
Avanti Steak Tartar	$23.95
raw filet seasoned with anchovies, egg yolk, lemon capers, brandy etc...	

Back Stage

Backstage, a fun and relaxing place, sits overlooking the beautiful gardens and fountains of Scottsdale Civic Center Plaza. Tucked away next to the Scottsdale Center for the Arts, Backstage has been serving visitors and locals alike for the past 15 years. This beautiful restaurant prides itself for offering over 60 world class domestic and imported beers, exotic beverages as well as many fine domestic and imported wines.

Backstage offers truly an innovative cuisine in addition to world famous lahvosh, a combination for a truly wonderful experience you won't want to miss.

Appetizers

Sahuaro Dip — $5.95
Spinach, red pepper, chipotle, onions and garlic in a creamy cheese sauce. Served with fresh tri-color corn tortilla chips.

Foccacio — $6.95
Topped with smoked chicken, fresh basil and rosemary.

Garden Greens

Smoked Chicken Salad — $7.95
Crisp romaine greens tossed with tender slices of hickory smoked chicken breast, parmesan cheese and our own Caesar salad dressing.

Cobb Salad — $8.95
Fresh salad greens with sliced turkey, bacon, avocado, blue cheese, tomato, onions and eggs. Your choice of dressing.

Shanghai Salad — $7.95
Mixed greens, chunks of chicken, mushrooms, red cabbage, celery, carrots and mandarin oranges. Served with crispy rice noodles and secret house dressing.

Dinner Entrees

Tuscany Meat Loaf — $8.95
Slices of fresh ground beef seasoned in the Tuscany style and served with mushroom and rosemary sauce, mashed potatoes and vegetable of the day.

Penne Arrabbiatta (100% meat free) — $8.95
Fresh garlic, olives, sweet peppers, basil, buffalo mozzarella and sun-dried tomatoes.

Chicken Chimichanga — $8.95
Enchilada sauce, fried flour tortilla, jack and cheddar cheese, tomatoes, green chiles, red onions, wild rice, sour cream, guacamole and black beans.

Grilled Lemon Chicken — $8.95
Fresh herbs, field greens, key lime vinaigrette and julienne potatoes.

Chicken Fettuccini Alfredo (Blackened) — $9.50
Blackened chicken breast, fettuccini Au Alfredo sauce.

Grilled Pork Chop — $9.95
Roasted tomato, mint salsa, mashed potatoes and vegetables.

Filet Mignon Merchand De Vin — $13.95
Sautéed filet, beurre rouge, fresh vegetables and mashed potatoes.

Lahvosh

Pesto — $8.95
Chicken, sun-dried tomatoes, pine nuts, parmesan, havart cheese and pesto.

Rosemary Red Potato — $8.95
Rosemary roasted baby red potatoes, grilled chicken breast, red onions, sweet peppers, fresh herbs and havarti cheese.

Spinach & Mushroom (100% meat free) — $8.95
Fresh marinated spinach, sautéed mushrooms, tomato, red onions, havarti, herbs.

Southwestern — $8.95
Smoked chicken, havarti, sweet peppers, black beans, cilantro, herbs.

Margarita (100% meat free) — $8.95
Tomato, green chiles, red onions, jack, cheddar and havarti cheeses and cilantro. Served with salsa on the side.

Teriyaki or BBQ Chicken — $8.95
Sweet peppers, red onion, marinated chicken and havarti cheese.

Shrimp Curry — $9.95
Originiol style curried pacific shrimp, exotic herbs, sweet onions and havarti cheese.

The Godfather (100% meat free) — $9.95
Slices of grilled eggplant, mushrooms, onions, mozzarella, parmesan, havarti and marinara sauce.

Smoked Salmon — $10.95
Goat cheese, tomato, green onion, havarti cheese and assorted fresh herbs.

Sandwiches

Vegetable Sandwich — $7.50
Avocado (in season), sautéed mushrooms, yellow squash, eggplant with tomatoes and havarti cheese.

Guadalajara Fajita — $6.75
Grilled tequila peppered beef wrapped in a double flour tortilla with onions, sweet peppers and chipotle mayo.

Salmon Club — $8.95
Smoked salmon, bacon, swiss cheese, lettuce, tomato. Your choice of toasted white or wheat bread, shoestring potatoes and chipotle mayonnaise.

Back Stage

PHONE
949–1697

HOURS
Sunday–Thursday
11:00 am–10:00 pm
Friday & Saturday
11:00 am–2:00 am

LOCATION
7373 Scottsdale Civic Center Mall (Upstairs next to Scottsdale Center for the Arts)

CUISINE
Eclectic American

ATTIRE
Casual

ENTERTAINMENT
Friday, Saturday & Sunday

PATIO DINING

AFTER THEATER DINING

TAKE OUT

VEGETARIAN MEALS

RESERVATIONS
Suggested (6 or more)

CREDIT CARDS
MasterCard, Visa, American Express, Discover

SMOKING
Section Available

HANDICAP FACILITIES
Elevator to upstairs

Baby Kay's Cajun Kitchen

PHOENIX
LOCATION
955-0011
HOURS
Lunch
Monday–Saturday
11:00 am–3:00 pm
Dinner
Monday–Thursday
5:00 pm–10:00 pm
Friday & Saturday
5:00 pm–11:00 pm
Sunday
4:00 pm–9:00 pm
LOCATION
20th & Camelback
Town & Country
Shopping Center

CUISINE
Cajun
ATTIRE
Casual
ENTERTAINMENT
Lunch
12:00 am–2:00 pm
Dinner
Monday–Saturday
7:30 pm–11:00 pm
TERRACE DINING
AFTER THEATRE DINING

RESERVATIONS
For Parties Of
Six Or More
CREDIT CARDS
MasterCard, Visa,
American Express,
Diners
CHECKS ACCEPTED
With Guarantee Card
SMOKING
No Cigars or Pipes
HANDICAP FACILITIES

28

For Starters...

RENE WINGS 4.95
Chicken Wings deep fried in peanut oil topped with a spicy homemade vegetable B-B-Q sauce. Just like Grandpa Rene served every Sunday.

SHRIMP REMOULADE (ROOM-alaude) ... 6.95
A Baby Kay's favorite! Butterflied shrimp in a Cajun horseradish-based sauce served chilled with a round of garlic toast.

SHRIMP COCKTAIL 6.95
A great traditional starter with a Cajun flair.

KRAB BITES .... small 4.95 ..... large 6.95
Cajun Krab salad served chilled with a round of garlic toast. For the tender taste buds.

Gumbo by the Cup

CHICKEN 4.95

CHICKEN & ANDOUILLE SAUSAGE 5.45

A La Carte

RED BEANS & RICE 2.75

DIRTY RICE 2.75
Seasoned groundbeef and hot pork sausage simmered with onions, bell peppers, celery, and long grain white rice. Cher, this was not swept off the kitchen floor.

CHICKEN & ANDOUILLE 3.95
SAUSAGE JAMBALAYA

GARLIC BREAD 1.00

GREEN OLIVE COLESLAW 1.00

POTATO SALAD 1.25

Entrees

GUMBO
A spicy soup-like dish mixed with onions, bell peppers, and celery, served over long-grain white rice. Gumbo is the brew that soothes the Cajun appetite.

Chicken 7.95

Chicken & Andouille 8.95
(On-DOO-e) Sausage

CRAWFISH ETOUFFEE (A-2-Fay) 13.95
Peeled Louisiana crawfish tails mixed with onions, bell peppers and celery, simmered in butter and served over long-grain white rice. This is for all those lazy Cajuns who don't want to peel crawfish and suck 'da heads.

RED BEANS & RICE 7.95
Red beans simmered all day with hamhocks, garlic, onions and Cajun seasonings. This is what a Cajun family sits down to after Mama's Monday washday. Try an ice cold Dixie with this specialty.

With Strips of Andouille sausage 8.75

B-B-Q-SHRIMP 13.95
Butterflied shrimp baked in a cayenne lemon butter sauce.

WHOLE CORNISH GAME 12.95
HEN WITH DIRTY RICE
A game hen dusted with Cajun seasonings and deep fried in peanut oil. Bite the hen, chew the rice...mighty nice.
*Choice of salad can be substituted with red beans and rice, dirty rice or jambalaya for just 75¢.

CAJUN COMBINATION 13.95
A combination of Chicken Gumbo, Chicken & Andouille Sausage Jambalaya, and Crawfish Etouffee. A good choice for the undecided.

CATFISH
A fresh filet of catfish lightly dusted with Cajun seasonings, deep-fried in peanut oil and topped with your choice of...

Courtbouillon (coo-BEE-yon) 11.95
Hand-chopped catfish in a tomato sherry-based sauce.

Crawfish Sauce 13.95
Sweet Louisiana crawfish tails in a seasoned sauce.

CHICKEN & ANDOUILLE 10.95
SAUSAGE JAMBALAYA
A traditional Cajun rice dish.

Salads

SHRIMP REMOULADE SALAD 7.95

HOUSE SALAD 2.95
Choice of Homemade Dressings: Creole Vinaigrette, Blue Cheese, Rasberry Vinaigrette, Remoulade

Desserts

BREAD PUDDING 3.75
WITH WHISKEY SAUCE

PECAN PIE 3.75

A LA MODE 4.25

PRALINE SUNDAE 3.75
Praline Liqueur, Chocolate Bourbon Sauce

KEY LIME PIE 3.25
Please ask about any new dessert selection

Don't forget to ask about Baby Kay's Daily Specials

Baby Kay's Cajun Kitchen

SCOTTSDALE LOCATION
990–9080

HOURS
Monday–Saturday
4:00 pm–1:00 am
Sunday
4:00 pm–9:00 pm

LOCATION
7216 East
Shoeman Lane
Scottsdale, AZ

CUISINE
Cajun

ATTIRE
Casual

ENTERTAINMENT
Nightly

TERRACE DINING

AFTER THEATRE DINING

RESERVATIONS
Suggested

CREDIT CARDS
MasterCard, Visa, American Express

CHECKS ACCEPTED
With Guarantee Card

SMOKING
No Cigars or Pipes

HANDICAP FACILITIES

THE BAMBOO CLUB
Pacific Rim Cuisine

We invite you to dine The Bamboo Club's way. Our service is Asian style. Your server will be happy to assist you in ordering. A tip from "The Big Bamboo:" Looking for an appetizer? Try any of our Deep Fried, Barbecued, or Steamed dishes!

Vegetarian

Vegetarian Egg Rolls	$5
Seasoned Vegetables with Garlic & Chili	$8
Cantonese Noodles with Mixed Vegetables	$9
Asian Tofu with Seasonal Vegetables	$8
Thai Yellow Curry with Bean Cake	$8
Sizzling Spicy Tofu	$9

Steamed

Chardonnay Steamed Green Mussels with Ginger & Green Onions	$8
Siew Mai-Cantonese Pork Dumplings on a Bamboo Leaf	$6
Bamboo Steamed Vegetables	$6
Chicken & Vegetable Dumplings on Napa Cabbage	$6

Woked

Pork & Vegetable Pot Stickers	$7
Chicken Chop Suey Bamboo Style	$8
Thai Yellow Curry Chicken with Coconut Milk	$10
Beef with Black Bean & Garlic Sauce	$9
Bangkok Shrimp with Bamboo Shoots & Mushrooms	$13

Sizzled

Crispy Whole Red Snapper with Ginger & Green Onion Infused Oil	$19
New Zealand Green Mussels with Black Bean & Garlic Sauce	$9
Hawaiian Sweet & Sour Pineapple Chicken	$9
Beef with Ginger & Green Onion	$10
Ahi Tuna with Black Bean & Garlic Sauce	$18
Tempura Shrimp with Spicy Green Pepper Sauce	$15

Salad

Caesar Salad with Crispy Wonton	$6
Spicy Crackling Calamari Salad	$9
BBQ Duck Salad with Cucumber in Rice Vinegar	$8
Indonesian Style Peanut Chicken Salad	$8
Korean Kim Chi Shrimp Cocktail	$8
Thai Spicy Beef Salad with Greens & Crispy Rice Noodles	$9
Spinach Salad of Shrimps, Fresh Mushrooms and Water Chestnuts in Orange Vinaigrette	$9
Warm BBQ Pork & Bean Salad with Honey Mustard Dressing	$8

Big Bamboo's Favorites

Wonton Sop with Spinach & BBQ Pork	$6
Soft Shell Crab Tempura Style	$9
Sea Scallops & Snow Peas in a Garlic White Sauce	$13
Orange Scallops or Shrimp on Crispy Spinach	$18
Maui Volcano Beef on a Broccoli Island	$16
Hawaiian Macadamian Nut Chicken	$16
Tempura Chicken in a Lemon Sauce	$10
Lemon Grass Chicken or Beef	$12
Dr. Kates' Honey Garlic Ribs	$9
Orange Chicken or Orange Beef	$12
Phoenix Shrimp in a Broccoli Nest	$18
Pacific Rim Bouillabaisse with Curry & Lemon Grass	$15
Steamed Whole Red Snapper with Ginger & Green Onion	$22

Accompaniments

Crispy Spinach	$5
Thai Cucumber Salad	$4
Kim Chi-Korean Spicy Cabbage	$5
Three Kinds of Woked Mushrooms	$6
Stir Fried Bean Sprouts & Green Onions	$4
Five Vegetable Fried Rice	$6
Chicken or BBQ Pork or Duck Fried Rice	$6
Club Special Fried Rice in a Pineapple Boat	$9

Deep Fried

Coconut Shrimp with Daikon Salad	$8
Calamari with Jalapeno Mayo	$7
Cantonese Pork Dumplings with Thai Cucumber Salad	$7
Chicken & Vegetable Spring Rolls with Vietnamese Dipping Sauce	$5

Barbecued

BBQ Pork with Hot Mustard	$7
BBQ Duck with Spicy Plum Sauce	$10
BBQ Chicken Livers with Cucumber Salad	$7
BBQ Long Spare Ribs Cantonese Style	$8
BBQ Chicken with Shrimp Chips	$7
Mixed BBQ Platter Hong Kong Style	$12

Noodles

Pad Thai-Thai Rice Noodles with Chicken & Shrimp	$11
Stir Fried Sesame Citrus Noodles with Seasonal Vegetables	$8
Singapore Style Rice Noodles with Curry, Shrimp & BBQ Pork	$11
Cantonese Noodles with Shrimp & Chicken	$11
Asian Rice Noodles with Shrimp, Chicken & Snow Peas	$12
Korean Style Beef or Chicken on Crispy Rice Noodle	$11

Dessert

The Big Bamboo's Banana Split	$4
Double Happiness Chocolate Mousse Torte	$5
Mango & Raspberry Ice with Cookie Crisp	$5
White Chocolate Macadamia Nut Cheesecake	$5
Deep Fried Coconut Ice Cream	$4
Chocolate Dipped Fortune Cookies	$3

Bamboo Club

PHONE
955-1288

HOURS
Monday–Thursday
11:30 am–11:30 pm
Friday–Saturday
11:30 am–Midnight
Sunday
5:00 pm–10:00 pm

LOCATION
2596 East
Camelback Road
Phoenix, AZ 85015

CUISINE
Pacific Rim

ATTIRE
Casual

TERRACE DINING

VEGETARIAN MEALS

RESERVATIONS
Suggested

CREDIT CARDS
MasterCard, Visa,
American Express,
Discover, Diners Club

CHECKS ACCEPTED

SMOKING
Section Available

HANDICAP FACILITIES

This charming restaurant is Scottsdale's only authentic Irish/American Restaurant & Pub, featuring traditional Irish food and decor. Rated "4 Star" by the Arizona Republic, the menu includes traditional Irish specialities. In the pub, Harp Lager, Bass Ale and Guiness Stout are served on draft, along with a world claass selection of spirits, wine and beer. Patio dining with working fireplace.

STARTERS
($1.75–$4.50)

OUR FAMOUS BAKED POTATO AND SOUR CREAM SOUP

MACHACA STYLE BLACK BEAN CHILI
Served with flour tortillas.

HOUSE SALAD
Fresh garden green and cherry tomatoes with your choice of dressing.

FIVE PEPPERCORN CAESAR SALAD
Traditional Caesar salad with a blend of zesty peppercorns.

BASKET OF IRISH SODA BREAD

APPETIZERS
($5.00—$8.00)

IRISH STUFFED POTATO SKINS
Stuffed with shredded corn beef, seasoned cabbage and topped with melted Vermont white cheddar cheese.

PEPPERED BUFFALO STYLE DRUMMETTES
Chicken drummettes, served with our own blue cheese dressing & french fries.

BLACK BEAN CAKES
Grilled crisp, topped with sour cream and salsa.

GRILLED ANDOUILLE SAUSAGE
With red lentils & goat cheese crumbles.

SPICY CHICKEN AND CHILI EGG ROLLS
With green chili sauce.

SMOKED PACIFIC MARLIN
With red chili roumoulade.

GRILLED CABRILLA CAKES
(Sea bass cakes)
With red and green chili sauces.

BASKET OF ONION RINGS
Thick sliced bermuda onion rings, dipped in guiness batter and deep fried. Served with ranch dressing.

SALADS
($6.00—$8.00)

GRILLED CHINESE CHICKEN SALAD
Served on top of mixed greens, rice noodles, and sesame soy dressing.

SPICY CHICKEN CAESAR SALAD
Our traditional caesar with grilled cajun chicken.

BLACK ROSE "HEARTS" SALAD
Boston bibb lettuce, hearts of palm, artichoke hearts, boiled eggs, tomatoes and toasted almonds tossed in a creamy Italian dressing.

SMOKED MARLIN SALAD
Hickory smoked pacific marlin on a bed of mixed field greens and with raspberry vinaigrette.

SANDWICHES AND BUERGER'S
($5.50-$8.00)

ROSE BURGER
Topped with sauteed onions and mushrooms, bacon and melted Vermont white cheddar cheese.

BASIC BURGER
Pure and simple. With your choice of jarlsberg swiss, mozzarella or Vermont white cheddar.

CHILI BURGER
Open faced 1/2lb. burger topped with our homemade chili and shredded cheddar cheese.

G.O.'S GRILLED MEATLOAF WITH VEGGIES AND MASHES
Open faced topped with jalapeno gravy served with veggies and mashes.

SPICY TERIYAKI BREAST OF CHICKEN
Marinated with red chilies and rice wine.

CORNED BEEF SANDWICH
Thin slices of corned beef and seasoned cabbage with jarlsberg swiss cheese. Served on rye bread.

FRESH MOZZARELLA & TOMATO WITH PESTO MAYO
Served on a grilled french roll.

"MILLIONAIRE" CLUB
Huge triple decker served on toasted whole wheat bread.

BBQ PORK SANDWICH
Tender pork loin grilled with a spicy southwestern BBQ sauce.

ENTREES
Cup of soup or house salad add $2.00

SHEPHERD'S PIE
The pride of our pub. Braised beef simmered with fresh herbs in a rich burgundy sauce with carrots, onions and celery. Served in a crock and covered with golden brown potato cheese crust. Many say "Tis really what's at the end of the rainbow."

CORNED BEEF AND SEASONED CABBAGE
Made from Charlie Finnegan's own family recipe and the boast of her husband Andy. Tender corned beef and specially seasoned cabbage, served with boiled red potatoes and a dollop of whole grain mustard.

McSORLEY'S FISH AND CHIPS
Icelandic cod fillets, guiness battered and deep fried with our own homemade chips. The perfect accompaniment to a well pulled pint.

AMES McGAREY'S CHICKEN AND DUMPLINGS
The favorite Sunday supper of the Robey McGarey family. Pulled boiled chicken and herbed dumplings in blond chicken gravy.

A MEDLEY OF MIXED GRILL
Andouille sausage, terriaki chicken and five peppercorn filet.

PORK CHOPS WITH FRESH APPLE CHUTNEY
Boneless center cut chops, boiled and served with apple chutney.

BACON WRAPPED BBQ SHRIMP
Jumbo, gulf shrimp wrapped with hickory smoked bacon and basted with our homemade BBQ sauce.

AHI TUNA
Grilled fresh pacific tuna topped with papaya/cilantro salsa.

STEAK SANDWICH DIABLO
Thinly sliced beef tenderloin with red pepper marinade. Served on grilled baguette.

Black Rose

PHONE
941-0040

HOURS
Lunch
Monday–Friday
11:00 am–5:00 pm
Dinner
Monday–Thursday
5:00 pm–10:00 pm
Friday & Saturday
5:00 pm–11:00 pm
Sunday
Available private parties

LOCATION
4341 North
75th Street
Scottsdale, AZ 85251

CUISINE
Irish American

ATTIRE
Casual

ENTERTAINMENT
Friday & Saturday

TERRACE DINING
SUNDAY BRUNCH
AFTER THEATRE DINING

RESERVATIONS
Suggested

CREDIT CARDS
MasterCard, Visa,
American Express,
Diners Club

SMOKING
Section Available

HANDICAP FACILITIES

Bagels 'n Bialys

PHONE
991-3034
HOURS
Daily
5:30 am–8 pm
LOCATION
6990 East
Shea Boulevard
Scottsdale, AZ 85254

CUISINE
Deli
ATTIRE
Casual
PATIO DINING
VEGETARIAN DISHES

CREDIT CARDS
MasterCard, Visa,
American Express,
Discover
CHECKS ACCEPTED
SMOKING
Section Available
HANDICAP FACILITIES

Best of Phoenix, Readers Choice 1992

Arizona Best Bagels 1992

Sandwiches, Etc.

Singles on Bialy Breads — Small / Large

1. Corned Beef — $3.99 / $5.99
2. Pastrami — $3.99 / $5.99
3. Roast Beef — $3.99 / $5.99
4. Turkey Breast — $3.99 / $5.99
5. Brisket of Beef — $3.99 / $6.99
6. Tongue — $4.99 / $6.99
7. Salami — $3.99 / $5.99
8. Hard Salami — $3.99 / $5.99
9. Bologna — $3.99 / $5.99
10. Baked Virgina Ham — $3.99 / $5.99
11. Tuna Salad — $3.99 / $5.99
12. Chicken Salad — $3.99 / $5.99
13. Egg Salad — $3.99 / $5.99
14. Chopped liver — $3.99 / $5.99
15. Veggie — $3.99 / $4.99

Starlet Special — $5.99
small sandwich and cup of soup

Combos

16. Reuben — $6.95
17. Racheal — $6.95
18. Open Tuna Melt — $6.95
19. Brisket Delight — $6.95
20. Philly Steak — $6.95
21. Chicken Club — $6.95
22. Marty's Trio — $6.95
23. Hawaiian Chicken Sandwich — $6.95
24. Marty's Trio — $6.95
25. Patty Melt — $6.95
26. Triple Decker — $6.95
27. Pastrami & Tongue — $7.25
28. Corned Beef & Tongue — $7.25
29. Pastrami & Corned Beef — $7.25
30. New Yorker — $7.25
31. Strickly Schwartz — $6.95
32. Hearty Chicken — $6.95
33. Bacon, lettuce, tomato — $6.95

Also Available

- Deli or Cold Salad Platters
- Smoked Fish Fantasies
- Charbroiled, Fresh Seasoned Hamburgers, Chilli or Hot Dogs
- New York Style Pizza, on Bialy Dough

Breakfast

"Fluffy Deli Eggs Your Style"
Corned Beef and Eggs — $5.95
Pastrami and Eggs — $5.95
Salami and Eggs — $5.95
Lox, Eggs and Onions — $5.95
Fluffy Egg Omelettes — $5.95
Cheese, Western, Ham, Spanish, Ham & Cheese, Denver, Bacon, Deli, Sausage, Turkey Bacon & Avocado, Spinach Or, Create your own

From the Griddle

Challa toast (3) — $3.95
Pancakes — $4.95
Plain, Strawberry or Blueberry
Matzo Brie — $4.95
Early Bird Special
2 Eggs or Egg Beaters any style, Bacon or Ham, Homefries, choice of Bagel or Bialy or Cheese (Mon–Fri only, 6am–10am)
Jewish Breakfast Burritos
Egg — $4.95
Spinach — $5.95
Mushroom — $5.95
Chicken — $5.95

Appetizers

Chopped Liver — $3.95
Cheese Blintzes — $5.95
Stuffed Cabbages — $3.95
Potato Kinish — $2.50
Potato Pancakes — $4.95

Cool Salads

Grilled Chicken Caesar Salad — $5.95
Chinese Chicken Salad — $5.95
Chicken Delight — $5.95
Hearty Chicken Sandwiches, Yogurt & Fruit — $5.95

Dinner Entrees

Served after 4:00 pm. Includes Soup or Salad, choice of One Side, served with Freshly Baked Dinner Rolls & Butter. Choice of Fries, Mashed Potatoes, Potato Pancake, Steamed Vegetable, Cole Slaw, Potato Salad, or Clarmont Salad, Pasta Salad and Dessert of the Day.

Chicken in the Pot — $9.95
1/2 Roast Chicken — $8.95
Stuffed Cabbage (sweet & sour) — $8.95
Brisket of Beef — $8.95
Open Faced Roast Beef, or Turkey Breast — $8.95
Chicken Filets — $8.95
Franks & Beans — $8.95
Early Bird Dinner (4pm-6pm, M-F) — $6.95

The Only Mexican Restaurant in Phoenix
Approved By Heart Smart Restaurant International™

Mexican Food Redefined

"Food and Service, 3 Stars"
—Elin Jeffords, Scottsdale Progress

"Americas Best Meal Deals"
—Zagat Survey Guide for 1995-1996

"Big on Flavor...I Like the Blue Burrito."
—Donald Downers,
Phoenix Magazine Rest. Critic

Blue Burrito Grille

PHONE
955-9596

HOURS
7 Days a Week
11:00 am–11:00 pm

LOCATION
3118 East
Camelback Rd
Safeway/Biltmore Plaza
Phoenix, AZ 85016

CUISINE
Mexican

ATTIRE
Casual

PATIO DINING

TAKE OUT

VEGETARIAN MEALS

CREDIT CARDS
MasterCard, Visa,
American Express

HANDICAP FACILITIES

Partial Menu

BURRITOS ORGINALES our house specialty

Shredded Chicken Machaca Burrito $4.15
Tender Breast White Meat sauteed with Onions & Tomatoes, with Cheese & Lettuce

Shredded Beef Machaca Burrito $4.15
Lean Tenderloin sauteed with Onions & Tomatoes, with Cheese & Lettuce

Chicken or Beef Fajita Burrito $4.35
Breast of Chicken or Mexican Spiced Steak, Sauteed Peppers & Onions & Cheese

Green Chili Steak Burrito $4.35
Chunks of Shredded Tender Steak, Smothered in a Thick Homemade Green Chili Sauce, with Cheese

Carne Asada Burrito $4.95
Charbroiled Lean Skirt Steak with Cheese, Guacamole, Lettuce & Tomatoes

Vegetarian Burrito $3.25
No Lard Black Beans, Cheese, Grilled Peppers & Onions, Lettuce & Tomatoes

Black Bean & Cheese Burrito $2.75
No Lard Black Beans with Cheese

THE BIG BLUE BURRITO $5.50

(Mucho! Serves 2)
A Double Size Burrito with your choice of Charbroiled Steak or Chicken with No Lard Black Beans, Rice, Guacamole, Sour Cream, Cheese, Lettuce & Tomatoes

TACOS A LA PARILLA white corn tortillas

FISH - Tacos del Mar (2 tacos) $4.95
Two Tacos Filled with Tender Chunks of Grilled White Cod in Soft, Double Layer White Corn Tortillas with Shredded Red & White Cabbage, & a Tangy White Cilantro Sauce. Served with Tri-Colored Chips.

VEGETARIANOS

Blue Corn Quesadillas $2.95
3 Folded Blue Corn Tortillias (6") Filled with Cheese and Sauteed Peppers & Onions

#5 Tamales Mexicanos $4.95
One 8 oz. Green Corn Tamale or Garden Vegetable Tamale with Rice & No Lard Black Beans

Vegetarian Burrito $3.25
No Lard Black Beans, Cheese, Grilled Peppers & Onions, Lettuce & Tomatoes

Black Bean & Cheese Burrito $2.75
No Lard Black Beans with Cheese

PLATILLOS MEXICANOS COMBINACIONES

#1 El Dos Tacos Combo $4.95
Two Hard Shell Tacos, Choice of Chicken Machaca, Beef Machaca, or Ground Beef with Rice & No Lard Black Beans

#2 Enchiladas Rancheras $5.25
Two Blue Corn Enchiladas with Charbroiled Chicken, Melted Cheese, Rice & No Lard Black Beans

#3 Chicken Fajita Burrito $5.95
Grilled Marinated Strips of Chicken with Cheese, Sauteed Peppers & Onions, Served with Rice & No Lard Black Beans

#4 Machaca Chicken Tostada & $4.95
Chicken Taco
One Machaca Chicken Tostada & One Hard Shell Chicken Taco, Rice & No Lard Black Beans

#5 Tamales Mexicanos $4.95
One 8 oz. Green Corn Tamale or Garden Vegetable Tamale with Rice & No Lard Black Beans

#6 Chimichanga (Beef or Chicken) $5.95
Deep Fried, Golden Brown Flour Tortilla filled with either Beef or Chicken & topped with Sour Cream, Guacamole, Tomatoes & Cheese, served with Rice & No Lard Black Beans

Chicken Fajita Rice Bowl $4.50
Grilled Marinated Chicken Strips with Sauteed Peppers & Onions in a Bowl of Mexican Rice, with one Flour Tortilla

Brunello

Brunello
RISTORANTE
FINE ITALIAN CUISINE

Brunello's offers one of the most pleasant dining experiences in the East Valley. You'll come to appreciate our intimate setting, which includes a magnificent water front view, attentive service and traditional Italian meal.

PHONE
897-0140

HOURS
Lunch
Monday–Friday
11:30 am–3:00 pm

Dinner
Sunday
4:30 pm–10:00 pm
Monday–Thursday
5:00 pm–10:00 pm
Friday & Saturday
5:00 pm–11:00 pm

LOCATION
1954 South
Dobson Road
Mesa, AZ 85202

CUISINE
Italian

ATTIRE
Casual
(No tank tops for men)

TERRACE DINING
PATIO DINNING
AFTER THEATRE DINING
TAKE OUT
VEGETARIAN MEALS

RESERVATIONS
Suggested

CREDIT CARDS
MasterCard, Visa,
American Express,
Diners Club

SMOKING
Section Available

HANDICAP FACILITIES

Appetizers

Antipasto Brunello	6.75
Escargots De Borgogne	6.75
Stuffed Clams	6.95
Stuffed Eggplant	5.25
New Zealand Mussels	6.95
(Garlic, Wine or Marinara)	
Fried Mozzarella in Marinara	4.75
Calamari Luciana	5.25
Shrimp Cocktail	7.50
Prosciutto Melon	5.95
Stuffed Mushrooms	6.95

Soups

Stracciatella	3.00
Tortellini in Brodo	3.00
Pasta E Fagioli	3.00

Salads

Caesar Salad	4.00
Hearts of Palm and Artichoke	5.25
Tomato Basil	4.00

Pastas
(Served with Salad)

Tortellini Brunello	9.50
(Round Pasta filled with Meat in Cream Sauce with Peas and Prosciutto)	
Fettuccine Alfredo	9.50
(Egg Noodles in Cream Sauce with Parmesan Cheese)	
Cannelloni Fiorentina	9.50
(Pasta filled with Meat and Spinach, topped with Cheese, Bechamel and Meat Sauce)	
Linguini with Clam Sauce	9.50
(White or Red Sauce)	
Ravioli	9.50
(Filled with Cheese and topped with Meat Sauce or Marinara)	

Chicken and Italian Specialties
(Served with Salad and Vegetables)

Chicken Picatta	11.50
(Butter, lemon and white wine)	
Chicken Valdostana	11.95
(Stuffed Breast of Chicken with Prosciutto and Cheese in Marsala and Mushroom Sauce)	
Chicken Parmigiana	11.50
Broiled Marinated Chicken	11.50
(Marinated in Olive Oil and Fresh Herbs)	
Eggplant Parmigiana	9.95
Sausage and Pepper	9.95
Chicken Scarpariella	11.95
(White Wine, Lemon and Sausage)	

Veal and Beef
(served with Salad and Vegetable)

Veal Piccata	13.95
(Butter, Lemon and White Wine)	
Veal Marsala	13.95
(Fresh Mushrooms and Marsala Wine)	
Veal Parmigiana	13.95
Veal Francese	14.25
(Deep Egg Batter, sauteed with White Wine, Lemon, Butter and Capers)	
Veal Saltimbocca	14.50
(Marsala Wine, Spinach, Prosciutto and Cheese)	
Veal Brunello	14.75
(Brandy, Cream and Tarragon)	
Veal Bruscetta	14.25
(Breaded with Fresh Tomato, Onion, Olive Oil and Basil)	
Filet Mignon Green Peppercorn	17.25
New York Steak	15.95

Seafood
(Served with Salad and Vegetable)

Fresh Daily Catch	(Ask Your Server)
Scampi	15.95
(Garlic, Butter and White Wine)	
Shrimp Fra Diavilo	16.95
(Spicy Red Sauce with Mussels and Clams over Linguini)	
Shrimp Michelangelo	15.95
(Sauteed with Cream, Cognac, Shallots, Mushrooms and Tarragon)	
Angel Hair Pescattori	15.95
(Shrimp, Calamari, Scallops, Clams and Mussels in Red Sauce)	
Calamari Marinara	11.95
(Served over Pasta)	
Fettuccini Brunello	15.95
(Shrimp Alfredo Sauce and Broccoli)	
Seafood Brunello	17.95
(Combination of Clams, Mussels, Shrimp, Scallops and Calamari in Red Sauce over Linguini)	

Carolina's PARADISO
CUCINA ITALIANA

"A major league meal from beginning to end!"

—Tony La Russa
Oakland A's Baseball

Antipasta
(tantalizing beginnings)

Calamari Fritti or Alla Griglia 5.95
Fried Calamari or grilled, spicy Marinara Sauce.

Mozzarella Romana 3.95
Fried Mozzarella

Funghi Ripieni 6.95
Stuffed Mushrooms, fresh Crab Meat, sweet Red Peppers, chives, creamy Cognac Shallot Sauce.

Antipasta Caldo Orchestra 8.95
Hot antipasta combo–stuffed Clam, stuffed Mushroom, Eggplant, Artichoke, Shrimp.

Insalata
(Salads)

Caprese 6.50
Buffalo Mozzarella, fresh Basil, Plum Dried Tomatoes drizzled with extra-virgin Olive Oil, Balsamic Vinegar, roasted whole Garlic Cloves

Insalata Cesare
Traditional Caesar 4.95
with grilled Chicken Breast 7.95

Pasta Della Casa
(Savory Flavors of Pasta)

Spaghetti Marinara or Bolgnese 7.95
(tomato or meat sauce)
With Mild or Hot homemade Italian Sausage 8.95

Fettuccine Alfredo or Pesto 8.95
Rich blend of Cream, Butter and imported Cheese or the famed Basil Garlic Sauce from Genoa.

Gnocchi Tricolore 8.95
Potato Dumplings bathed in Alfredo with hints of Marinara and Pesto.

Capellini Portofino 13.95
Angel Hair Pasta tossed with fresh Shrimp, Scallops, Broccoli, Basil, light Marinara Sauce.

Tortellini con Funghi 10.95
Stuffed with imported Porcini Mushrooms, smothered in Mascarpone Creame Sauce.

Linguini Vongole 13.95
Delicate blend of extra-virgin Olive Oil, fresh Clams, Italian Parsley, served Red or White.

Tagliatelli Affumicata 13.95
Imported Egg Pasta, Smoked Salmon, roasted Peppers, fresh Dill, sun-dried Tomatoes, light Vodka Cream Sauce, garnished with tri colored Caviar.

This is a small sample of the wonderful array of food available at Carolina's Paradiso

Manicotti Mondense con Arrogosta 14.95
Pasta stuffed with Ricotta, imported Cheese, Canadian Lobster Sauce Cardinale.

Pollo Marsala 13.95
Sauteed Breast of Chicken, Shallots, Mushrooms, imported Marsala Wine.

Pollo Genovese 13.95
Tender Breast of Chicken, sauteed Artichokes, Capers in a light Lemon White Wine Sauce.

Pollo Parmigiana 13.95
Breaded Chicken Breast, imported Cheese, baked in Marinara Sauce.

Cannelloni 10.95
Delicate blend of Veal, Chicken, Turkey Breast and Herbs, wrapped in Crepe, lavished in Bachamel Sauce.

Vitello Piedmontese 15.95
Veal, thinly sliced marinated in Tomato Citrus, served with braised Belgium Endive and Radicchio.

Scampi 15.95
Jumbo Shrimp sauteed in a luscious Sauce of Garlic, extra-virgin Olive Oil, Scallions, Parsley, Butter and White Sauce.

Gamberi Fra Diavolo 16.95
For the spicy pallet–Jumbo Shrimp sauteed in Herbs, Basil, extra-virgin Olive Oil and spicy Marinara, garnished with fresh Clams and New Zealand over a bed of Linguini.

Speciale Paradisio
(Special Favorites of the House)

Vitello Cuscienetto 15.95
Scallopini of Veal stuffed with Prosciutto, imported Cheese, lavishly served in a Madeira Wine and Mushroom Sauce.

Cioppino Posillipo 18.95
Shrimp, Scallops, Calamari, Clams, Mussels, Fresh Catch braised in Plum Tomato and Saffron, served over a bed of Linguini.

Pesce Spada Balsamico 15.95
Center cut fresh Swordfish loin, grilled with Sweet Peppers, carmelized Pearl Onions with a delicate touch of Balsamic Vinegar.

Maiale (Pork) Milanese 14.95
Superb Pork Tenderloin lightly breaded, pan sauteed and adorned with roasted Garlic Cloves, Capers, fresh Thyme and Lemon.

Agnello (Lamb) Braciole 16.95
Top Round of Lamb stuffed with ground Lamb, Veal hard boiled Egg, Pine-Nuts served in a Lamb Garlic stock and accompanied by Gnocchi.

Anatra (Duck) Ravioli 14.95
Fresh Pasta with roasted Duck and Ricotta served in a succulent Juniper Berry and wild Mushroom Sauce.

Carolinas Paradiso

PHONE
391-3339

HOURS
Lunch
Monday–Friday
11:00 am–2:00 pm
Dinner
Sunday–Thursday
5:00 pm–10:00 pm
Friday–Saturday
5:00 pm–11:00 pm

LOCATION
10155 East Via Linda
(at Mountain View)

CUISINE
Italian

ATTIRE
Casual

ENTERTAINMENT
Week-ends

TERRACE DINING

PATIO DINING

BANQUET FACILITIES

AFTER THEATRE DINING

FULL SERVICE CATERING

VEGETARIAN MEALS

RESERVATIONS
Suggested

CREDIT CARDS
MasterCard, Visa, American Express, Diners Club, Discover

SMOKING
Section Available

HANDICAP FACILITIES

Café Terra Cotta
TUCSON ■ SCOTTSDALE

Cafe Terra Cotta is one of Arizona's critically acclaimed restaurants. Overseen by Donna Nordin, a James Beard nominee for Best Chef: Southwest, Cafe Terra Cotta serves flavorful "Contemporary Southwest Cuisine" in a casual setting. Recommended by the New York Times as the place to go for Southwestern cuisine and featured in articles in Gourmet Magazine and Bon Appetit, placed Cafe Terra Cotta on Arizona's culinary map. Most recently Donna Nordin was named by The Academy of Restaurant and Hospitality Sciences as one of Americas' top 100 chefs and Cafe Terra Cotta as one of the top 10 Southwestern restaurants in the United States.

STARTERS

Shrimp Flautas with Chipotle Chile, ... $7.25
Lightly Deep Fried and Served on a Tomatillo Sauce

Garlic Custard with Warm Salsa Vinaigrette $6.50
and Herbed Hazelnuts

Buffalo Carpaccio with Infused Chili Oil, ... $7.50
Arugla and Shaved Parmesan

Seafood Ceviche Margarita with Tortilla Strips $6.75

Chili Glazed Duck Quesadilla with $7.25
Smoked Gouda and Caramelized Onions

Grilled Portabello Mushroom on a $6.25
Risotto Cake with Cilantro Oil

SALADS

Smoked Acorn Squash Soup, ... $5.75
Chipotle Crema & Scallions

Jennifer's Tortilla Soup $5.25

Mixed Greens, Garlic Croutons, ... $4.95
Citronette Dressing

Southwestern Whole Leaf Caesar Salad $7.25
with Red Chile Croutons

with Grilled Chicken Breast $8.95

Crispy Breaded Calamari on Baby Greens $7.50
with Avocado, Tomato, Red Onion, Queso Fresco
& a Horseradish Tabasco Crema. Served with a
Papaya Tequila Dressing

SMALL PLATES & PASTA

Grilled Shrimp Tostada with Black Beans, ... $12.95
Greens, Red Onion, Tomatoes, Avocado, Pico de Gallo,
Orange Chipotle Dressing and Cilantro Crema

Guajillo-Maple Glazed Rabbit on Baby Greens $11.95
with Carrots and Corn with Chili Oil Dressing

Penne Pasta with Baby Vegetables, ... $12.95
Roasted Garlic, Wild Mushrooms in a
Tomato-Lemon Sauce

Pan-Fried Crabcakes on Hot Basil Slaw $11.75
and Cilantro Tartar Sauce

Chile Rubbed Sea Scallops over Red Pepper $13.75
Fettucine with a trio of Peppers in a saffron-Tequila Butter

Arbol Shrimp Fritters over Cavatapi Pasta $14.25
with Smoked Gouda Cream Sauce, Proscuitto,
Cilantro and Red Chiles

BIG PLATES

Lamb Chops on Sun-Dried Cherry-Ancho $19.00
Mole with Tortilla Lasagne and Whipped Sweet Potatoes

Large Prawns Stuffed with Herbed $16.25
Goat Cheese on a Southwestern Tomato Coulis

Pork Tenderloin Adobado with $15.95
Black Beans and Apricot-Chile Conserve

New York Certified Angus Strip Steak, ... $18.95
Tomatillo-Scallion Butter with Roasted Garlic
Chipotle Mashed Potatoes

Chile Relleno Platter- One Chicken & $14.95
One Shrimp Stuffed Poblano Chile on Red
Pepper Chipotle Sauce, Served with Black Beans

Tortilla Crusted Chicken Breasts with Roasted $14.95
Garlic & Goat Cheese Sauce and Red Pepper Flan

Vegetable Platter of Tortilla Lasagna, ... $13.95
Risotto Cake, Red Pepper Flan, Grilled Portabello
& Spicy Vegetable Flauta

Pacific Coast Salmon Crusted with Sunflower $17.75
Seeds on a Yellow Mole. Served with a
Wild Mushroom Shrimp Tamale and Basil Butter

This Evening's Seafood .... Market Price

PIZZAS FROM THE WOOD BURNING OVEN
(No Substitutions, Please)

BBQ Rabbit Salad on a Pizza $11.95

Grilled Eggplant, Roasted Peppers, Pesto, ... $10.95
Pine Nuts and Smoked Tomato Sauce

Southwestern Duck with Peppers, Spinach, ... $11.45
Pepper Jack and Mozzarella on Honey-Thyme
Whole Wheat Crust

Mesquite Smoked Bacon with Wild $10.95
Mushrooms, Roasted Poblanos and Fontina Cheese

Grilled Chicken with Rosemary, Feta Cheese, ... $10.95
Black Olives, Crushed Chiles & Roasted Garlic

Your Choice - Pepperoni, Black Olives, ... $11.50
Peppers, Tomatoes, Mushrooms, Onions, and/or
Spinach (Chicken and Rabbit extra)

SANDWICHES
(Choice of Fries, Black Beans, Orzo Pasta, or Marinated Vegetables)

Grilled Vegetable Sandwich with $6.95
Fire-Roasted Chiles, Herbed Cheese, Arugula
served on Foccacia

Chicken Breast with Melted Jarlsberg and $7.95
Salsa Mayonnaise

Grilled Mesquite Smoked Ham with Green Chile $7.95
Rajas, Jack Cheese and Rosemary-Habanero Aioli

Sirloin Burger on Onion-Basil Roll or French Bread $7.95

Grilled Salmon BLT Sandwich on $7.95
Onion-Basil Roll with Lime Chipotle Sauce

Side of Salsaq $1.75

DESSERTS

Chocolate Mousse Pie $5.50

Creme Brulee (Vanilla or Fresh Fruit) with Biscotti .. $5.00

Winter Tulipe with Caramel $5.50
Toasted Pinon Ice Cream

Orange Tequila Pear Tart $5.00

Cocoa Pumpkin Cake Brandied Peach Ice Cream $500

Chocolate Marquis with Frangelico and Hazelnuts .. $5.50

Glazed Apple Tart ala Mode $5.00

BEVERAGES

Coffee $1.75

Lemonade $1.75

Espresso $2.25

Ty'nant Sparkling Mineral Water (330ml) $2.25

Sole Still Water (330ml) $2.00

Cappuccino, Cafe Latte, Iced Mocha Latte $2.75

Coke, Diet Coke, Sprite, Ginger Ale, ... $1.25
Milk, Bencheley Teas

Cafe Terra Cotta

PHONE
948-8100

HOURS
Sunday–Thursday
11:30 am–10:00 pm
Friday–Saturday
11:30 am–11:00 pm

LOCATION
6166 North
Scottsdale Road
#100
Scottsdale, AZ 85253

CUISINE
Contemporary
Southwestern

TERRACE DINING

RESERVATIONS
Suggested

CHECKS ACCEPTED

CREDIT CARDS
MasterCard, American Express, Discover, Visa, Diners Club

SMOKING SECTION

HANDICAP FACILITIES

Coyote Springs

20TH ST. LOCATION
PHONE
468-0403
LOCATION
S.E. Corner
20th St. & Camelback

WASHINGTON LOCATION
PHONE
256-6645
LOCATION
122 E. Washington
Phoenix, AZ

HOURS
Lunch (Daily)
11:00 am–5:00 pm
Dinner (Daily)
5:00 am–close

CUISINE
Southwerstern
Brewpub

ATTIRE
Casual

ENTERTAINMENT
Thursday–Sunday

PATIO DINING

BANQUET FACILITIES

FULL SERVICE CATERING

TAKE OUT

VEGETARIAN MEALS

CREDIT CARDS
MasterCard, Visa,
American Express,
Carte Blanc

SMOKING
Section Available
(no pipes, cigars, or cloves)

HANDICAP FACILITIES

"We proudly serve the finest handcrafted ales & lagers, brewed on the premises in our micro brewery located behind our antique bar."

We gladly conduct tours of our brewery and our brewmeister will answer any questions you may have. Please ask your server for details.

In addition Coyote Springs also serves a full bar, with happy hour specials PLUS one or more "guest" beers & ales on a weekly basis; from around the country and the world.

Coyote Springs Brewing Company
Phoenix's Oldest Brewery

Appetizers

Red, White & Blue Nachos $5.45
   add Grilled Chicken $1.25
Sonoran Sausage Roll $3.95
Beer Batter Onion Rings 3.75
Hot Pretzel Basket 3.75
(cheese sauce .75¢)
Squaw Peak Skins $4.25
Beer Batter Mushrooms $3.45
Chilies con Queso 4.25
Coyote Springs Wings
12pcs. $3.95   24pcs. $6.95   36pcs. $795
★ "Best of Show", Arizona Wing Fest '94

Soups & Salads

Sun Chili .... cup $1.95 .... bowl $3.95
pork chunks, ground sirloin, beans & spices, topped with jack & cheddar, with chips
Coyote Caesar $5.95
with romaine lettuce, chili croutons creamy Caesar dressing
Chicken Caesar $7.95
with grilled 7-herb chicken
Salmon Caesar $7.95
grilled salmon filet
Manchurian Chicken Salad $6.95
chicken breast marinated with Asian flavors & grilled, on crisp greens with water chestnuts, mandarin orange, sprouts & crisp noodles, Manchurian dressing
Grilled Vegetable Salad $6.50
grilled seasonal vegetables on crisp greens, tossed with balsamic vinaigrette
Soup of the Day .... cup $1.95 ... bowl $3.95
(ask server for today's creation)

Sandwiches

All sandwiches served with your choice of one side: brew city fries, southwestern pasta salad, jalapeno pineapple slaw, borracho beans, cottage cheese
(after 5pm, baked potato or rice pilaf)

The Coyote club $6.25
tender ham & turkey piled high with swiss & american, bacon, lettuce, tomato, & mayo
The "Real" Reuben $6.50
NY style corned beef piled high with beer-braised sauerkraut & swiss, served with handmade 1000 island on marble rye
7-herb Chicken $6.50
2 breasts marinated in our secret blend of 7 herbs & spices, char-grilled & served with tomatoes, bacon & monterey jack

Coyote's Link Sausage $5.75
our own turkey fajita sausage, grilled, served with peppers, onions & mushrooms, jalapeno jack, with beer horseradish mustard
Caesar Steak $6.95
char-grilled rib-eye steak with romaine lettuce, tomatoes, peppers on toasted baguette with Caesar mayonnaise
Cajun Chicken $6.25
2 breasts, blackened & covered with melted cheddar, on a hoagie roll with lettuce, tomato, red onion on baguette
Texas Tri-Tip $5.95
choice beef marinated in west texas spices & our own ale, grilled, on a potato bun w/jalapeno jack, choice of 3-pepper catsup or red bear BBQ
Smoked Turkey Cobb $5.95
mesquite smoked turkey, tomato, lettuce & bacon on marble rye with bleu cheese mayo
Pastabilities .... (priced right)
always different, always delicious! ask your server for today's creation served with dinner salad

Burgers

The Burger 5.50
1/2 lb. sirloin burger char-grilled to order
BBQ Burger 6.25
with bacon & cheddar, in red bear BBQ sauce
Cheesey Burger 5.95
3 types of cheese melted on 1/2 lb. patty
Texas Red 6.50
1/2 lb. open face, sun chili, cheddar, red onions
New Mexico 6.25
1/2 lb., green chiles, bacon, Jack cheese, salsa
The Gardenburger 5.50
char-grilled veggie burger (no soy), lettuce, tomato, sprouts, Jalapeno Jack, 3 Pepper catsup

Entrees

Served with fresh vegetables & your choice of 1 side plus spent grain bread

Ranch Steak 10.95
11oz. choice rib-eye, char-grilled, side of salsa
Red Bear Ribs 8.95
baby back ribs, grilled, basted w/red bear BBQ
Tri-Mustard Chicken 8.95
2 breast halves, deglazed w/white wine, shallots, mushrooms, simmered in beer mustard, dijon, english mustard & sweet cream
Chicken Relleno 8.95
jumbo breast stuffed w/cilantro pesto & green chiles, grilled, topped w/Jack & cheddar
Grilled Salmon 10.95
fresh salmon honey glazed, w/black bean salsa
Fish & Chips 7.95
icelandic cod deep fried in beer batter, w/crispy brew fries, Jalapeno tartar sauce & malt vinegar

CAFESTIA
Cosmopolitan Coffeehouse · Patisserie · Bar

Already all our local, national and international friends and among them the most prominent visitors that have visited the Greekfest have labeled Cafestia the most beautiful coffee house in Phoenix.

A visit to Cafestia above everything else, will also be an aesthetic experience

Cafestia

Once upon a time "cafeneio": a coffee house was the place for relaxation and companionship where people gathered to discuss and solve small and not so small problems. Now people have changed and with them many and beautiful things have changed. But not at the coffee house CAFESTIA that is housed in the Greekfest Center

CAFESTIA derives its name from the word cafe and Estia, the Hellenic goddess of the hearth, of the centre to which life returns to be replenished, the essence of things, even the center of the center of the world.

At CAFESTIA the older generation will find whatever was lost in the "transition" and the younger generation will discover an environment purely European with the style and architectural reminders of Greece.

CAFESTIA is the place for an all day affair. The day starts with a variety of coffees, teas, juices and on premises baked goods, fruits and cheeses, it continues on through mid-day with light snacks, European desserts and canapes, and it turns into a civilized cafe-bar in the evening, with uniquely prepared "Ouzomezethes" or appetizers to match your drinks.

The decor of Cafestia incorporates many of the design elements of the Byzantine Era in a harmonic synthesis where the granite, the marble, the bronze and the wood dominate.

Morning
- Housemade Yogurt, mild & creamy with nuts & honey or fresh fruit
- Seasonal fresh fruit plate with selected imported cheeses
- Petite Greek dougnuts (loukoumathes)

Midday
- Roasted chicken & vegetable sandwich on housebaked bread
- Roasted lamb & vegetable sandwich on housebaked bread
- Grilled vegetable & cheese sandwich on housebaked bread

Traditional Tea Time
- Sweet Tea—a two cup pot of your choice of beverage and a selection of cream cheese and preserve sandwiches and fresh baked cookies.
- Mixed Tea—a two cup pot of your choice of beverage, Cafestia smoked fish and minted cheese sandwiches, cream cheese and preserve sandwich and fresh baked cookie

Evening
- Hot "ouzomezethes"
- Baked stuffed eggplant
- Pita Bites®
- Smoked fish
- Minted feta dip with bread
- Marinated red pepper and eggplant
- Aegean roasted salad

Cafestia

PHONE
265-5509
CAFESTIA
Daily
7:00 am–Midnight
LOCATION
1940 East
Camelback Road
Phoenix, AZ 85016

CUISINE
Greek
ATTIRE
Elegant Casual

RESERVATIONS
Suggested
CREDIT CARDS
MasterCard, Visa, American Express, Diners Club, Discover
SMOKING
Section Available
HANDICAP FACILITIES

Chances Are !! Restaurant-Lounge

Chances Are Restaurant has been heralded as one of Scottsdale's finest eating places...and with sensible prices! Our executive chef and staff are award winnning experts. Our experience and skills are your assurance of superb food...whether a business luncheon, or a sumptuous special occasion gourmet meal. For entertainment, relax in our wonderful lounge with quiet music and dancing.

APPETIZERS

JUMBO SHRIMP COCKTAIL — $6.50
Gulf shrimp served with cocktail sauce.

ESCARGOT — $6.50
Giant snails, baked in garlic, shallots and white wine with mushroom caps.

OYSTERS ROCKEFELLER — $6.75
Baked in a classic spinach and sherry sauce.

OYSTERS ON THE HALF SHELL — $6.00
Served with cocktail sauce.

SCAMPI — $6.50
Jumbo Gulf Shrimp sautéed in garlic, shallots, white wine and butter.

SOUPS

FRENCH ONION GRATINEE — $3.50
THE SOUP-OF-THE-DAY CUP — $2.50
BOWL — $3.50

SALADS

CAESAR SALAD — $4.50
Crispy romaine tossed in a creamy Caesar dressing with croutons and Parmesan cheese.

HOUSE SALAD — $2.50
Crispy garden greens. Choice of dressing.

PASTAS

Our pastas are served with the soup of the day or salad with bread.

FETTUCCINI MILAN — $11.50
With spicy sausage, pepper, onions, and mushrooms.

LINGUINI — $11.50
White or red clam sauce.

PASTA BELLA — $13.50
Scallops, shrimp and salmon sautéed with fresh tomato, artichoke hearts and basil in a light pink sauce over linguini.

PASTA MARINARA — $9.50
With sausage or meatballs. — $11.50

ENTREES

Served with your choice of baked potato, mashed potatoes, or rice with vegetables.

NEW YORK SHRIMP STEAK — $13.50
Broiled to your liking, served with mushroom caps.

TENDERLOIN FILET — $14.50
PETITE CUT — $12.50
The most tender of meats, broiled, served with bernaise or bordelais sauce.

PORK CHOPS — $11.50
Center cut, broiled, served with fresh apple, raisin and apple brandy sauce.

LAMB CHOPS — $17.50
Broiled French Lamb, served with mint jelly.

HOUSE SPECIAL STEAK — $14.50
Broiled New York strip, topped with sautéed mushrooms and onions in brandy sauce.

Chances Are Prime Rib

Served with choice of:
rice, mashed potatoes, or baked potato

Regular Cut — $13.50
English Cut — $12.50

Served Friday and Saturday

FISH

Served with your choice of baked potato, mashed potatoes, or rice with vegetables.

SHRIMP SCAMPI — $14.00
Jumbo Gulf Shrimp sautéed in garlic, shallots, and white wine butter.

BEER BATTERED SHRIMP — $14.00
Dipped in light beer batter and deep fried. Served with two tone sauce.

SHRIMP GABRIELLE — $14.50
Mushrooms, Scallions and Tomatoes sautéed in a butter and white wine sauce.

FILET OF SALMON — $13.00
Fresh from the Pacific, broiled or baked. Served with lemon caper or dill hollandaise sauce.

RUBY RED TROUT — $12.50
Fresh trout, grilled, served with toasted almond sauce or lemon caper butter.

SCALLOPS — $12.50
Sautéed or deep fried.

CHICKEN

Served with your choice of baked potato, mashed potatoes, or rice with vegetables.

BROILED HALF CHICKEN — $10.50
Marinated with herb and white wine. Broiled crispy.

CHICKEN SCALOPPINI — $10.95
Chicken breast, sautéed with mushrooms, red wine sauce.

CHICKEN PICCATTA — $11.50
Chicken breast sautéed in lemon, garlic, and white wine topped with capers.

CHICKEN CHARDONNAY — $11.50
Boneless chicken breast sautéed in butter, white wine, mushrooms, lemon, and shallots sauce.

VEAL

Served with your choice of baked potato, mashed potatoes, or rice with vegetables.

VEAL PICCATA — $13.50
Tender loin medallion, sautéed with mushrooms, capers, in white wine and lemon butter.

VEAL MARSALA — $13.50
Tenderloin medallions sautéed with mushrooms in marsala wine butter.

VEAL PARMIGIANA — $12.50
Cutlet lightly breaded, pan fried, topped with Marinara and mozzarella and baked.

ASSORTED DESSERTS — $2.50

Chances Are

PHONE
994–4338

HOURS
Lunch
Monday–Sunday
11:00 am–5:00 pm

Dinner
Monday–Sunday
5:00 pm–10:00 pm

LOCATION
7570 East 6th Avenue
& Miller Road
Scottsdale, AZ

CUISINE
Continental

ATTIRE
Semi-Casual

LOUNGE
11:00 am–1:00 am

ENTERTAINMENT
Dancing & Live Music Nightly

BANQUET FACILITIES

FULL SERVICE CATERING

TAKE OUT

VEGETARIAN MEALS

RESERVATIONS
Suggested

CREDIT CARDS
MasterCard, Visa, American Express, Diners Club, Discover

NON-SMOKING
Section Available

HANDICAP FACILITIES

CHIANTI
RISTORANTE

Come enjoy the real taste of Italy at Chianti. We offer a wide variety of authentic Italian dishes at affordable prices, in a friendly relaxed atmosphere where you'll really feel at home. Chianti is conveniently located on the southwest corner of 40th street and Camelback. Come see us soon!

APPETIZERS & SALADS

CAESAR SALAD	3.95
FOR TWO	5.50

Traditional Caesar Salad with Parmesan Croutons

NEAPOLITAN SALAD	3.50

Tomato, Onion, Olives and Fresh Basil Dressing

COLD ANTIPASTO	7.95

A Combination of Italian Gourmet Meats and Cheeses on a Bed of Mixed Greens, Garnished with Marinated Artichoke, Tomato Wedges, Black Olives with Chianti's Special Herb Dressing

MOZZARELLA CAPRESE	5.95

Fresh Mozzarella, Tomato, Basil and Olive Oil

MOZZARELLA FRITTA	4.50

Topped with Fresh Tomato Sauce and Basil

PASTA AS YOU LOVE IT
Served with a Fresh Garden Salad

SPAGHETTI WITH MEATBALLS OR SAUSAGE	7.95

Spaghetti Served with Meat Sauce and Meatballs or Sausage

CANNELLONI FIORENTINA	7.95

Crepes Stuffed with Chicken, Veal, Spinach and Parmesan Cheese

ANGEL HAIR POMODORO E BASILICO	6.95

Angel Hair with Fresh Tomato and Basil Sauce

FETTUCCINI ALFREDO	7.95

Egg Pasta with Cream Sauce and Parmesan Cheese

BAKED LASAGNA	8.95

Baked Pasta Layered with Ricotta, Sausage and Meat Sauce

TORTELLONI PRINCIPESSA	9.95

Pasta Filled with Chicken and Prosciutto. Served in Alfredo Sauce with Mushrooms, Parmesan Cheese and Walnuts

HOMEMADE CHEESE RAVIOLI	7.95

Ravioli Stuffed with Ricotta Cheese and Topped with Marinara or Meat Sauce

LINGUINI WITH CLAM SAUCE	9.95

Linguini with Baby Clams Sauteed in Garlic, Olive Oil and Parsley

PIZZA

PIZZA MARGHERITA	8.95

Fresh Tomato, Mozzarella, Fresh Basil and Olive Oil

PIZZA ROMANA	10.95

Onion, Mushrooms, Pancetta, Mozzarella, Romano Cheese and Tomato

PIZZA PUTTANESCA	9.95

Black Olives, Capers, Anchovies, Mozzarella and Fresh Tomato

PIZZA DIAVOLA	10.95

Tomato, Garlic, Pepperoni, Sausage, Mozzarella and Fresh Herbs

CHIANTI FAVORITES
Served with fresh garden salad, pasta of the day and fresh vegetables

BREAST OF CHICKEN PARMIGIANA	$8.95

Sauteed Chicken Cutlet Topped with Marinara Sauce and Mozzarella Cheese

STUFFED EGGPLANT WITH RICOTTA	9.95

Sauteed Slices of Eggplant Stuffed with Ricotta Cheese and Baked with Marinara Sauce and Romano Cheese

BREAST OF CHICKEN MARSALA	$9.95

Sauteed Chicken with Mushroom and Marsala Wine Sauce

VEAL PICCATTA	12.95

Sauteed Veal Scaloppine with Lemon and Butter Sauce

VEAL PARMIGIANA	12.95

Sauteed Veal Cutlet with Marinara Sauce and Mozzarella Cheese

FRUTTI DI MARE	12.95

Fresh Mussels, Clams, Scungilli and Calamari, Braised with White Wine, Garlic and Tomato. Served Over Linguini

ANGEL HAIR PESCATORE	12.95

Calamari, Scallops and Shrimp Braised with Garlic in Our Special Fresh Tomato Basil Sauce Served over Angel Hair Pasta

CALAMARI FRADIAVOLO	11.95

Sauteed Calamari Braised with Garlic, Olive Oil and White Wine. Served on a Bed of Linguini in spicy marinara sauce

---

Chianti

PHONE
957-9840

HOURS
Monday–Friday
11:30 am–10:00 pm
Saturday & Sunday
5:00 pm–10:00 pm

LOCATION
3957 East
Camelback Road
Phoenix, AZ 85018

CUISINE
Italian

ATTIRE
Casual

TAKE OUT

VEGETARIAN MEALS

RESERVATIONS
Suggested

CREDIT CARDS
MasterCard, Visa,
American Express

CHECKS ACCEPTED

SMOKING
Section Available

HANDICAP FACILITIES

Christopher's

Christopher's, the ultimate in dining elegance, spotlights the classical yet innovative presentations of Chef Christopher Gross honored as Best Chef of the Southwest, James Beard Foundation, Mobil 4 Stars and as a member of the Fine Dining Hall of Fame by Nation's Restaurant News, Christopher's offers guests Chef Christopher's contemporary French cuisine, unique presentations and spectacular wine list in a luxuriously appointed European setting. Both a la carte and prix fixe menu dining are available combined with Christopher's award winning wine list featuring an extensive wine by the glass program.

STARTERS

Caviar (Osetra) — 42.00

Salad of Greens with Forest Mushrooms — 11.50
SALADE AUX CHAMPIGNONS DE FORET

Soup of Wild Mushrooms with Foie Gras — 14.00
SOUPE DE CHAMPIGNONS SAUVAGES AU FOIE GRAS

Salad of Foie Gras with Yams and Mushroom Chips — 20.00
SALADE DE FOIE GRAS AUX PATATES DOUCES ET CHAMPIGNONS FRITS

Terrine of Hudson Valley Foie Gras A.B.C. Prepared Three Ways — 20.00
TERRINE DE FOIE GRAS DE LA VALLEE DE L'HUDSON PREPAREE DE TROIS FAÇONS

Ravioli of Petit Gris in a Mild Garlic Sauce — 14.00
RAVIOLES DE PETIT GRIS AVEC UNE SAUCE LEGERE A L'AIL

Roasted Arizona Squab Served with Quinoa — 14.00
PETIT PIGEON ROTI D'ARIZONA AU QUINOA

MAIN COURSES

Roasted Halibut with Forest Mushrooms — 29.00
FLETAN ROTI AUX CHAMPIGNONS DE FORET

Sautéed California Striped Bass with Bokchoy in a Carrot Sauce — 29.00
LOUP DE MER SAUTE AVEC DU BOK CHOY ET UNE SAUCE AUX CAROTTES

Steamed Salmon with Peashoots, Beets in a Lemon Sauce — 29.00
SAUMON A L'ETUVE AVEC DES POUSSES DE PETITS POIS ET BETTERAVES

Duck with Roasted Pears in a Red Wine Sauce — 29.00
CANARD AUX POIRES ROTIES AVEC UNE SAUCE AU VIN ROUGE

Sautéed Sweetbreads with Black Trumpets — 29.00
RIS DE VEAU POELES AVEC DES TROMPETTES DE LA MORT

Sautéed Lamb with Ratatouille and Turnip Dauphinoise — 29.00
AGNEAU POELE AVEC UNE RATATOUILLE ET UN GRATIN DAUPHINOIS AUX NAVETS

Faux Filet with Fareki, in a Red Wine Sauce — 29.00
FAUX FILET AU FAREKI AVEC UNE SAUCE AU VIN ROUGE

Roast Squab with Girolles and Bouillon of Foie Gras — 29.00
PIGEON ROTI AVEC SES GIROLLES ET FOND DE FOIE GRAS

ALL MAIN COURSES ARE AVAILABLE AT HALF-PRICE AS APPETIZERS

We would like to invite you to adjourn to our Patio to enjoy your dessert, coffee and after dinner drinks. Please ask your server for details.

CHRISTOPHER'S DESSERT MENU

Plateau de Fromages — $7.50
ASSORMENT OF CHEESES

Vanilla Flan — $7.50
SERVED WITH FRESH FRUIT

Parnassienne de Mousse au Chocolat — $7.50
CHOCOLATE TOWER

Soufflés — $7.50
CHOICE OF FLAVORS

Nougat Glacé — $7.50
WITH RASBERRY SORBET

Gateau de Fromage — $7.50
CHEESE CAKE WITH FRUIT HONEY SAUCE

Fruits Frais en Saison — $7.50
SEASONAL FRESH FRUITS

Chaud et Froid au Chocolat — $7.50
HOT AND COLD CHOCOLATE

Crèmes Glacées Assorties — $7.50
ASSORTMENT OF ICE CREAMS

CHRISTOPHER'S OPORTO

1032 Dow's Crusted Oporto	$11.00
1049 Dow's Vintage 1977	$26.00
1054 Dow's Vintage 1983	$16.00
1052 Warre's Vintage 1980	$14.00
1039 Gould Campbell Vintage 1970	$14.00

DESSERT WINES

1207 Christopher's "Pierced Cuvée" ($8.25)
Bonny Doon Vineyard (Santa Cruz)

1206 Vin de Glacier, Bonny Doon ($8.50)
Muscat (Santa Cruz)

1232 Dolce, Far Niente ($20.00)
Semillon (napa)

MADEIRA

1084 Leacock's 10 Year Bual	$9.50
1080 Blandy's 10 Year Malmsey	$8.50
1088 Cossart Malmsey 1952	$18.00
1087 Cossart Sersial 1940	$20.00

See Wine list for a complete list of: Cognacs, Armagnacs, Eaux de Vie, Ports, Madeiras and Sherrys

Christopher's Blend Coffee
Freshly Roasted and Custom Blended for Christopher's

Menu Dégustation
The Participation of Your Entire Dining Party is Required for the Menu Dégustation

AMUSE-GUEULES
Petit Amour with Snow Peas

Lobster Ravioli with Tomatoes and Cucumber
RAVIOLI DE HOMARD AUX TOMATES ET CONCOMBRES
Castello Gancia, Sparkling Wine (Italy)

Salad of Sauteed Foie Gras with Yams and Mushroom Chips
SALADE DE FOIE GRAS SAUTE AVEC DES POMMES DE TERRE
Vouvray, Barton & Guestier (France)

Roasted Halibut with Forest Mushrooms
FLETAN ROTI AUX CHAMPIGNONS DE FORET
Bourgogne "Les Satilles" O.Leflaive
(Burgundy, France)

Roasted Arizona Squab Served with Quinoa
PETIT PIGEON D'ARIZONA ROTI AU QUINOA
Calera, Pinot Noir (Central Coast)

Sauteed Sweetbreads with Black Trumpets
RIS DE VEAU POELES AVEC DES TROMPETTES DE LA MORT
Bonny Doon, Vin Gris de Cigare (California)

Plateau de Fromages
(Maytag Blue Cheese, St. André and Tete de Moine)
Sandeman Oporto (Founders Reserve)

DESSERTS

Christopher's Apricot Tower
PARNASSIENNE AUX ABRICOTS
Bonny Doon, Christopher's "Pierced Cuvée",
Marsanne (Santa Cruz)

MIRANDISES
TARTES AU CHOCOLAT
CAFE

MENU PRESTIGE $75.00
WITH WINES OF THE WORLD $115.00

Christopher's

PHONE
957-3214

HOURS
Dinner
Tuesday– Sunday
6:00 pm–10:00 pm

LOCATION
2398 East
Camelback Road
Phoenix, AZ 85016

CUISINE
French Contemporary

ATTIRE
Jacket Required

VALET PARKING

FULL SERVICE CATERING

VEGETARIAN MEALS

RESERVATIONS
Suggested

CREDIT CARDS
MasterCard, Visa,
American Express,
Diners Club, Discover,
Carte Blanche

HANDICAP FACILITIES

Christopher's Bistro

Christopher's Bistro, ideal for more relaxed dining combines the spontaneity of a French bistro with the very best of American International cuisine. The Bistro has been lauded as "4 Stars. Exceptional" by Food & Wine and as "two of this country's best dining rooms" by the New York Times. The finest and freshest of ingredients, the deceptively simple yet elegant presentations of Chef Christopher, the highly trained professional staff and the award winning wine list combine to create a uniquely memorable dining experience.

BISTRO DINNER STARTERS

CAVIAR (OSETRA) 1/2oz. 21.00 1oz. 42.00
with tortillas españolas and fresh cream
Louis Roederer, Brut Premier
(Montagne de Reims) $11.00

CREAM OF WHITE BEAN SOUP　　5.25
WITH ESSENCE OF WHITE TRUFFLE
Santa Margherita, Pinot Grigio, (Italy) $ 7.50

SOUP OF RED BELL PEPPERS　　5.25
(Original Creation Published in "Bon Appetit" 1984)
Hugel "Gentil" (Alsace) $ 5.00

CREAM OF LOBSTER SOUP　　6.95
Scharffenberger, Sparkling Wine (Mendocino) $ 8.00

ESCARGOTS "CLASSIC"　　10.25
(please allow 15 minutes for baking time)
Calera, Pinot Noir (Central Coast) $ 7.50

SALAD OF HOT SAUTÉED　　14.95
FOIE GRAS
Vouvray, Barton & Guestier (Loire) $ 6.00

WARM ONION TART　　6.95
WITH A GOAT CHEESE SAUCE
Morgan Winery, Sauvignon Blanc (Sonoma) $ 6.00

ANGEL HAIR PASTA　　8.95
WITH SHITAKE MUSHROOMS AND
ESSENCE OF WHITE TRUFFLE
Trimbach, Riesling (Alsace) $ 6.75

ROASTED GOAT CHEESE　　9.95
WITH GARLIC, THYME AND BACON
ON A BED OF GREENS
Grgich Hills, Fume Blanc (Napa) $ 9.00

PANACHE OF VINE RIPENED　　9.95
TOMATOES AND FRESH
MOZZARELLA SERVED WITH
A BOUQUET GARNI OF MIXED
GREENS AND BASIL
Chateau de Sancerre, Sancerre (France) $ 8.75

FIELD GREENS SALAD　　5.25
WITH CONFIT VEGETABLES
Hugel "Gentil," an Alsatian Blend (France) $ 5.00

VEGETABLE SIDE DISHES

Straw Potatoes	2.50
Gratin Dauphinois	3.50
Pommes Frites	2.50
Mashed Potatoes	2.50
Mixed Vegetables	3.50
Shallot Risotto (with mushrooms) 3.50	
Onion Rings	3.50
Broccoli	3.50

DINNER MAIN COURSES

GRILLED FILET OF PRIME　　22.95
BEEF WITH ONION RINGS WITH A
CHOICE OF RED WINE, BEARNAISE
OR AU POIVRE SAUCE
Heitz, Cabernet Sauvignon (Napa) $ 9.00

GRILLED PRIME USDA SIRLOIN　　22.95
WITH POMMES FRITES WITH A
CHOICE OF RED WINE, BEARNAISE
OR AU POIVRE SAUCE
Clos du Val, Cabernet Sauvignon (Napa) $ 7.00

GRILLED RACK OF LAMB,　　22.95
FLAVORED WITH ROSEMARY AND
SORGHUM GLACE SERVED WITH
A GRATIN OF POTATOES
Sterling Three Palms, Merlot (Napa) $ 10.00

MARINATED VEAL CHOP　　22.95
WITH MASHED POTATOES
Armida, Pinot Noir (Russian River) $ 7.00

CASSOULET OF DUCK WITH   16.95
MASHED POTATOES, SAGE AND
ESSENCE OF WHITE TRUFFLE
Bonny Doon, Le Cigare Volant (California) $ 9.00

SMOKED AND BRAISED LAMB   20.95
SHANKS WITH A 'BRICK' OF GREEN
LENTILS AND WHEATBERRIES
Storybook Mountain, Zinfandel (Napa) $ 8.00

SMOKED OSSO BUCO   20.95
WITH MUSHROOM RISOTTO
Tinto Pesquera, Ribera del Duero,
Tempranillo (Spain) $ 8.25

GRILLED ONGLET STEAK   17.95
WITH SAUTÉED SHALLOTS
AND A RED WINE SAUCE
SERVED WITH POMMES FRITES
Frog's Leap, Zinfandel (Napa) $ 8.25

PASTA WITH WILD MUSHROOMS   15.95
Trimbach, Gewürztraminer (Alsace) $ 7.50

GRILLED SALMON WITH   18.50
CUCUMBER AND DILL
Logan, Robert Talbott Vineyard, Chardonnay
(Monterey) $ 8.75

GRILLED AHI TUNA WITH   20.95
PANCETTA, CABBAGE AND SHIITAKE
Robert Mondavi Pinot Noir,
unfiltered (Napa Valley) $ 8.50

GRILLED COD SERVED IN A   17.95
TOMATO SAUCE WITH PROVENÇAL
VEGETABLES
Bourgogne "Les Satilles" O.Leflaive (Burgundy) $ 6.75

GRILLED HALIBUT WITH BOK   17.95
CHOY AND BABY CARROTS IN
A SAFFRON SAUCE
Markham, Chardonnay (Napa) $ 7.75

ALL FISH AND MEAT PREPARED AT
MEDIUM RARE TEMPERATURE UNLESS
OTHERWISE REQUESTED

DESSERT MENU

Banana Split $ 5.75

Tarte Bressanne $ 5.75

Assortment of Cheeses $ 6.75

Fresh Fruit in Season $ 6.50

Assortment of Ice Creams $ 4.75

Vanilla Flan $ 5.75

Chocolate Tower $ 5.75
(With Illycaffé Espresso Sauce)

Soufflés $ 5.50
(Flavor? If we have it we'll make it)

Cheesecake $ 5.75
(Served with Fruits, Champagne Honey Sauce and Almonds)

Croustillant of Strawberries $ 5.25

Cookies and Ice Cream $ 5.50
Chocolate Chip Cookies with Assorted Ice Creams

Chocolate Festival $ 5.75

Apple Tart with Vanilla Ice Cream $ 5.50

Cannelés de Bordeaux with Vanilla Ice Cream $ 5.75

Assortment of Sorbets $ 4.75

MAY WE RECOMMEND

Christopher's Suggested Wine by the Glass to Complement Menu. Selected by Paola Gross, Wine Director

See Our Wine List for a Complete Selection of Over Seventy Wines By The Glass From $4 - $19

Christopher's Bistro

PHONE
957-3214

HOURS
Luncheon
Monday–Saturday
11:00 am–5:00 pm
Dinner
Nightly
5:00 pm–10:00 pm

LOCATION
2398 East
Camelback Road
Phoenix, AZ 85016

CUISINE
American International

ATTIRE
Casual

PATIO DINING

VALET PARKING

FULL SERVICE CATERING

VEGETARIAN MEALS

RESERVATIONS
Suggested

CREDIT CARDS
MasterCard, Visa,
Amerinan Express,
Diners Club, Discover,
Carte Blanche

HANDICAP FACILITIES

Different Pointe of View

PHONE
863-0912

HOURS
Daily
6:00 pm–10:00 pm

LOCATION
11111 North 7th Street
Phoenix, AZ 85020
The Pointe Hilton
Resort at Tapatio Cliffs

CUISINE
Classical Cuisine

ATTIRE
Casual

LOUNGE
5:00 pm until 1:00 am

SUNDAY BRUNCH
10:00 am–1:30 pm
(except June–Sept.)

TERRACE DINING

ENTERTAINMENT
Wednesday–Saturday
9:00 pm–1:00 am

DANCING
Wednesday–Saturday
9:00 pm–1:00 am

VEGETARIAN MEALS

RESERVATIONS
Suggested

CREDIT CARDS
MasterCard, Visa,
American Express,
Diners Club, Discover

SMOKING
Section Available

HANDICAP FACILITIES

This award-winning mountaintop restaurant features elegance above all. Gourmet selections featuring garden fresh cuisine, breathtaking views, first rate service and an internationally acclaimed wine cellar combine to create one of the Valley's most memorable dining experiences. The menu is based on Classical Cuisine and features the daily harvest from the mountainside Chef's Garden including Rack of Lamb with Rosemary and Thyme, French-style Veal Chop with Mushroom-Foie Gras Stuffing and Tarragon Beurre Blanc and Chef's selection of Wild Game of the Day.

Classical à la Carte Cuisine

Starters

Escargot Bourguignonne
Garlic - Shallots - Fresh Herbs
$8.00

Oysters Rockefeller
Spinach - Bacon - Tomato - Mornay Sauce
$8.00

Shrimp Cocktail
Traditional Red Sauce
$10.00

House-Smoked Salmon
Herbed Creme Fraiche
$8.00

Fresh Oysters on the Half Shell
Spiced Sun-Dried Tomato-Herb Vinaigrette

Soup du Jour
$4.00

French Onion Soup Gratinée
$4.00

Caesar Salad
Prepared for Two
$12.00

Mixed Baby Greens Salad
Lingonberry Vinaigrette
$4.00

Smoked Mozzarella Cheese Salad
Apples and Pecans with Orange Mint Dressing
$7.00

Entrees

Filet Mignon
"Chateau-Style" Bordelaise and Béarnaise Sauce
"Traditional-Style" Sautéed Onions and Wild Mushrooms
"Garlic-Roasted" Portabella Demi Glaze
$26.00

Rack of Lamb
Rosemary and Thyme
$28.00

Shrimp Provencale
Sauteed with Garlic, Tomatoes and Fresh Herbs
$24.00

Filet of Salmon
Baked in Parchment Paper with a Julienne of Vegetables
$24.00

French-Style Veal Chop
Wrapped in House-Smoked Bacon - Mushroom-Foie Gras Stuffing - Tarragon Beurre Blanc
$26.00

Grilled Marinated Lamb Chops
Tomato-Basil Relish
$28.00

Double-Roasted Smoked Duck Breast
Lingonberry Sauce - Sautéed Mixed Greens
$24.00

Wild Game of the Day
Chef's Choice of Preparation
$29.00

DON AND CHARLIE'S
American Rib & Chop House

Happy Hour
Best of Phoenix, New Times, '87, '88, '89
Best of Phoenix, New Times, Readers Choice, '90

New York Strip
Best of Phoenix, New Times, '88

BBQ Ribs
Best of Phoenix, New Times, Readers Choice, '88, '89
Best of Phoenix, New Times, '88, '89

Garlic Chicken
Best of Phoenix, New Times, '87

Appetizers
Fried Calamari, Lemon, Cocktail sauce	$5.95
Onion Strings (serves 2)	$4.45
Jumbo shrimp Cocktail (serves 5)	$8.95
Shrimp De Jonghe	$8.95
Frogs' Legs, Garlic Butter	$7.95
Don's Garlic Cheese Toast (serves 2)	$3.50
House Salad	$3.50
Cole Slaw (creamy or deli-style)	$2.50

Entree Salads
Caesar Salad*	$7.95
Cajun Chicken Caesar Salad*	$8.95
Garbage Salad*	$8.95
Salmon Pasta Salad*	$12.95

Fresh salmon, sun-dried tomatoes, hearts of palm, artichoke hearts, fresh asparagus, capers, black olives, roma tomatoes, and rainbow pasta.

Children's Portions
12 years or younger. Children's portions come with a choice of coleslaw or salad, and french fries.

BBQ Ribs	$7.95
Hamburger	$5.50
Cheeseburger	$5.50
BBQ Chicken	$5.95
Grilled Cheese	$4.95

Side Dishes/Vegetable
Sauteed Mushrooms	$3.45
Creamed Spinach	$3.95
Cauliflower Au Gratin	$3.95
Baked Macaroni	$2.95
Cajun Rice	$2.50

Chicken
Garlic Chicken, Cajun Rice (half chicken)	$11.95
Garlic Chicken, Cajun rice (whole chicken)	$14.95
Garlic Chicken, Peppers, Onions and Mushrooms	$15.95
BBQ Chicken (half chicken)	$11.95
BBQ Chicken (whole chicken)	$13.95
Chicken Schnitzel, Lemon Butter Sauce	$13.95
Chicken & Pasta	$12.95
Southwestern Style BBQ Chicken (whole chicken)	$13.95

Our Famous Barbeque
Slow smoked over hickory wood.

BBQ Baby Back Ribs (full slab)	$15.95
BBQ Rib and Chicken Combination	$15.95
BBQ Rib and Filet Mignon Combination (8 oz.)	$19.95
Southwestern Style Back Ribs (full slab)	$15.95
BBQ Pork Chops (full pound)	$14.95

Prime Rib
Carefully selected and aged, then slow roasted to perfection. Cooked fresh daily—served until we run out.

Small Cut, Horseradish Sauce	$16.95
Large Cut, Horseradish Sauce	$18.95
Prime Rib Bones, Horseradish Sauce	$12.95
Prime Rib Bones, BBQ Style	$12.95

Prime Steak
Filet Mignon (12 oz.)	$19.95
Prime New York Sirloin (16 oz)	$23.95
Prime New York Sirloin (fresh garlic)	$24.95
Prime Ribeye Steak (14 oz.)	$18.95
Top Sirloin (14 oz.)	$16.95
Rib Lamb Chops (3)	$23.95
Grilled Veal Chop (14 oz.)	$22.95
Calves Liver, Peppers, Onions and Mushrooms	$12.95
Chopped Steak (16 oz.)	$11.95
Mumsie's Chopped Steak, Onions, Peppers	$12.95

Fish and Seafood Pasta
Fresh Fish of the Day (consult our server)	Market
Shrimp De Jonghe	$14.95
Fried Shrimp, cocktail Sauce	$14.95
Frogs' Legs, Garlic Butter	$14.95
Pasta Primavera*	$10.95
Pasta Primavera (with shrimp) *	$13.95

Entrees and specialties include chopped liver, bread basket, cole slaw (deli-style or creamy) or salad, with your choice of dressing, House Anchovy Dressing, 1000 Island, Creamy Garlic, Bleu-Cheese, Vinaigrette, and Lo-Cal spa Vinaigrette, (Caesar salad with entree, $2.50 extra) and choice of au gratin, baked, double-baked or french fries. (*Does not include potato)

Don & Charlies

PHONE
990-0900

HOURS
Monday–Thursday
5:00 pm–10:00 pm
Friday & Saturday
5:00 pm–10:30 pm
Sunday
4:30 pm–9:00 pm

LOCATION
7501 East
Camelback Road
Scottsdale, AZ 85251

CUISINE
American

HAPPY HOUR
Monday–Friday
5:00 pm–6:30 pm

EARLY EVENING MENU
Monday–Friday
5:00 pm–6:00 pm

BANQUET FACILITIES

TAKE OUT

RESERVATIONS
Suggested

CREDIT CARDS
MasterCard, Visa, American Express, Diners Club, Discover

CHECKS ACCEPTED

HANDICAP FACILITIES

El Choro Lodge

PHONE
948-5170

HOURS
Monday–Friday
11:00 am–3:00 pm &
5:30 pm–11:00 pm
Friday & Saturday
9:00 am–3:00 pm &
5:30 pm–11:00 pm

LOCATION
5550 East
Lincoln Drive
Scottsdale, AZ 85252

CUISINE
Mexican
ATTIRE
Casual
TERRACE DINING
BANQUET FACILITIES
Up to 250 People
FULL SERVICE CATERING
VEGETARIAN MEALS

RESERVATIONS
Suggested
CREDIT CARDS
MasterCard, Visa,
American Express,
Diners Club, Discover
SMOKING
Section Available
HANDICAP FACILITIES

EL CHORRO LODGE

Ask the locals; ask the movie, television and sports celebrities; and ask the first-time visitor who was there just last night. The answers will all be the same: "You have not been to the Valley unless you have experienced their fine dining or sat under an Arizona moon on their spacious patio."

"Outwardly little has changed at El Chorro Lodge over the past 50 plus years. A juniper fire still glows on the outdoor hearth and the Gruber's sticky bun recipe still gets raves. Most important, the family feeling continues. Guests recognize it in the longtime staff that operates the rambling restaurant. Finally, they sense it in the attitude of the regular patrons who still see El Chorro as a kind of private lodge.

"We are sort of a club for many of our guests," Joe and Evie Miller say with a smile."

–Author Pam Hait

"Best Place to Eat Outdoors"
Reader's Choice
Best of Phoenix

Award Winning Cuisine

Historic Landmark

Best Sticky Buns
Phoenix Cuisine '93

FRANCO'S TRATTORIA

CUCINA TOSCANA

Not a trace of momentum was lost when Franco was forced to move from his mountain view location to his beautiful new premises on Hayden Rd. Rave reviews from his faithful clientele, and ever growing number of new customers welcomed the opening of his even larger and more beautiful premises.

ANTIPASTI

BOCCONCINI CON PROSCIUTTO — $5.50
mozzarella with tomato, prosciutto, olive oil, basil

ZUCCHINI FRITTI — $3.95
fried zucchini sticks with lemon

GRILLED AND ROASTED VEGETABLES — $7.00
radicchio, zucchini, peppers, plumb tomato, eggplant and fennel

BRUSCHETTA
with sauteed greens and garlic — $3.95
with tomatoes and ricotta — $3.95

INSALATA MISTA — $3.95
mixed greens

INSALATA DI PESCE — $7.00
shrimp, scallop, fish, squid, celery, shallot, olive oil, lemon

INSALATA TRICOLORE — $4.75
arugala, radicchio, belgian endive

INSALATA CAPRICCIOSA — $5.25
fennel, goat cheese, sun dried tomato, beans, arugala, radicchio, red onion

ZUPPA ORTOLANA — $4.50
vegetable soup with pancetta and toasted bread

TORTELLINI IN BRODO — $4.50
chicken and prosciutto filled dumplings in veal broth

PASTA

CAPELLINI POMODORO E BASILICO — $10.25
organic tomato, basil and garlic

SPAGHETTI BOLOGNESE — $10.75
meat sauce

FUSILLI ALLA PIRATA — $11.75
tomato, anchovy, caper, olive paste, garlic, hot pepper

PENNE PAESANA — $11.75
cream, onion, homemade sausage

FETTUCINE SALSA CRUDA — $11.75
fresh tomato, escarole, garlic, sundried tomato, beans

PENNE SHRIMP AND RADICCHIO — $13.75
with tomato and a touch of cream and hot pepper

LINGUINE FRUTTI DI MARE — $14.50
clams, shrimp, scallop, squid, fish, garlic, tomato, touch of hot pepper

RISOTTO FUNGHI PORCINI — $14.50
tomato, garlic, porcini mushroom

RISOTTO COI CARCIOFI — $14.50
fresh baby artichokes and pancetta
please allow 1/2 hour to prepare risotto

ENTREES

CHICKEN PAILLARD — $14.75
chicken breast, pounded, marinated and grilled, topped with arugala, radicchio, onion and tomato

MEZZO POLLO AL FORNO — $12.75
half chicken roasted with garlic, rosemary and sage

CONTADINA — $14.75
skinless/boneless chicken and homemade sausage with garlic, rosemary, peppers and mushrooms

SCALOPPINE CON FUNGHI — $16.75
pounded veal with tomato, basil, mushrooms and garlic

BATTUTA DI VITELLO — $16.75
pounded grilled veal, olive oil, balsamic vinegar and sage

ORECCHIE D'ELEFANTE — $20.50
pounded breaded veal chop topped with tomato, onion, basil, oil and vinegar

LOMBATINA AL CARCIOFO — $23.75
14 oz. loin veal chop with white wine, artichoke and mushroom

FILETTI DI MANZO AL ROSMARINO — $19.75
filet of beef with garlic, sage, rosemary & mushrooms

BISTECCA FIORENTINA — $19.75
17 oz. grilled Black Angus porterhouse, with sliced tomato and onion

PESCE DEL GIORNO — market price
entrees served with vegetable and potato

to split an entree $2.00 additional

Franco's Trattoria

PHONE
948-6655

HOURS
Monday–Thursday
5:00 pm–10:00 pm
Friday & Saturday
5:00 pm–10:30 pm
Sunday
4:30 pm–9:30 pm

LOCATION
8120 North
Hayden Road
Scottsdale, AZ 85285

CUISINE
Italian

ATTIRE
Casual

PATIO DINNING

VEGETARIAN MEALS

RESERVATIONS
Required

CREDIT CARDS
MasterCard, Visa, American Express

SMOKING
On Patio Only

HANDICAP FACILITIES

Greekfest

Greekfest means Greek Festival "panegeri" that is to say, a symposium—a celebration of food, wine, spirited music, good company, debate, conversation and all things that make life more enjoyable in a cosmopolitan atmosphere.

PHONE
265-2990

GREEKFEST
Lunch
Monday–Saturday
11:00 am–2:30 pm
Dinner
Monday–Thursday
5:00 pm–10:00 pm
Friday & Saturday
5:00 pm–11:00 pm
Sunday
5:00 pm–9:00 pm

LOCATION
1940 East
Camelback Road
Phoenix, AZ 85016
(NW Corner on 20th Steet)

CUISINE
Greek

ATTIRE
Elegant Casual

RESERVATIONS
Suggested

CREDIT CARDS
MasterCard, Visa, American Express, Diners Club, Discover

SMOKING
Section Available

HANDICAP FACILITIES

Festive Ambiance

With research and good taste, we have brought the perfect prosopopoeia of the authentic archipelago atmosphere and architecture. Rough white stucco walls, ceilings made from large polished wood beams.

Greek wavy marble and wooden polished floors, large monastery like arches, decorated with traditional eclectic folklore, all created a warm, romantic, colorful ambiance full of fantasy, memories and proof of the Hellenic history.

Festive Food

Above all though, the main attraction is the meal itself that is meticulously prepared always with pathos, devotion, attention to details and with respect to nature and tradition, using the best ingredients and herbs from our gardens and family recipes.

Festive Memories

For many years we have been prized as the best Greek restaurant in Phoenix and our guests come back to Greekfest for the food, the taste memory, the cultural and gastronomic experience and personalized service.

With the attractive, romantic and elegant style of the Greekfest as well as the ceremonious performance of Greek cooking and presentation of the meal, we assure you that your Greek dining experience will remain unique and memorable.

Gianni
CUCINA ITALIANA

Best Pasta House

Those who cannot remember the pasta are condemned to repeat it.

Thank Goodness. This way we get to go back again and again to Gianni Cucina Italiana. Lets see, what is the subliome pappardelle con porcini we enjoyed so much on our last visit? The dish features homemade broad noodles in a voluptous cream sauce studded with with heady porcini mushrooms.

Maybe it was the Tagliatelle Bolognese, highlighted by a defty seasoned meat sauce with the aroma of the Mediterranean on a summer afternoon.

Or perhaps it was the superb gnocchi, light potato dumplings, scented with an intense tomato sauce.

It doesn't matter. You can't live in the pasta. Except at Gianni Cucina Italiana.
—**Best of Phoenix, New Times, 1995**

Antipasta: Appetizers

Bresaola della Valtellina $7.50
dry aged beef drizzled with virgin olive oil

Mozzarella in Carrozza 4.75
fried mozzarella with tomato sauce

Salciccia Griglia e Pomodoro 4.50
grilled sausage and tomato

Melanzane Mario 5.25
grilled eggplant and a touch of garlic oil

Prosciutto e Melone 7.95
italian prosciutto e melon

Calamari Fritti 6.50
fried calamari

INSALATA: Salads

Contadina   Small 3.50   Large 5.50
variety of imported greens

Caprese 6.95
fresh mozzarella di bufala with tomatoes and sweet basil

Insalata di pollo 7.50
with grilled breast of chicken

Insalata di Montagna 6.95
with mortadella, salame

PASTA: Homemade

Ravioloni di Magro 9.50
ricotta cheese & spinach

Capelli Salsa Cruda 7.95
fresh chopped tomato & olives & herbs

Penne arrabiatta 8.95
spicy tomato and mushrooms

Rotelle di prosciutto Cotto 11.50
rolled pasta with ham, cheese and tomato

Fusilli Primavera 9.95
fresh vegetables

Paglia Fieno 9.50
cream, peas and ham

Pappardelle con Porcini 11.95
pocini, mushrooms and cream

Tagliatelle Salciccia 7.95
sausage, tomatoes and bell peppers

Maccheroni al Pesto 8.95
sweet basil and cream

Capelli Pomodoro e Basilico 7.50
sweet basil and tomatoes

Lasagna al Forno 8.95
pasta sheets layered with meat, cheese and tomatoes

Gnocci Pomodoro 8.50
potato dumplings with tomato

Farfalle Salmone Affumicato 12.50
smoked salmon and cream

Spaghetti Vongole al Cartoccio . 13.50
clams and tomatoes

Risotto Primavera 12.50
Italian arborio rice with mixed vegetables

SECONDI: Entrees

Salciccia e polenta 11.50
sausage & polenta

Petti di Pollla Alla Griglia 13.50
grilled breast of chicken

Tubi di Melanzane 11.95
rolled eggplant with ham and cheese

Vitello al Pepe 14.95
veal with cream and pepper

Cotoletta Milanese 14.95
breaded veal

Pesce del Giorno 15.95
fish of the day

The above menu is just a small sample of the wonderful dishes available at Gianni.

Gianni Cucina Italiana

PHONE
998–2507

HOURS
Lunch
Monday–Friday
11:00 am–2:00 pm
Dinner
Monday–Sunday
5:00 pm–10:00 pm

LOCATION
8320 North
Hayden Road #103
Scottsdale, AZ 85258

CUISINE
Italian

ATTIRE
Casual

TAKE OUT

VEGETARIAN MEALS

RESERVATIONS
Suggested

CREDIT CARDS
MasterCard, Visa,
American Express,
Diners Club, Discover

SMOKING
Section Available

HANDICAP FACILITIES

Goldie's Neighborhood Sports Cafe

After one year Goldie's has become the premier Neighborhood Sports Restaurant in Scottsdale. Known for its great selection of outstanding food, including fresh pasta dishes, roasted chicken Bar B Que Ribs and homemade Epicurean desserts. The burgers, either hamburger or turkey burger, served on whole grain buns that are baked in an old world, wood fire oven, are a treat. All of the sandwiches are huge and really hit the spot.

The focus of Goldie's is the European wood fired oven. Exhibition pizza spinning and preparation entertain you while you sip a coldie, brew that is, at Goldie's.

The Thai pizza, made fresh from scratch with old world care and quality, homemade crust, a delicious peanut sauce, delicate herbs, fresh vegetables and a touch of cilantro, is a heady experience. My favorite though, is the fresh roma tomato and basil pizza, its pizza at it's traditional best.

With three, 10-foot TV screens and 17 TV monitors, Goldie's is the best sports viewing spot in town. There is not a bad seat in the house, four pool tables, and a video game room makes Goldie's a favorite for the family.

APPETIZERS

CRAB QUESADILLA $6.95
Fresh sauteed snow crab, cilantro, roma tomatoes, cream cheese, spinach and fresh squeezed lime juice, folded inside a 13" flour tortilla.

GRILLED SEA SCALLOPS $7.95
Scallops seasoned and grilled to perfection, laid atop a steaming order of angel hair pasta with a champagne cream sauce and fresh basil.

GREEN CHILI CHICKEN ROLLS $4.75
Marinated and roasted white meat and fresh Anaheim chilies stuffed into a rice wrapper, deep fried, and served with a sweet jalapeno dipping sauce.

PEEL AND EAT SHRIMP $6.95
Half pound of our delicious shrimp that you peel and eat, served with cocktail sauce (about 12 to 15 shrimp).

BUFFALO WINGS $4.95
One dozen of our fresh chicken wings deep fried and prepared with an authentic buffalo sauce. Medium, Hot, or X-Hot.

SALADS

	Full	Half
ORIENTAL CHICKEN SALAD	$7.95	$5.95

Sesame marinated chicken breast, grilled and sliced laid atop fresh chopped greens, and dressed with a spicy peanut sauce and a sesame oil and vinegar, garnished with fresh roasted chopped peanuts.

THAI PASTA SALAD .... $7.95 .... $6.45
Chilled egg fettuccine tossed with snow peas, red and yellow peppers, cilantro, fresh grilled chicken breast, tossed with Goldie's spicy peanut sauce.

CAESAR SALAD
  Chicken or tenderloin .... $7.95 .... $6.45
  Traditional .... $5.95 .... $3.95
A traditional Caesar salad as is or add fresh grilled chicken breast, regular or Cajun style, or marinated tenderloin and grilled onions.

SOUTHWESTERN CHICKEN SALAD $7.95
Grilled Cajun chicken breast, sour cream and guacamole, cheddar and jack cheese, salsa and our own Sweet Jalapeno salad dressing served in a tortilla shell.

CHICKEN

GRILLED CHICKEN SANDWICH. $6.95
8 oz. of trimmed chicken breast, grilled and served with your choice of side dish.

CAJUN CHICKEN SANDWICH $6.95
8 oz. of trimmed chicken breast grilled and seasoned Cajun style, served with a side of guacamole, choice of side dish.

CHICKEN FOCACCIA $6.95
Honey mustard marinated chicken breast grilled and sliced, then rolled inside a fresh pizza dough with a touch of honey garlic mayo.

BUFFALO CHICKEN FOCACCIA $6.95
Grilled chicken breast sliced and rolled into a fresh baked pizza dough with buffalo sauce, bleu cheese and celery.

FROM THE DELI
(all deli sandwiches are served on a hard crusted roll)

CLUB $6.50
Turkey, Ham, Bacon, Lettuce, tomato and mayo and choice of side.

PIZZAS

MIXED SEAFOOD $9.95
Shrimp, scallops, snow crabs, roma tomatoes, cilantro. garlic on a olive oil covered crust.

CARMELIZED ONION AND GORGONZOLA $7.25
Slow roasted white onions with a touch of honey and rosemary dotted with gorgonzola cheese on fresh garlic and olive oil.

EGGPLANT AND LAMB $7.75
Fresh grilled eggplant and marinated leg of lamb with roasted red pepper and feta cheese on fresh garlic and olive oil.

ANDOUILLE SAUSAGE $7.25
This one is hot, red and green bell peppers, cajun spices, jalapenos on a red sauce.

GRILLED VEGGIE $7.25
Fresh grilled seasoned vegetables, mozzarella, provolone on our red sauce.

MEATBALL $7.00
Goldie's meatballs and our marinara covered with provolone and mozzarella cheeses.

GRILLED SCALLOPS $9.25
Grilled scallops, fresh roasted red and yellow peppers on a fresh garlic and olive oil.

ROASTED PEPPER $7.25
Fresh roasted red, green and yellow bell peppers, with mozzarella, provolone and feta cheese.

TERIYAKI CHICKEN $7.95
Marinated and grilled chicken breasts, red onions, roasted red pepper, pineapple, and teriyaki sauce.

HOT SICILIAN $7.25
Hot capicola, prosciutto, salami, mortadella, and provolone with an Italian dressing on fresh garlic and olive oil.

PINWHEEL $9.95
Four selections that we have chosen for your dining enjoyment, Teriyaki chicken, roasted pepper, sundried tomato and prosciutto.

ROMA AND BASIL $7.25
This pizza is covered with chunks of marinated Roma tomatoes and fresh basil. The crust is brushed lightly with crushed garlic and olive oil and topped with a blend of cheeses.

LEEKS, PANCETTA AND GOAT CHEESE $7.75
Sauteed leeks and pancetta on top of a garlic and olive oil crust with a touch of pesto, dotted with goat cheese.

ROASTED BBQ CHICKEN $7.25
Fresh roasted chicken cooked in our own BBQ sauce on top of a BBQ covered crust with red onion, red pepper, cilantro, and provolone cheese.

ROASTED CHICKEN & POTATO PIZZA $7.95
Red potato sliced and sauteed with rosemary and roasted chicken on top of a garlic & olive oil pie with feta cheese.

SUNDRIED TOMATO AND GOAT CHEESE $7.95
A garlic and olive oil crust covered with sundried tomatoes and goat cheese sprinkled with mozzarella and provolone.

SHRIMP SCAMPI $8.25
Sauteed Shrimp on top of a garlic and olive oil crust with roma tomatoes, red onions, and mushrooms.

GORGONZOLA WALNUT $7.95
A pesto covered crust with mozzarella, provolone dotted with imported gorgonzola cheese. Crisp walnuts and fresh roma tomatoes.

SALMON PIZZA WITH PESTO $7.95
Grilled salmon flaked over a pesto covered crust with pinenuts and smoked provolone cheese.

THAI CHICKEN PIZZA $7.95
Sesame marinated chicken, fresh roasted peanuts, red and yellow peppers, and cilantro on a peanut sauce covered crust.

VEGETABLE SANDWICHES

Veggie Focaccia $6.25
Marinated cucumbers and onions rolled inside a fresh baked pizza dough with spinach, roma tomatoes, and alfalfa sprouts. Served with your choice of side dish.

STEAK SANDWICHES

Tenderloin Focaccia $7.25
6 oz. of tenderloin in garlic, rosemary and balsamic vinegar, grilled then rolled inside a fresh pizza dough with grilled onions and a touch of honey garlic mayo.

PASTA

	Full	Half
ANGEL HAIR	$8.95	$6.95

Blackened sea scallops with a roasted garlic sauce

LINGUINI	$7.95	$5.95

Bolognese meat sauce with onions, bell peppers, mushrooms, garlic

Fettuccini
Alfredo (available Cajun style)	$6.95	$4.95
Chicken & Shrimp	$8.95	$6.95
Smoked Salmon, pine nuts, fresh basil pesto.	$9.25	$7.25

PENNE
Spicy Sausage marinara, provolone cheese, oregano, garlic.	$7.95	$5.95

TORTELLINI
Smoked salmon, pesto, champagne cream sauce	$7.95	$5.95

Goldies Sports Bar

PHONE
451-6269

HOURS
Monday–Sunday
11:00 am–1:00 am

LOCATION
10135 East Via Linda
Scottsdale, AZ
(Corner of Via Linda & Mountain View)

CUISINE
Eclectic

ATTIRE
Casual

BAR
11:00 am–1:00 am
Menu Service
Monday–Saturday
11:00 am–12:00 am
Sunday
11:00 am–11:00 pm

PATIO DINING

AFTER THEATRE DINING

TAKE OUT

VEGETARIAN MEALS

RESERVATIONS
Not Required

CREDIT CARDS
MasterCard, Visa, American Express, Diners Club, Discover

SMOKING
Section Available

HANDICAP FACILITIES

The above is just a small sample of the wonderful menu available at Goldies.
Be sure to ask about our fresh desserts, and our childrens menu.

Golden Swan

PHONE
991-3388

HOURS
Seasonal

LOCATION
7500 East
Doubletree Ranch Rd.
Scottsdale, AZ 85258

CUISINE
Regional American

ATTIRE
Proper Dress

OUTSIDE TERRACE DINING

GAZEBO DINING

SUNDAY BRUNCH

BANQUET FACILITIES

VEGETARIAN MEALS

RESERVATIONS
Suggested

CREDIT CARDS
MasterCard, Visa,
American Express,
Diners Club, Discover

SMOKING
Ouside Terrace and
Gazebo Sections Only

HANDICAP FACILITIES

Dine indoors or out, overlooking blooming gardens and a lagoon filled with black swans and Japanese Koi fish. With its casual elegance, Golden Swan features regional American cuisine with a distinctively native influence.

For a "Backstage" look at the innovative Sunday "Chef's Brunch", and a fun interaction with the Chefs, guests are invited into the kitchen, where the food is served buffet-style.

Appetizers

Cured Salmon Tartar and Potato Napoleon with Maple Bacon Dressing on Beet Carpaccio
7.25

Iceberg Taco with Vegetable Slaw Curried Duck Satey and Peanut Dressing
6.25

Crab and Piñon Nut Cakes with Roasted Corn Chowder and Mango Jicama Slaw
7.50

Oysters on the half shell with Caviar and Horseradish Créme Fraîche
6.25

Chilled Gulf Shrimp with Vine Ripened Red and Yellow Tomato Relish
9.50

Barbecued Arizona Quail Breast on a White Bean Cake, Frisse and Cilantro Dressing
6.75

Soups and Salads

Lobster Bisque with Fennel Créme Fraîche
4.25

Coriander Carrot Vichyssoise
4.75

Young Smooth Mountain Greens with Julienne Pears, Maytag Blue Cheese and Oven Fried Pecans
4.50

Gainey Caesar Salad with Fresh Corn, Tomatoes and Chipotle Croutons
4.95

Vine Ripened Red and Yellow Tomato Salad with Goat Cheese Fritter
5.75

Crisp Soft Shell Crab with Fresh Poached Artichokes Garlic and Olive Dressing
7.50

Specialities

Herb Roasted Pork Loin with Crisp Panchetta and Garlic Mashed Potatoes
19.50

Herb Marinated Range Chicken Baked in Arizona Red Clay with Pecan Bread Stuffing and Roasted Garlic Butter
22.50

Grilled Lamb Chop Glazed with Jalapeño Honey Mustard, Rolled in Toasted Pistachios with Broiled Herb Potatoes
22.50

Herb Marinated Salmon Fillet with Orange Honey Barbecue Sauce
21.50

Grilled Shrimp and Scallop Kabob on Masa, Mushroom Cannelloni
22.50

Grilled Herb Marinated Ranch Chicken on Cilantro Couscous, Mango Salad
19.75

Potato Crusted Orange Roughy, Crawfish Chili on Warm Fennel Salad and Field Greens
21.50

Grilled Swordfish Steak with a Crab and Shrimp Stuffed Pasilla Chili
21.50

Grilled Lobster, Crisp Soft Shell Crab and Baby Abalone in Cider Jus
Market Price

Sautéed Veal Medallion with Goose Liver, Artichoke Hearts and Oregon Mushrooms, Cilantro Spatzle
22.50

Steamed Halibut Roll with Chayote Squash and Cucumber Ginger Relish
21.50

Grilled Filet of Beef with Southwest Herb Butter, Asparagus, Mushroom Chimichanga
22.50

Guido's CHICAGO MEAT & DELI RISTORANTE

Submarines
On a 9" roll. Includes lettuce, tomatoes, onions and our own Italian dressing, mustard or mayonnaise.

Cold Sandwiches
Also can be heated at your request.

		WHOLE	HALF
1	Italian Sub	3.95	2.25
2	American Sub	3.95	2.25
	Ham, Turkey and American Cheese		
3	Imported Ham and Provolone Cheese	3.50	1.95
4	Imported Ham & Swiss	3.50	1.95
5	Capocollo, Hard Salami & Provolone	3.95	2.25
6	Hard Salami & Provolone	3.95	1.95
7	Capocollo & Provolone	3.95	1.95
8	Corned Beef	3.95	2.25
9	Pastrami	3.95	2.25
10	Turkey Breast & Provolone	3.50	1.95
11	Prosciutto (aged Italian ham)	4.50	2.50
12	Cheese	2.95	1.75
13	Chicken Salad Sandwich	3.95	2.25
14	Italian Roast Beef	3.95	2.25
15	Fresh Tuna Salad	3.95	2.25

Special Italian Hot Sandwiches on Italian Bread

16	Fried Homemade Italian Sausage	3.95	2.25
17	Homemade meatball	3.95	2.25
18	Hot Roast Beef		3.95
	In Italian juices with peppers and onions.		
19	"Chicago Style" Combo		4.98
	Italian beef & sausage with peppers & onions.		

Entrees

Spaghetti with meatballs or sasuage 6.95
in Guidos own Marinara sauce

Eggplant parmesean 7.95
Baked with marinara sause and mozzarella

Lasagna al a Guidos 7.95
Cheese and meat or spinich and cheese

Gnocchi Parmadoro 7.95
Red and white cream sauce, pine nuts and fresh basil and garlic

Perciatelli All Ametriciana 8.95
Tube shape pasta, seasoned red sauce with panchetta and sausage

Linguini and Clam Sauce 7.95
Fettuccine Alfredo 7.95
Spinach fettuccine in a white cream sauce

Paglia E Fieno 8.95
Green and white tagliarini seasones sausage and mushrooms in cream sauce

Chicken Marsalla 8.95
Chicken breast braised in brown Marsalla wine with mushrooms, served with a side order of pasta

Linguini Bolognese 7.95
Linguini in a delicious meat sauce

Angel Hair Pasta 6.95
Smoothered in fresh Roma tomatoes, basil and classic Italian garlic sauce

Chicken Picatta 8.95
Chicken breast cooked in a butter and white wine sauce with lemon and caper, served with a side order of pasta

Chicken Parmesean 7.95
Italian style breaded chicken breast topped with marinara sauce and mozzerella

Pasta Mista Guido 8.95
Italian flag: tri colored pasta with pesto, alfredo and marinara

Mostaccioli Al Forno 6.95
Mostacciohi with olive oil, parsley and guido's seasonings

Puttanesca Grande 7.95
Lunguini with olives, capers and delicious spices

Tortallini Alla Noce 8.95
Fresh tortalini in a special cream sauce with walnuts and mushrooms

Pasta Primavera 7.95
Fresh pasta in a delicious mix of cauliflower, broccoli, onions, zucchini and carrots with choice of olive oil, cream sauce or red sauce

Chicken Dinners

The Original Broasted Chicken Dinner 6.95
Four pieces of broasted chicken, coleslaw or salad, broasted potatoes or potato salad, with bread and butter

Family 16.95
12 pieces of broasted chicken, coleslaw or salad, broasted potatoes or potato salad with bread and butter

Tub 21.95
16 pieces of broasted chicken, coleslaw or salad, broasted potatoes or potato salad with bread and butter

Barrel 26.95
24 pieces of broasted chicken, coleslaw or salad, broasted potatoes or potato salad with bread and butter

---

Guido's Chicago Ristorante

PHONE
951-0636

HOURS
Monday–Thursday
8:00 am–9:00 pm
Friday & Saturday
8:00 am–10:00 pm
Sunday
9:00 am–7:00 pm

LOCATION
10893 North
Scottsdale Rd.
Scottsdale Shea
Center

CUISINE
Meat & Deli Restaurant

ATTIRE
Casual

TERRACE DINING

CREDIT CARDS
MasterCard, Visa

HANDICAP FACILITIES

Hops Bistro & Brewery

HOURS
Daily
Lunch and Diner
Late Night Lounge

CUISINE
American/Micro Brewery

ATTIRE
Casual

BAR
Daily
Lunch , Diner and Late night

LATE NIGHT MENU
Friday & Saurday

VEGETARIAN MEALS

RESERVATIONS
Accepted

CREDIT CARDS
MasterCard,Visa, American Express, Diners Club, Discover

SMOKING
Bar area only

HANDICAP FACILITIES

HOPS! has escalated the image of the brew pub. Its distinguished reputation for quality, service and the unprecedented high standard of food and spirits have made it a top contender in the Valley's restaurant world.

APPETIZERS

Soup du Jour — 3.25
ask your Server for our daily soup selection

♥ Vegetarian Black Bean Soup — 3.25
with pico de gallo, tortilla strips and creme fraiche

Carmelized Onion Tart — 5.95
beer crust carmelized onions, pancetta and goat cheese

Chicken Wings — 5.75
with celery, carrots and blue cheese dip

Stuffed Jalapeno Chilies — 5.95
filled with spicy cream cheese and served with cool Ranch Dressing

Chicken Tenders — 6.50
with Chipotle Aioli, celery and carrots

Black Bean Quesadilla — 6.50
goat cheese, chipotle sauce and black beans

Bite Size Shrimp — 7.50
cajun dusted flash fried and served with lemon tartar

Chicken Quesadllla — 6.95
chile rubbed chicken, onions, peppers, with jack cheese, pico de gallo and guacamole

Warm Salted Pretzels — 3.75
with a combination of honey and spicy golden mustard

Tortilla Chips — 4.75
Tri color tortilla chips with guacamole and salsa

Black Beans & Beer Croutons — 5.50
mild boursin cheese, tomato-basil relish ,black beans & beer croutons

SALADS

Field Green Salad — 4.50
goat cheese toast, roma tomatoes, jicama, lemon-walnut vinaigrette

Calamari Salad — 8.95
light cornmeal breading, goat cheese, balsamic vinaigrette

Caesar Salad — 5.95
fleshly grated parmesan and garlic croutons

Chinese Chicken Salad — 9.95
marinated chicken, toasted almonds, mixed vegetables and oriental dressing

Chicken Caesar — 9.95
hearts of palm, tomatoes, black olives, croutons topped with grated parmesan cheese

VEGETABLE SPECIALTIES

Thai Pasta — 8.95
julienne vegetables sauteed in teriyaki sauce, tossed with angel hair pasta and fresh ginger

Vegetable Calzone — 8.95
a pizza pocket filled with fresh vegetables, black beans and herbed ricotta cheese

♥ Vegetable Burrito — 6.95
seasonal vegetables, spicy jack cheese and black beans

♥ Grilled Vegetarian Sandwich — 6.95
assorted grilled vegetables on a nine grain roll

Mediterranean Plate — 9.95
ratatouille, green chile polenta and garlic wilted greens

A HOPS! CLASSIC

Oven Roasted Chicken — 9.95
Roasted garlic whipped potatoes, creamed spinach, natural chicken sauce

PASTA

Salmon & Shrimp Penne — 9.95
shallots, garlic and lemon cream sauce

Penne Arrabbiatta — 8.95
onion and pancetta in a spicy marinara sauce

❤ Angel Hair Pasta — 8.95
mushrooms, spinach, cured tomatoes sauteed in garlic, olive oil and vegetable broth

Tortellini Alla Panna — 9.95
asparagus tips and pancetta in a Parmesan cream

Chicken Fettucine — 9.75
with spinach, shiitake mushrooms, red onions and garlic alfredo sauce

PIZZA

Four Cheese — 8.95
mozzarella, smoked mozzarella, parmesan, spicy jack, sweet peppers, sundried tomato, basil and rosemary cream

Jamaican Spiced Chicken — 8.95
salsa, roasted garlic Paste and spicy jack cheese

Sedona — 8.95
smoked sausage, spicy jack cheese, serrano peppers on top of our black bean sauce

Vegetarian — 7.95
fresh vegetables, mozzarella, marinara sauce

Thin Crust — 7.95
marinara, roma tomatoes, basil and buffalo mozzarella

Frizzled Pepperoni — 8.95
fresh marinara, mozzarella and asiago cheeses

SANDWICHES

Hops! Hamburger — 6.95
choice of asiago, swiss, spicy jack or cheddar

Grilled Chicken Sandwich — 8.95
sonoma jack cheese, avocado, sprouts and pasta salad

Achiote Grilled Ahi Tuna — 8.95
jalapeno cabbage, spicy jack cheese and chipotle sauce

Philly Cxheese Steak — 7.95
angus beef beer braised onions, american cheese, french fries

❤ Turkey Sandwich — 6.95
turkey, tomatoes, sprouts, lettuce, honey mustard

Turkey Burger — 7.95
choice of asiago, swiss, spicy jack, or cheddar

Blackened Catfish — 8.95
cilantro aioli, tartar sauce, cajun fries

SPECIALTIES

Chicken Margarita — 12.95
double boneless breast with grilled spring vegetables, polenta and a tequila lime butter sauce

Grilled Atlantic Salmon — 13.95
served on a bed of angel hair pasta, seasonal vegetables and a dill beurre blanc

Spicy Shrimp Marinara — 13.95
seared in amber beer with artichokes, wild mushrooms, spinach, chipotle peppers and angel hair pasta

Grilled Pork Chops — 14.95
maple whipped sweet potatoes, zucchini and golden squash with honey mustard glaze

Sauteed Snapper — 10.95
with shrimp, finished in a sherried cream served over dirty rice

New York Strip Steak — 14.95
ancho chile butter, served with crsipy cajun fried onions, barbequed black beans and a roasted corn salad

❤ Puttanesca Linguine — 11.95
shrimp, ahi tuna, capers, olives and spicy marinara

❤ *the 'Heart Smart' designates that this item meets the guidelines of the 'Heart Smart Smart Restaurants International' which are: 30% or less in fat, 10% or less calories from saturated fat, 150mg or less cholesterol and 1100mg or less sodium.*

James Salter, Brewmeister; Alan Skeversky, Executive Chef; Jay Edwards, Director of Staff Training

Hops! Bistro & Brewery

SCOTTSDALE LOCATION

PHONE
945–4677

LOCATION
Scottsdale
Fashion Square
7000 East
Camelback Road
Scottsdale, AZ 85251

PHOENIX LOCATION

PHONE
468–0500

LOCATION
Biltmore Fashion Park
2584 East
Camelback Road
Phoenix, AZ 86016

NORTH SCOTTSDALE LOCATION

PHONE
468–0500

LOCATION
Pima Crossing
8668 East Shea Blvd.

Hole-in-the-Wall

PHONE
870–1977

HOURS
Daily
Breakfast & Lunch
7:00 am–3:00 pm

Dinner
Sunday–Thursday
5:00 pm–10:00 pm
Friday & Saturday
5:00 pm–11:00 pm

LOCATION
7677 North
16th Street
Phoenix, AZ
The Pointe Hilton
Resort at Squaw Peak

CUISINE
Western

ATTIRE
Casual

LOUNGE
7:00 am until 1:00 am

TERRACE DINING

ENTERTAINMENT
Thursday–Saturday
9:00 pm–12:30 am

FULL-SERVICE CATERING

TAKE OUT

VEGETARIAN MEALS

RESERVATIONS
Suggested

CREDIT CARDS
MasterCard, Visa,
American Express,
Diners Club, Discover

SMOKING
Section Available

HANDICAP FACILITIES

A favorite hideaway, Hole-in-the-Wall Eatin' and Drinkin' Place is known for its authentic Western style and down-home cookin'. Guests can dig in and enjoy some of the best mesquite-smoked-cooked Western fixin's for breakfast, lunch or dinner in the whole state of Arizona. Trout and eggs, catfish, cowboy steaks, barbecue beef sandwiches, corn, homemade biscuits, ranch-style beans and apple pie are just a few specialties. Dine inside or enjoy patio dining featuring the view of the resort's water feature and fire pit. A sunken bar with live guitar music completes this authentic Western experience.

APPETIZERS

Sautéed Mushrooms 4.25
Sautéed in wine and garlic sauce
Buffalo Wings 4.25
Buffalo Breasts 4.95
Famous "Hole" Fundito 4.95
Traditional Spanish cheese fondue with chips and salsa
Homemade Deep-Fried 3.95
Onion Rings
Bear Claws 4.75
Rattlesnake (seasonal) 8.95
Rattlesnake T-Shirt 12.00
Rattlesnake and T-Shirt 18.95

Every "Hole" plate dinner comes with:
A mountainous plate of salad, topped with the 'Hole' house dressing (Lemon-French), Thousand Island, Bleu Cheese or Ranch. Homemade biscuits, the best bakin' soda biscuits this side of the Pecos, served with butter and honey. Roastin' ears (corn-on-the-cob), hot and mouth-waterin', a real rancher's treat. The West's best ranch-style beans. Cowboy relish, crackers and butter.

HANGMAN'S NOOSE
A full pound of T-bone broiled 15.95
over mesquite coals

DESPERADO'S DELIGHT
This enormous 22-oz. 18.95
porterhouse is for the real man. Seasoned and treated in Jose's secret formula. Broiled over mesquite coals

BANDIT'S BEST BEEF
Tender and juicy 10-oz. filet mignon, ... 17.95
broiled over mesquite coals
For the smaller appetite, 8-oz 15.95

PRIME RIB
Oven-roasted seasoned to perfection. For extra flavor, let Gabby sear your cut over mesquite wood.
Cattleman's Cut, 16-oz. 16.95
Wrangler, 12-oz. 13.95

THE 'HOLE' SPECIALTY
Mouth-waterin' mesquite-broiled bar-b-que back pork ribs:
Full slab 15.95
One-half slab 11.95
The best bar-b-que beef ribs an outlaw can handle 10.95
All you can eat 13.95

THE 'HOLE' COMBO
A combination for the vaqueros who can't decide:
Sirloin steak and baby-back ribs 15.95
Sirloin steak and beef ribs 13.95
Quarter chicken and baby-back ribs 14.95
Filet and beef ribs 19.95
Filet and shrimp 21.95

WAGON BOSS
What a steak sandwich oughta be 10.95
8-oz. top sirloin, broiled over mesquite coals and served with Texas garlic toast and sliced tomatoes

BRANDIN' IRON
Choice chunks of seasoned 11.95
sirloin on a skewer with mushrooms, green peppers, onions and cherry tomatoes, broiled over mesquite coals and served on a bed of rice pilaf

CHICKEN 'N' DUMPLIN'S
Jose's down-home dumplin's to 9.95
warm a cold bandit's heart

POACHER'S PLEASURE
A half of a bar-b-que'd baked chicken 9.95

CHICKEN-FRIED STEAK
Served with mashed potatoes and 8.95
homemade country gravy

THE LOOT
Sautéed shrimp and a delicious 8-oz. 16.95
top-sirloin steak, broiled over mesquite coals

THE MARK OF ZORRO
Succulent swordfish, broiled 15.95
over mesquite coals

LOS SHRIMP
Large shrimp sautéed in butter, garlic, ... 15.95
shallots and white wine. A ranch hand's delight

WESTERN CATFISH WITH HUSH PUPPIES
Specially seasoned pan-fried catfish. 11.95
Served with homemade hush puppies

GRAZER
Jose puts together a vegetarian meal 8.95

This is just a small selection of the wonderful items available at the Hole-in-the-Wall.

the Impeccable Pig
Scottsdale

*D*ee Ann Skipton graces her customers with her unique eye for a era gone by. The simplistic beauty gives ambience that is unmatched in the valley. The open kitchen will touch your senses with every visit, for the menu changes daily, but the favorites stay the same. Serving food and fun to guests for over fifteen years, the Impeccable Pig is the established favorite.

Impeccable Fun

The entrance gives you a little taste of all the enjoyment you are about to experience. Wander through the meandering shops adjacent to the dining area, you will find them to be full of pleasant surprises. A delightful array of home decorating items, colorful fashions, southwestern accessories and country antiques are mixed in a visually exciting, eclectic ensemble. If you are looking for a perfect package for a fun filled afternoon, the Impeccable Pig will satisfy all of your needs.

Impeccable Dinning at Affordale Prices

The Impeccable Pig beckons one to explore...to experience the sights, sounds and tastes of an adventure in dining. The dining rooms have a comfortable, cozy ambience created by their warm antiques and charming decor, procured from The Impeccable Pig gift shops. The open air kitchen is inviting and the chef encourages an audience; questions and comments, about the original recipes are welcome. Repeat visitors and locals alike have discovered a visit to Scottsdale isn't complete without a delightful dining experience at the Impeccable Pig.

The Impeccable Pig

PHONE
941-1141

HOURS
Lunch
Monday–Saturday
11:00 am–3:00 pm

Dinner
Tuesday–Saturday
5:00 pm–10:00 pm

LOCATION
7042 East
Indian School Road
Scottsdale, AZ 85251

CUISINE
American Creative
ATTIRE
Casual
TERRACE DINING
OPEN KITCHEN
SUNDAY BRUNCH
ART WALK EVERY THURSDAY

RESERVATIONS
Suggested
CREDIT CARDS
MasterCard, Visa, American Express
CHECKS ACCEPTED
SMOKING
Section Available
HANDICAP FACILITIES

63

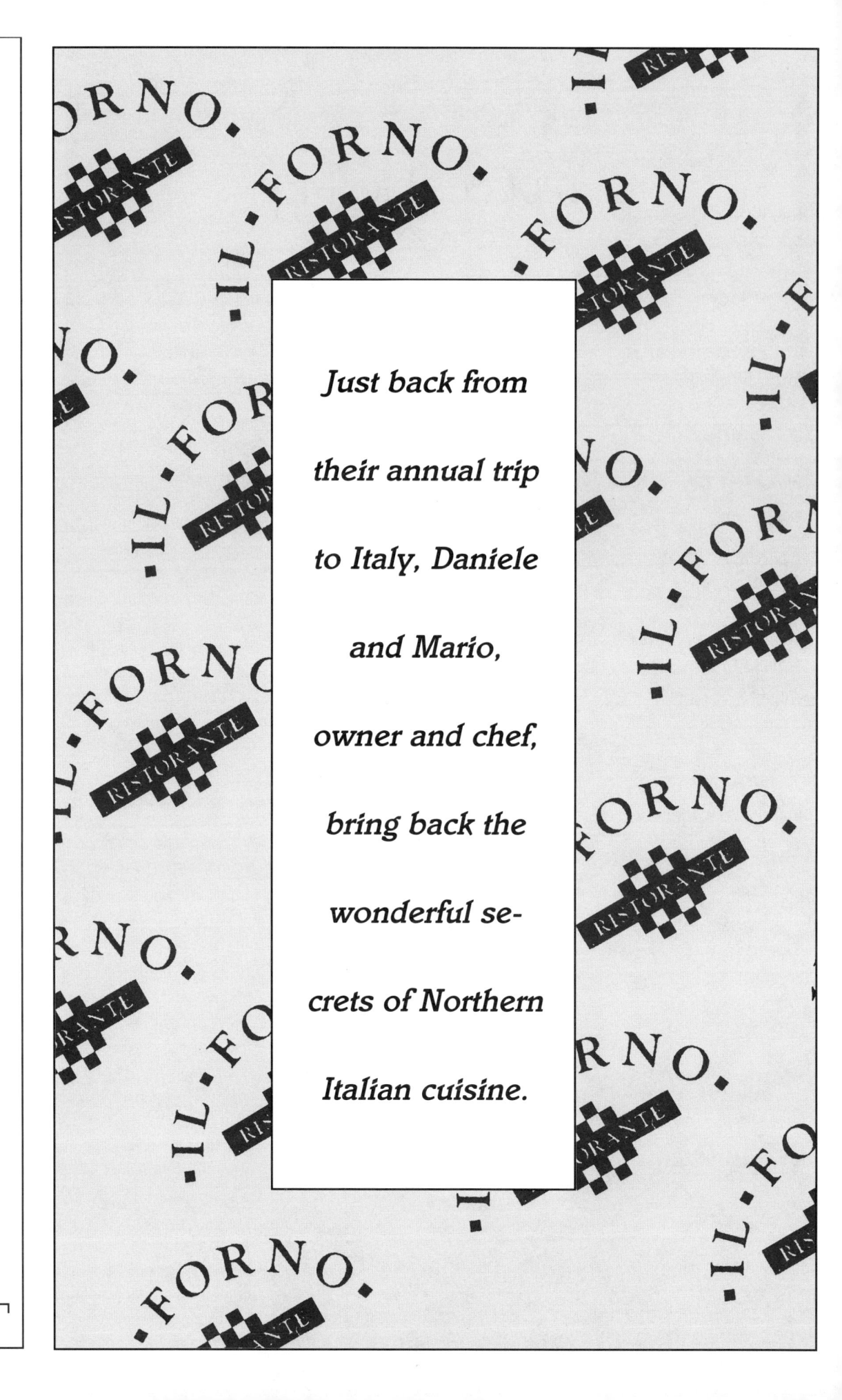

Just back from their annual trip to Italy, Daniele and Mario, owner and chef, bring back the wonderful secrets of Northern Italian cuisine.

Antipasta

Proscuitto
Cured Italian Ham.

Crostini All'Orvietana
Toasted Tuscan Bread with different toppings.

Antipasto
Assortment of Italian Meats and cheeses

Carpaccio
Sliced Prime Beef Tenderloin with capers and Dijon sauce.

Insalata Di Pesce Fresco Con Fagioli Sgranati
Fresh seafood and bean salad.

Calamari Fritti Della Casa
Fried Calamari tossed with fresh spices.

Pepperoni Al Forno Con Acciughe
Roasted peppers in our wood burning oven with anchovies.

Porcini Freschi Alla Griglia
Grilled fresh Porcini mushrooms.

Fettuccine Ai Funghi Porcini Freschi
Fettuccini with fresh porcini

Fettuccine Con Mentucha
Fettuccine with wild mint

Zuppe

Minestrone Tipico Orvietano

Pasta E Fagioli Alla Fiorentina

Ribollita alla Contadina (House Special)
Twice cooked soup.
Thanks to Ernesto and Giovanni from "Trattoria Etrusca," Orvieto, for the recipes.

Insalata

Tri Colori
Arugula, Belgium Endive, Radicchio and walnuts.

Di Cesare
Caesar Salad.

Caprese
Mozzarella and Tomato.

Romana
Tomatoes, Cucumbers and Red Onions.

Primi Piatti

Pappardelle Bolognese Ai Funghi Porcini Freschi
Wide ribbon pasta with fresh Porcini mushrooms in our house meat sauce.

Lasagna Con Salciccia Di Vitella
Lasagna with veal sausage.

Ravioli Di Magro
Cheese and spinach ravioli.

Gnocchi Di Patate Al Pomodoro
Potato dumplings in tomato sauce.

Penne Alla Cacciatora Con Pollo
Penne pasta with chicken in a hunter style sauce.

Secondo Piatti

Bisteca Alla Fiorentina
1 pound T-bone steak grilled over hot coals.

Scampi Della Casa
Large shrimps sauteed in olive oil, white wine and herbs.

Agnello Al Forno
Roasted lamb.

Scaloppine Di Vitella Al Limone
Veal scaloppine cooked in a lemon capers sauce.

Scalloppine Di Vitella Alla Marsala
Veal scaloppine cooked in marsala wine and fresh mushroom sauce

Cacciuco Alla Livornese
Livorno Fish Stew.

Pollo Alla Diavola
Chicken marinated in lemon, sage and garlic. Roasted in our own woodburning oven.

Linguini Pescatore
Medley of seafood on a bed of Linguini.

Pollo in Fricassea Coi Funghi
Chicken casserole with fresh Porcini mushrooms.

Pesce Speciale Della Casa
Chilean seabass in fresh tomato sauce with roasted peppers, capers and black olives.

Il Forno Ristorante

PHONE
952-1522

HOURS
Lunch
Monday–Friday
11:00 am–2:00 pm
Dinner
Monday–Saturday
5:00 pm–10:00 pm
Sunday
5:00 pm–9:00 pm

LOCATION
4225 East
Camelback Road
Phoenix, AZ 85018

CUISINE
Tuscan–Etruscan

ATTIRE
Casual

PATIO DINING

FULL SERVICE CATERING

TAKE OUT

VEGETARIAN MEALS

EXTENSIVE WINE LIST

DAILY SPECIALS

RESERVATIONS
Suggested

CREDIT CARDS
MasterCard, Visa,
American Express,

Jet Lag Lounge & Dinnerclub

PHONE
837-8000

HOURS
Sunday–Thursday
11:00 am–9:00 pm
Friday & Saturday
11:00 am–10:00 pm

LOCATION
8340 East
McDonald Drive
Scottsdale, AZ 85250

CUISINE
French Provincial

ATTIRE
Casual

LOUNGE
Piano Bar
5:30 until closing

TERRACE DINING

SUNDAY BRUNCH

BANQUET FACILITIES

AFTER THEATRE DINING

ART WALK EVERY THURSDAY

FULL SERVICE CATERING

TAKE OUT

VEGETARIAN MEALS

RESERVATIONS
Suggested

CREDIT CARDS
MasterCard, Visa,
American Express

NO CHECKS ACCEPTED

SMOKING
Section Available

"American comfort food" is the best way to describe the menu at the Jet Lag Lounge, also known for their ribs and walleye pike. We are known city-wide for our dining and dancing atmosphere for the 40-and-over crowd, and lunch is also a favorite with this neighborhood bar and grill.

Nightly entertainment, Tuesday–Saturday, keeps your feet moving with your friends every Tuesday through Saturday starting at eight till midnight. You're a guest when you enter and a friend when you leave. Located on the corner of Hayden and Chaparral, in the Chaparral Plaza in Scottsdale.

Salads

Tossed Salad	$2.95
Garden fresh greens	
Chef Salad	$4.95
Garden greens, turkey, ham, cheese and your choice of dressing	
Char-Grilled Chicken Salad	$5.25
Garden greens, tomato and cucumber wedges walnuts and mandarin slices, topped with sliced chicken breast and our own honey-mustard sauce.	
Seafood Salad	$5.25
Garden greens topped with shrimp & crab with your choice of dressing	
Caesar Salad Sm. $3.50 Lg. $4.95	
Romaine lettuce, croutons, cheese and our special dressing	
Add Shrimp and Crab	$6.95
Add Grilled Chicken	$6.25
Add Cajun shrimp	$6.25

Appetizers

Buffalo Wings	$4.5Q
Served B.B.Q., Hot or Mild	
Shrimp Cocktail	$6.75
5 Jumbo Shrimp	
Chicken Strips	$5.00
Served with Honey Mustard Sauce	
Potato Skins	$4.00
Filled with Cheddar Cheese, Bacon & Onions	
Vegetable Platter	$4.00
Variety of Daily Vegetables	
Blazin' Wings	$4.50
Spicy and Breaded	
Calamari Rings	$4.50
Stuffed Jalapeno Poppers	$4.50
Onion Rings	$3.50

Burgers
Half-pound Prime Beef served with French Fries

Basic Burger	$5.00
Cheese Burger	$5.25
Black Forest Burger	$5.95
Mushroom & Swiss Burger	$5.95
San Antonio Burger	$5.95
Pork Tenderloin on Grilled Bun	$5.95
Prime Dip Au Jus	$5.95

Entrees
*All entrees include rolls, baked potato or fries.
Add $1.25 for soup or salad.*

Filet Mignon		$13.95
Bacon wrapped and covered in mushrooms		
New York Strip Loin	8oz	$8.95
	10oz cut	$10.95
Baby Back Rib	Full Slab	$12.00
with our spicy B.B.Q. sauce		
Grilled Pork chops		$7.00
Three chops grilled to perfection		
Chopped Sirloin		$6.00
with sauteed mushrooms		
Chicken Piccata		$8.00
Boneless breast covered in mushrooms		
Country Fried Chicken		$7.00
Breaded chicken breast with country gravy.		
Teriyaki Chicken		$7.00
Marinated and grilled		
Deep Fried Shrimp		$9.00
Breaded and butterflied		
Catfish		$9.95
Blackened or grilled		
Northern Walleye		Market Price
Pan seared or deep fried		

Chicken Breast Sandwiches
Served on a Grilled Bun with French Fries

Grilled Chicken Breast	$5.00
Tomato, lettuce and mayo	
Teriyaki Style	$5.25
Cajun Style	$5.25
Ham & Swiss Cheese	$5.95
Country Chicken Breast	$5.95

Friday & Saturday Special

Prime Rib	10oz cut	$10.95
	12oz cut	$12.95
Friday Fish Fry		$5.95

고 려 원
KOREAN GARDEN

"Simplicity has its charms, and this is a prime example. The medium-size building is clean inside and out. The menu isn't extensive, but it is uncompromising..."
—Elin Jeffords, Arizona Republic

Korean Garden

PHONE
967-1133

HOURS
Lunch
Monday–Saturday
11:00 am–2:30 pm
Dinner
Monday–Saturday
5:00 pm–10:00 pm
Sunday
5:00 pm–10:00 pm

LOCATION
1324 South
Rural Road
Tempe, AZ 85281

CUISINE
Korean

ATTIRE
Casual

RESERVATIONS
Suggested

CREDIT CARDS
MasterCard, Visa,

SMOKING
Section Available

HANDICAP FACILITIES

DINNER MENU
Most entrees are served with a bowl of rice and vegetable side dishes.

1. Galbeee 갈비 $10.95
   Korean Bar B-Que short ribs
2. Bool Goki 불고기 9.95
   Thin sliced Bar-B-Que beef seasoned with special sauce
3. Dak Bool Goki * 닭불고기 9.95
   Thin sliced Bar-B-Que chicken breast seasoned with spicy sauce
4. Daegee Bool Goki * 돼지불고기 9.95
   Thin sliced Bar-B-Que pork seasoned with spicy sauce
5. Jap Chae 잡채 8.95
   Clear noodles mixed with pan fried vegetables & beef
6. Bibim Bob 비빔밥 8.95
   Rice mixed with beef, vegetables and hot sauce
7. Ojinguh Bokum * 오징어볶음 8.95
   Pan fried squid and vegetables with spicy seasoning
8. Sae Woo Bokum * 새우볶음 10.95
   Pan fried shrimp and vegetables with spicy seasoning
9. Hae Mool Chigae * 해물찌게 10.95
   Crab, squid, clam, shrimp & vegetables with hot spicy soup
10. Fish Soup * 생선매운탕 9.95
    Fish with hot spicy vegetable soup
11. Broiled Fish 생선구이 9.95
    Broiled fish seasoned
12. Yookgae Jang * 육개장 8.95
    Boiled, shredded beef soup with hot seasoning
13. Soon Doo Boo* 순두부찌게 8.50
    soft tofu with oysters, vegetables soup
14. Kimchi Chigae * 김치찌게 8.50
    Kimchi with tofu, bits of pork stew
15. Doenjang Chigae * 된장찌게 8.50
    Soybean paste stew with vegetables, tofu, clams soup
16. Duk Mandu Guk 떡만두국 8.95
    Dumplings with rice cake, beef, egg drop soup
17. Mool Naengmyun 물냉면 8.95
    Cold noodles with sliced beef & vegetables in icy broth
18. Bibim Naengmyun * 비빔냉면 8.95
    Cold noodles mixed with sliced beef vegetables and hot sauce

* Indicates hot spicy

SIDE DISHES
All side dishes are served chilled.

1. Kimchi * 김치 $ .65
   Korean style pickled cabbage (spicy)
2. Gakkduki * 깍뚜기 .65
   Korean style pickled diced radish (spicy)
3. Salad 샐러드 .65
   Romaine lettuce with Korean dressing
4. Bean Sprout 숙주나물 .65
   Boiled & seasoned bean sprout
5. Spinach 시금치나물 .65
   Boiled & seasoned spinach
6. Occasional / Seasonal side dishes .65
   Broccoli, Tofu, Potato, Fish Cake, Kelp, Garlic, etc....
7. Sang Choo 상추 2.50
   Lettuce leaves with seasoning sauce

APPETIZERS

1. Mandu Tuigim 만두튀김 $ 4.95
   Deep fried meat & vegetable dumplings
2. Bindae Duk 빈대떡 4.95
   Korean style bean sprout bean pan cake with bits of pork
3. Kim Bob (spring rolls) 김밥 4.95
   Vegetables, beef, rice rolled with seaweed paper

MESQUITE CHARRED TABLE B.B.Q.
Served with a bowl of rice, vegetable side dishes and Sang Choo (Lettuce leaves with seasoning sauce).

1. Galbee 갈비 $12.95
   Korean Bar-B-Que short ribs seasoned with special sauce
2. Bool Goki 불고기 $11.95
   Thin sliced Bar-B-Que beef seasoned with special sauce
3. Dak Bool Goki * 닭불고기 $11.95
   Thin sliced Bar-B-Que chicken breast(boneless, skinless) seasoned with special sauce
4. Daegee Bool Goki* 돼지불고기 $11.95
   Thin sliced Bar-B-Que pork loin seasoned with hot and spicy sauce
5. K.G.Bool Goki 등심구이 $11.95
   Unseasoned special choice boneless short ribs

La Fontanella
ITALIAN RESTAURANT
Originally from Chicago

Chef Owned

Bertos's Gelato Specialties

Full Bar

Awarded ✓ ★★★
by Mobile Travel Guide

Awarded Excellence in Zagut Survey

"Combination of quality and value"
—*New Times*

Appetizers

Mozzarella Caprese	4.50
Suppli' for Two	3.00
Prosciutto & Melon (in Season)	4.50
Focaccia for Two	3.00
Roasted Red Peppers	4.50
Artichokes alla Greca (in Season)	4.50
Marinated Artichokes	4.50
Stuffed Mushrooms	4.50
Marinated Eggplant	4.50
Mozzarella Marinara	4.50
Mixed Marinated Vegetables	5.50
Escargot	6.50
Antipasto for Two	8.50
Fried Calamari for Two	8.50
Dinner Salad	2.50
Soup	2.50

Entrees served with Hot Crispy Rolls and Herbal Olive Oil

Pasta

Spaghetti or Penne — 7.00
served with choice of Bolognese meat sauce or tomato sauce

Spaghetti al Sol — 7.00
garlic, olive oil, sundried tomatoes and sunflower seeds

Lasagne — 9.00
wide pasta baked with ricotta, meat sauce and mozzarella

Manicotti — 9.00
ricotta filled crepes with meat sauce or tomato sauce

Cannelloni — 9.00
veal filled crepes served with cream sauce and walnuts

Gnocchi alla Gorgonzola or alla Bolognese — 9.50
with a light gorgonzola cream sauce or with Bolognese sauce

Ravioli Florentine — 9.50
large cheese filled ravioli partly covered with fresh spinach, sauteed with cream sauce and grated cheese

Penne con Melanzane alla Sbambata   9.50
pasta quills tossed with eggplant in a hot red pepper tomato sauce

Penne con Broccoli Affugati   9.50
broccoli sauteed with diced tomatoes, garlic, olives, grated cheese, and sun dried tomatoes

Farfalle al Salmone   10.75
bowties tossed with pieces of salmon, mushrooms, peas and cream sauce

Today's Catch alla Puttanesca   10.75
linguettini with today's catch, tomatoes, oregano, olives, red pepper and capers

Poultry

Chicken alla Franca   10.75
split breast of chicken stuffed with garlic butter, dusted with fine bread meal and then baked

Chicken Vesuvio   10.75
split breast of chicken and potatoes, baked with lemon, garlic and butter

Chicken Cacciatore   10.75
split breast of chicken baked with tomato sauce, sausage, onions, mushrooms, olives and bell peppers, served with spaghetti

Charbroiled Chicken   10.75
split breast of chicken seasoned with herbs and charbroiled

Chicken Sorrentina   10.75
breast fillet layered with eggplant, covered with tomato sauce and melted cheese

Chicken Marsala   10.75
breast fillet sauteed with mushrooms and marsala wine

Chicken Piccata   10.75
breast fillet sauteed with lemon, butter and capers

Chicken Breast Paillard   10.75
breast fillet pressed thin, seasoned with herbs and charbroiled

Fish

Baked Norwegian Salmon   13.50
fillet baked with a little parmigiano and lemon butter

Salmon Reale   13.75
fillet of Norwegian salmon oven poached, topped with sea scallops in a sherry cream sauce with pine nuts

Today's Catch Piccata   13.75
Today's Catch (Steak Cut) broiled, served with lemon butter and capers

Imported Dover Sole alla Guido   17.75
whole sole from the Bay of Dover, seasoned with lemon, butter and parmigiano grana, de-boned tableside

Seafood

Calamari Romana   12.25
calamari in tomato sauce over linguettini

Uncle Roy's Fantasia   12.25
clams and mussels sauteed with garlic, shallots, a little diced tomato, and red pepper flecks over linguettini

Scampi   14.75
broiled with lemon, garlic and butter, in their shells

Stuffed Scampi   16.75
shrimp stuffed with a rich lobster scallop and shrimp filling

Seafood Reale   13.75
shrimp and scallops in a sherry cream sauce with pine nuts over fettucine

Pescatore Diablo   14.75
shrimp, scallops, clams, mussels and calamari in a semi-hot diablo sauce, over fettuccini

Meat Specialties

Veal Parmigiana   13.25
veal cutlet covered with tomato sauce, mushrooms and melted mozzarella

Veal Cutlet alla Milanese   13.25
veal, pounded thin, lightly breaded and crisply fried

Veal alla Berto   14.25
tender veal steak, charbroiled, then topped with spinach, pancetta and melted fontina cheese

Ossobuco di Vitellina   14.75
veal shank braised with wine, diced tomatoes and pancetta

Beef Braciole   13.25
flank steak roll, stuffed with prosciutto, peas, hard boiled egg, spinach, and cheese, braised in a light tomato sauce

Bistecca ai Ferri   15.75
Porterhouse steak charbroiled, garnished with sauteed mushrooms and red peppers

Lamb Agrassato   11.25
lamb shank braised with onions, tomatoes, raisins, pine nuts, potatoes, and marsala wine...Sicilian style

Rack of Lamb all'Isabella   22.75
individual rack of lamb seasoned with a light herbed crust

Too full for dessert? Take some home for later

Berto's Gelato
Box of Spumoni Wedges or 12 Tartufi   18.00
Also, 17oz. herbal olive oil   8.75

La Fontanella

PHONE
955-1213

HOURS
Lunch
Tuesday–Friday
11:00 am–2:00 pm
Dinner
Monday–Sunday
4:30 pm–9:00 pm

LOCATION
4231 East
Indian School
Phoenix, AZ

CUISINE
Italian

FULL BAR

EARLY BIRD DINNERS
up to 5:45 seating
(15% discount)

RESERVATIONS
Suggested

CREDIT CARDS
MasterCard, Visa, American Express, Discover

SMOKING
Section Available

HANDICAP FACILITIES

A Scottsdale Landmark

Welcome to Los Olivos Mexican Food Restaurant. Family owned, housed in a charming structure, it was originally built many years ago by Tomas Corral (the grandfather). The Corral family left its native Mexico for America in 1919, because Cecilia Corral (the grandmother) did not want her sons working in the mines. Old timers will remember it as a bakery, tavern, pool parlor, even a chapel at one time. Combining their native talents, the second generation of the Corral family has brought Los Olivos from a little adobe eating spot to its present dining experience.

APPETIZERS

Cheese Crisp	4.00
Flat or folded fresh flour tortilla with cheese	
Cheese Crisp	5.25
with green chili strips and onions	
Cheese Crisp with guacamole	6.25
Mexican Pizza	6.75
Cheese crisp with green chili strips, onions, spices, tomatoes, and black olives	
Mary Lou	6.75
Folded cheese crisp topped with red or green chili con carne	
Nachos	5.95
Crisp fresh corn tortilla chips with melted cheese, topped with jalapeno peppers	
Nachos with Beans	6.75
Nachos Supreme	7.25
Served with guacamole, sour cream and tomatoes	
Guacamole Dip and Chips	5.50

SALADS

Topopo Salad	6.95
Chef's special—a salad eaters favorite! Our mexican chef salad with mixed vegetables and surrounded with pieces of chicken, slices of ripe avocado, fresh jalapenos, fresh tomatoes, and cheddar cheese, and topped with cottage cheese	
Taco salad	6.75
Green Dinner Salad	1.75
Guacamole Dinner Salad	3.50
Albondigas Mexican meatball soup	2.50
Tortilla Soup	2.75
Beef broth topped with fresh corn tortilla chips, cheese and onions	
Gazpacho Fresh chilled vegetable soup	2.95

LOS OLIVOS COMBINATION SPECIALTIES

Taco, Tamale, Enchilada	9.45
Green Corn Tamale, Chile Relleno	8.25
Red or Green Chile	6.50
Two Cheese and Onion Enchiladas	7.40
Red or Green Burro	6.00
Enchilada Style	6.75
Beef and Chicken Flauta	9.95
Sour Cream Enchilada, Green Corn Tamale	7.95
Two Chicken or Beef Enchilada	11.50

CORRAL SPECIALS

Miniature Combo	7.95
Mini taco, enchilada, tostada, tamale, beans and rice	
Los Olivos Special	7.95
Two sour cream enchiladas served with beans and rice	
Mexican Flag	8.50
An unique combination of three enchiladas: One beef enchilada covered with red sauce, two cheese enchiladas covered with green sauce, one topped with sour cream, the other topped with a green pepper	
Chorizo con Huevos	7.25
Homemade Mexican sausage, scrambled with eggs, served with a side of beans, rice and fresh flour tortilla	
Huevos Rancheros	6.95
Fried or scrambled ranch eggs smothered with our green chili and tomato sauce, served with beans, rice and flour tortilla	
Machaca	7.95
Shredded dry beef, sauteed with fresh vegetable and spices, served with beans, rice and flour tortilla	
Mushroom Enchiladas	8.95
Two cheese enchiladas topped with sauce and fresh mushrooms, served with beans and rice	

BEEFEATER FAVORITES

Carne Asada — 10.95
Long-time steak favorite served with our special salsa, rice, fresh flour tortilla, and green salad

Steak Picado — 9.50
Bits of steak lightly sauteed in our special vegetable sauce, served with beans, rice and fresh flour tortilla

Carne Asada and Enchilada
A smaller version of our Carne Asada accompanied by a cheese and onion Enchilada, complimented with a green salad and our special salsa

Spanish Steak — 7.50
Ground sirloin topped with a delicious spanish tomato and vegetable sauce. Served with rice and beans

Fajitas — 10.25
Sauteed strips of steak, chicken breast, or both, marinated in our special sauce, garnished with green peppers, onions, served with beans, guacamole, sour cream and a fresh flour tortilla

New! Shrimp Fajitas — 13.50

A LA CARTE

Tacos
Crisp corn tortilla folded to hold meat, chicken or guacamole and garnished with cheese, lettuce and tomato

Shredded Beef	2.25
Cheese	2.00
Chicken	2.50
Guacamole	3.00
Beef and Guacamole	3.35
Beef and Sour Cream	3.35

Tostadas
Crisp, flat corn tortilla topped with a variety of Mexican favorites and garnished with cheese, lettuce and tomato

Bean	2.50
Guacamole	3.15
Red or Green Chili	3.15
Tomato Supreme	4.95

Beef, beans, Guacamole, and sour cream

Tamales
Soft seasoned cornmeal, steamed to perfection in a corn husk

Beef with red sauce	2.75
Green corn with green sauce	3.25

Enchiladas
Soft fresh corn tortilla rolled and stuffed with cheese or meat, and topped with your choice of a mild red or green sauce, melted cheese onion

Cheese and onion (red sauce)	2.95
Beef (red or green)	3.40
Sour Cream	3.40
Sour Cream Beef	3.85

Beef enchilada covered with green sauce and topped with sour cream

Chicken Enchilada (red sauce)	3.60
Mushroom and Cheese Enchilada	3.85

Sonora Enchilada — 3.00
Seasoned corn patty, deep fried, and topped with lettuce and tomato

Rellenos — 3.50
Green chili pepper stuffed with cheese, dipped in egg batter, then deep fried and covered with our delicious green sauce

Enchilada Style — 4.00
Topped with melted cheese and onions, and your choice of red or green sauce

Flautas — 4.50
Crisp corn tortilla, rolled and stuffed with your choice of shredded beef or chicken, topped with guacamole

Chalupas — 4.95
Seasoned corn meal patty, deep fried and topped with your choice of shredded beef, chicken, or guacamole, topped with lettuce and tomato

Chimichangas
Crisp, deep fried, flour tortilla rolled and stuffed with your choice of delicious fillings and topped with melted cheese

Beef	6.00
Chicken	6.00
Enchilada Style	6.50
Chimichanga Supreme	7.15

Enchilada style with sour cream and guacamole

Burritos or Burros
Fresh, soft flour tortilla rolled stuffed with your choice of delicious

Bean	2.95
Chili (red or green)	3.75
Mixed (red or green mixed with beans)	4.00
Any of the above enchilada style	add .85
Burro Supreme (not french fried)	5.75
Chorizo	4.50
Machca	4.50
Chicken	4.50
Supreme	6.60

Your choice of the above burros enchilada style, with sour cream and guacamole

AMERICAN DISHES

Hamburger	4.25
Cheeseburger	4.75
Avocado burger	4.95
Green Chili burger	4.95
Mushroom burger	5.25
Grilled Cheese Sandwich	3.95

Above served with fries

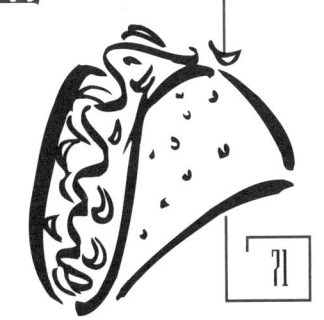

POSTRE

A wide variety to choose from

Los Olivos

PHONE
946-2256

HOURS
Sunday–Thursday
11:00 am–10:00 pm
Friday & Saturday
11:00 am–1:00 am

LOCATION
7328 2nd Street
Scottsdale, AZ 85281

CUISINE
Mexican

ATTIRE
Casual

ENTERTAINMENT
Friday & Saturdays
9:00 pm–1:00 am

TERRACE DINING

AFTER THEATRE DINING

RESERVATIONS
Suggested

CREDIT CARDS
MasterCard, Visa, American Express

SMOKING
Section Available

HANDICAP FACILITIES

Lo Cascio

PHONE
949-0334

HOURS
Lunch
Monday–Friday
11:00 am–2:00 pm
Dinner
Sunday–Thursday
5:00 pm–10:00 pm
Friday & Saturday
5:00 pm–11:00 pm
Call for Summer
Hours

LOCATION
2210 North
Scottsdale Road
Tempe, AZ 85281

CUISINE
Southern Italian

ATTIRE
Casual

AFTER THEATRE DINING
TAKE OUT
VEGETARIAN MEALS

RESERVATIONS
Suggested

CREDIT CARDS
We Welcome

Diners Club International

Diners Club and Other Major Credit Cards Accepted

SMOKING
Section Available

HANDICAP FACILITIES

Lo Cascio
Italian Restaurant

Enjoy a delightful dinner of southern Italian cuisine, with homemade pasta, lasagna, manicotti or ravioli, etc. Or try veal, chicken or pizza at affordable prices.

Parliamo italiano & siciliano–Aperto ogni giorno.

Pasta Dishes

All entrés served with soup or salad, bread and butter

YOUR CHOICE OF:
SPAGHETTI, LINGUINI OR MOSTACCIOLI:

WITH MEAT SAUCE	8.95
WITH TOMATO SAUCE	8.45
WITH AGLIO AND OLIO	7.95
Sauteed garlic in olive oil	
WITH WHITE CLAM SAUCE	8.95
A delicate blend of garlic, olive oil and clams.	
WITH RED CLAM SAUCE	8.50
WITH FRESH MARINARA SAUCE	8.95

FETTUCCINI ALFREDO — 9.95
Fettuccini tossed with white sauce and parmesan cheese.

FETTUCCINI BOSCAILOLA — 9.95
Fettuccini, white sauce with a touch of garlic, mushrooms and ham.

MOSTACCIOLI ALFORNO — 9.50
Mostaccioli with meat sauce, topped with mozzarella cheese and baked

RAVIOLI — 9.50
Homemade pasta pillow stuffed with meat or cheese.

RAVIOLI ALFORNO — 9.95
Homemade pasta pillow stuffed with meat or cheese, topped with sauce, mozzarella cheese and baked.

CANNELLONI — 9.95
Homemade egg noodles stuffed with three kinds of meat, baked with sauce and mozzarella cheese.

MANICOTTI — 9.95
Homemade egg noodles stuffed with three kinds of cheese, baked with sauce and mozzarella cheese.

LASAGNE — 9.95
Layers of pasta, two kinds of meat, sauce, ricotta and romano cheeses, baked with mozzarella cheese.

TORTELLINI MEAT SAUCE — 9.95

TORTELLINI ALLA PANNA — 10.95
Tortellini with white sauce.

Italian Specialties

VITELLO ALLA PARMIGIANA — 14.95
Sauteed veal cutlet baked with tomato sauce and mozzarella cheese.

COTOLETTA ALLA MILANESE — 14.50
Sauteed breaded veal cutlet.

VITELLO MARSALA — 15.75
Sauteed scallopini with butter, garlic, mushrooms and marsala wine sauce.

VITELLO PICATA — 14.50
Sauteed scallopini with butter, garlic, mushrooms, capers, lemon and white wine sauce.

VITELLO ALLA FRANCESE — 15.95
Sauteed egg dip scallopini with garlic, mushrooms, butter and white wine sauce.

VITELLO AL CARCIOFI — 16.95
Sauteed bite size veal with mushrooms, onion, garlic, lemon, white wine and artichoke hearts.

POLLO ALLA CACCIATORE — 12.95
Half chicken with mushrooms, green peppers, onion, white wine, sauteed in a special red sauce.

POLLO ALFORNO — 11.50
Half chicken baked with butter and spice.

POLLO FRITTO — 11.50
Half chicken dipped in Italian breading and fried.

CHICKEN MARSALA — 12.95
Sauteed chicken breast with mushrooms, garlic butter and marsala wine sauce.

CHICKEN PICATA — 12.95
Sauteed chicken breast with mushrooms, garlic, capers, lemon, white wine and butter sauce.

CHICKEN PARMIGIANA — 11.95
Sauteed breaded chicken breast, baked with tomato sauce and mozzarella cheese.

EGGPLANT PARMIGIANA — 10.95
Sauteed breaded eggplant baked with tomato sauce and mozzarella cheese.

Appetizers, Soups & Salads

DINNER SALAD	3.95	FRIED CALAMARI	6.95
ANTIPASTA FOR ONE	6.95	FORMAGGIO FRITTO	6.50
PATATINE FRITTE	2.70	MOZZARELLA MARINARA	6.50
FUNGHI FRITTE	6.50	GARLIC BREAD	1.50
ZUCCHINI FRITTE	5.50	PIZZA BREAD	2.50
ESPRESSO	1.95	SOUP	3.95
		CAPPUCCINO	3.50

MANCUSO'S

OF SCOTTSDALE
EST. 1969

It is more than a gourmet delight to experience the Northern Italian and Continental Cuisine at Mancuso's at the Borgota. In their double tiered building that resembles an Italian renaissance grand palace, their new menu features veal, seafood, fowl and homemade pasta. Enjoy their cappuccino and Espresso Bar. Piano music during dinner hour.

Mancuso's

PHONE
948-9988

HOURS
5:00pm-10:30pm

LOCATION
6166 North
Scottsdale Road
Scottsdale, Az 85253

CUISINE
Italian

ATTIRE
Moderate

LOUNGE
Piano Bar
5:30 pm-Closing

RESERVATIONS
Recommended

CREDIT CARDS
MasterCard, Visa,
American Expres,
Diners Club

SMOKING
Section Available

APPETIZERS (Cold)

CARPACCIO DI MANZO Sliced raw beef, mustard sauce & capers	$7.50
FRESH OYSTERS ON HALF SHELL Cocktail sauce	$6.95
BELUGA MALOSSAL CAVIAR And garni	$59.00

APPETIZERS (Hot)

OYSTERS ROCKEFELLER	$7.50
ESCARGOT BOURGOGNE Wine, butter & garlic	$7.50
SHRIMP SCAMPI Olive oil, butter & garlic	$7.95
STUFFED MUSHROOMS Alfredo sauce	$5.95
FROG LEGS Olive Oil, butter, garlic & chives	$7.50

SALADS (INSALATE)

INSALATA CESARE (Caesar salad)	$5.95
FRESH BUFALA MOZZARELLA Imported, tomato, olive oil & fresh basil	$7.25
INSALATE SPINACCA Wild mushrooms, lemon pepper dressing	$5.95
POMODORO E CIPOLLA Sliced tomato, sweet Maui onion and Italian vinaigrette	$4.95
SMOKED SALMON & HEARTS OF PALM	$7.95

PASTA

PENNE ARRABIATA Short tubular pasta, spicy marinara sauce & mushrooms	$13.50
GNOCCI Pasta, potato dumpling & sun dried tomatoes with rose sauce	$13.50
STRAW & GRASS FETTUCCINE Sausage meat, mushrooms, cheese, butter & cream	$14.50
CAPELLINI & POMODORO Angel hair, fresh tomatoes, garlic & basil	$12.95
FETTUCCINE SHRIMP & SCALLOPS Wine, mushrooms & tomato sauce	$16.95
COMBINATION Fettuccine, ravioli, lasagna, cannelloni, with tomato sauce	$14.50
CANNELLONI Spinach, beef, veal & cheese, Alfredo or tomato sauce	$13.50
PENNE & EGGPLANT Short tubular pasta with eggplant & tomato sauce	$13.95
LINGUINI & CLAMS Whole baby clams, red or white sauce	$13.50
ANGEL HAIR PASTA WITH SHRIMP Olive oil, basil, garlic & fresh tomatoes	$15.75

CHICKEN

CHICKEN & GRILLED EGGPLANT Garlic, basil & tomato concassee	$16.95
CHICKEN OSCAR Double boneless breast, crab meat, asparagus & bearnaise sauce	$16.95

DUCKLING

DUCK A L'ORANGE our special sauce	$18.95
DUCK A L'RASPBERRY raspberry sauce	$18.95

SPECIALTIES

FRENCHED LAMB CHOPS DIJON Dijon sauce	$22.95
FRENCHED LAMB CHOPS (DOUBLE) Garlic, olive oil & herbs	$22.95
FROG LEGS PROVENCALE Olive Oil, garlic, butter & tomato concassee	$18.95
SAUTEED EGGPLANT Eggplant, ricotta cheese & marinara sauce	$14.50

VEAL

VEAL MARSALA Wine, cheese & imported mushrooms	$20.95
VEAL & EGGPLANT Sun dried tomatoes, basil, wine cream sauce	$20.95
VEAL SALTIMBOCCA Prosciutto, wine, lemon & butter	$20.95

BEEF

TOURNEDOS THREE Medallions of beef, lamb & veal, bearnaise sauce	$20.95
TOURNEDOS DIJONNAISE Dijon mustard sauce	$19.50
FILET MIGNON AU POIVRE Brandy, cream & green peppercorns	$19.50

FISH & SEAFOOD

SHRIMP DIJONNAISE Dijon mustard sauce	$20.95
ORANGE ROUGHY Fresh tomato, basil & garlic sauce	$17.95
LOBSTER FRA DIAVOLO Lobster, shrimp, scallops, mussells, clams & marinara sauce on a bed of ligiuini	$23.95

marché Gourmet

The soul of France in the heart of Scottsdale, with an intimate, yet simple indoor-outdoor dining atmosphere associated with true Country French cuisine. Onion Soup, Chicken Dijonnaise, Lamb Rack, Boullabaisse & Tofu Provençale? Oui! C'est "Fameux!" Creme Brulee, Cappuccino, Cordials.

The only French Restaurant serving Breakfast Daily

Breakfast
(Served Until 2 pm on Sundays)

Blue Corn Pancakes	4.95
With syrup	
Original French Toast	4.95
With syrup	
Tofu Scramble	5.95
Vegetables, brown rice, and potatoes	
Smoked Salmon Bagel	7.95
Cream cheese, capers, tomatoes, etc...	

Toast & Herbed Red Potatoes Served with the following:

Nopaleggs	6.75
Nopales, onions, pimientos & 3 eggs scrambled	
Huevos Con Chorizo	6.95
Chorizo, & 3 eggs scrambled	
Indian Lamb Sausage	6.95
Lightly spiced	

Frittatas
open face, 3 egg omelettes with red potatoes & toast

Piperade Ham, peppers, mushrooms & tomato	6.95
Southwest Ham, onion, garlic, green chile, corn & cumino	6.50
Salmon Dill, mushroom, onion & red pepper	6.95

Herbed Red Potatoes served with the following:
Eggs Benedict

Regular with Canadian Bacon or tomato	6.95
Pesto with a Pesto Hollandaise	7.25
Louie with seasoned crab meat	7.95
Florentine on a bed of creamed spinach	6.95
Deluxe combination of Florentine and Louie	8.75

Lunch

Salads

Carribean Shrimp	9.95
Mixed greens with water chestnuts, peas, carrots, peanuts, and topped with Bay Shrimp, with curry vinaigrette.	
Nicoise	9.95
Mixed greens, brown rice, green bean, red potato, tuna, tomato and egg wedges, olives. Served with vinaigrette. Anchovies upon request.	
Caesar	6.95
Mixed greens, croutons, parmesan. (ANCHOVIES ?)	
Add grilled chicken	8.95
Add grilled duck breast	10.95

Specialties

Eggplant Marinara	6.95
With steamed brown rice and marina sauce	
Half Cornish Game Hen	7.95
With french fries and lunch salad	
Salmon Bearnaise	11.00
With steamed red potatoes, brown rice and vegetables	
Steamed Vegetables	7.50
In light olive oil & lemon, served with brown rice	
Duck Tamales	8.95
With mixed brown rice & Orange-Tomatillo sauce	

Pastas

Provençale	6.95
Bell pepper, tomato, black olives, onions & herbs	
Salmon	7.95
Creamy dill sauce with mushrooms, onions & red peppers	
Sonora	6.95
With onions, corn and green chili tossed in Tomatillo sauce	
Alsacian	6.95
Ham, onion & nutmeg tossed with parmesan	
Pesto	6.95
Basil dressing, parmesan & pinons	
Greek	6.95
Tossed in olive oil, with Kalamata olives, onion, garlic, and parmesan cheese	
Hungarian	7.25
In a creamy Paprika sauce with bacon, turkey, cabbage	

Marché Gourmet

PHONE
994-4568

HOURS
Sunday
7:30 am–2:00 pm
Breakfast only
Monday–Saturday
7:30 am–9:30 pm

LOCATION
4121 North
Marshal Way
Scottsdale, AZ 85251

CUISINE
Country French

ATTIRE
Casual

TERRACE DINING

SUNDAY BRUNCH

ART WALK EVERY THURSDAY

FULL SERVICE CATERING

RESERVATIONS
Suggested

CREDIT CARDS
MasterCard, Visa,
American Express,
Diners Club, Discover

SMOKING
Section Available

HANDICAP FACILITIES

Dinner
(Served Monday thru Saturday, 5:30 to 9:00 pm)

Starters

Sauteed Calamari	6.25
Olive oil, garlic, onion, parsley, tomato sauce	
Polenta Cote D'Azur	5.75
Topped with two cheeses, with marinara sauce	
Baked Brie with Pesto	8.95
Please allow 20 minutes	
Escargots	6.25
In garlic and shallot butter	
Miso Soup	4.50
Made to order, with red miso	
Onion Soup Gratinee	4.95
Topped with croutons and Swiss cheese	

Chicken Dishes
Served with vegetables, brown rice or red potatoes, steamed or Lyonnaise style.

Bordelaise	12.50
In red wine and mushroom sauce	
Provençale	12.50
In herbs de Provence, with lemon	
Parmesan	12.50
Battered in Parmesan	
Dijonnaise	12.50
In a creamy Dijon and white wine sauce	
Normandy	12.50
With fresh apples in Brandy sauce	
Hungarian	12.50
In a creamy Paprika sauce	
A L'Orange	12.50
In a zesty fresh Orange sauce	
Tarragon	12.50
In a light, Terragon sauce	

House Specialties

Merguez	13.50
Spicy lamb sausage & French fries	
Pepper Steak	15.00
Green peppercorn sauce & French fries	
Alsacian Choucroute	14.00
Sauerkraut in wine with garlic sausage, ham and frankurter; served with steamed red potatoes and dijon mustard	
Cassoulet Toulousain	15.00
A specialty from southern France made of slowly baked Northern style white beans flavored with tomato, onion, garlic; garnished with pork loin, sausage and our duck confit; then baked again	
Spanish Paella	16.00
Mediterranean delicacy made of richly flavored saffron rice baked with onion, tomato, peas and green peppers; garnished with scallops, shrimp, green lip mussel, calamari, chorizo and chicken	
Bouillabaisse "J-Mr's Style"	16.00
Tomatoes, onion, garlic, parsley, red potatoes, in a saffron and fennel flavored seafood broth with scallops, shrimp, white fish and mussel, Served with the traditional "Rouille" sauce	
Duck Confit	15.00
Baked with ham and imported peas	
Veal Blanquette	14.00
In white wine cream sauce with peas, carrots and mushrooms. Served with steamed red potato or rice	
Butterflied Tiger Shrimp	13.00
Spicy or mild, with mixed rice and vegetables	

From the Mesquite Grill
Served with vegetables and brown rice (mixed or steamed) or red potatoes, steamed or Lyonnaise style

New Zealand Lamb Rack	16.00
Individual rack, cooked medium rare	
Duck A L'Orange	14.00
Double breast, cooked medium rare	
Butterflied Quails (3 pc)	17.00
Served with a Tangy "Diable" sauce	
Cornish Game Hen	13.00
Served with "Diable" sauce	
Pork Tenderloin	13.00
With cranberry compote	
Salmon Filet	14.00
Served with Bearnaise sauce,	

Specialty Desserts...
Along with our pastry tray

Creme Brulee	4.75
Peach Melba	4.75
Coupe Normandie	4.75
Warm stewed apples over vanilla ice cream with Grand Marnier	

Maria's WHEN IN NAPLES

Maria makes FRESH pasta. If you know the difference between fresh pasta and regular pasta, you will appreciate Maria's. Decorated in a comfortable yet elegant style, this restaurant features old favorites, daily specials, gourmet foods, and antipasta to die for.

Buon Appetito

Antipasta, insalate e altre specialita'

BRUSCHETTA ALLA TOSCANA 4.95
Toasted country bread with garlic, olive oil, and fresh tomatos and arugola

INSALATA DI CESARE 4.95
Salad of romaine with Caesar dressing and toasted parmigiano croutons

CALAMARI FRITTI 6.95

CARPACCIO 7.95
Thin slices of raw filet mignon with arugola and freshly shredded parmigiano cheese and capers topped with a lemon-mustard sauce

CLAMS CASINO 7.95
Baked stuffed clams with Italian herbs, bacon and white wine

LA CAPRESE 7.95
Fresh buffalo mozzarella with tomato and basil

TRAMEZZINO DI POLENTA 7.95
CON FUNGHI DI BOSCO E FONTINA
Sliced polenta, wild mushrooms and Fontina cheese

PORTOBELLO OREGANATO 7.95
Baked with garlic, olive oil, Romano cheese and white wine sauce

ANTIPASTO MISTO 8.95
An assortment of Italian cold sliced meats, seasonal marinated vegetables and cheeses

From our wood burning oven

PIZZA MARGHERITA 7.95
Tomatoes, mozzarella cheese, oregano and olive oil

PIZZA CAPRICCIOSA 8.95
Fresh tomato, diced prosciutto, artichoke hearts, black olives, mozzarella cheese and arugola

PIZZA CON LA LUGANEGA 8.95
Italian sausage, roasted peppers, mozzarella, oregano and tomato sauce

PIZZA FAGOTTINO RUSPANTE 8.95
Folded pizza filled with chicken, mozzarella, provolone, ricotta, grilled zucchini, eggplant and mushrooms

PIZZA SCHIACCIATINA 8.95
CON CIPOLLA ROSSA
Thin oval pizza with Bermuda onions, gruyere and mozzarella cheeses, ham and sage

PIZZA VEGETARIAN 8.95
Artichokes, zucchini, fresh tomatoes, red onions, sweet peppers and tomato sauce

Zuppe

ESCAROLA IN BRODO 4.95
CON CAPELLINI TRINCIATI
Escarole soup with angel hair

PASTA E FAGIOLI ALLA NAPOLETANA 4.95
Bean soup with escarole and pasta

ZUPPA DI LENTICCHIE E VERDURA 4.95
Lentil soup with vegetables

RAVIOLETTI IN BRODO 6.95
Homemade vegetarian ravioli in a clear chicken broth

Pasta fatta in casa
Homemade Pasta
Served with fresh garden salad and baked bread

GNOCCHI AL POMODORO E BASILICO 11.95
Homemade potato dumplings with fresh tomato, and basil

FETTUCCINE ALLA BOLOGNESE 12.95
Homemade pasta with meat sauce and grilled sausage

FETTUCCINE CAMPINOSTRI 12.95
Fresh fettuccine with eggplant, peppers, mushrooms and peas in a light tomato sauce

LASAGNA ALLA BOLOGNESE 12.95
Fresh homemade pasta with bolognese sauce, bechamel sauce, mozzarella and parmigiano cheese

RAVIOLI DI RICOTTA 12.95
Ravioli filled with ricotta and spinach in creamy pesto sauce

CANNELLONI DELLA CASA 13.95
Filled with veal and chicken baked in bechamel sauce and topped with bolognese sauce

RAVIOLI DI ZUCCA AI 13.95
QUATTRO FORMAGGI
Ravioli filled with butternut squash in a four cheese sauce

FETTUCCINE "DI FABIO" 14.95
*Homemade pasta with wild mushrooms,
fresh tomato and arugola*

STROZZAPRETI AI GHIOTTONE 14.95
Homemade potato dumplings with sausage and spinach sauce

RAVIOLI DI ARAGOSTA 16.95
ALLE DOE SALSE
Ravioli filled with lobster meat in two sauces

TAGLERINI MARE & MONTI 17.95
*Homemade thin pasta with asparagus and shrimp sauteed with leeks
and tomatoes*

MARIA'S SPECIAL PASTA OF THE DAY
Please ask your server

Piatti Principali— Main Entrees

Served with fresh garden salad, fresh vegetables, potatoes, and fresh baked bread

MELANZANE PARMIGIANA 12.95
Layers of sliced eggplant with fresh tomatoes, parmigiano, mozzarella and fresh herbs

PAILLARD DI POLLO 14.95
Grilled chicken paillard with herbed olive oil and lemon

FRICASSEE DI POLLO AL BALSAMICO 15.95
Sauteed chicken with mushrooms in balsamic vinegar sauce with carrots, potatoes and mushroom caps

POLLO E SALSICCIA SCARPARIELLO 15.95
Sauteed chicken and sausage with garlic, olive oil and lemon

VITELLO ALLA MARIA 16.95
Sauteed veal with mushrooms, artichoke hearts, capers and lemon

VITELLO ALLA MARSALA 16.95
Veal scallopine sauteed with a mushroom marsala wine sauce

VITELLO PARMIGIANA 16.95
Sauteed veal scallopine with fresh tomato and mozzarella

MEDAGLIONI DI BUE ALLA CAPRESE 20.95
Sauteed medallion of filet mignon with tomato, basil and buffalo mozzarella

MEDAGLIONI DI BUE ALLA 20.95
CONTESSA MARIA
Grilled medallion of filet mignon with sauteed mushrooms in garlic and lemon sauce

PESCE PEL GIORNO   Please ask your server
"Catch of the day"

Altre specialita' di pasta— Other Pasta Specialities

Served with fresh garden salad and fresh baked bread

CAPELLINI AL POMODORO E BASILICO 9.95
Angel hair pasta with fresh tomato and basil sauce

CAPELLINI NAPOLETANA 12.95
Angel hair pasta with sausage, onions, mushrooms, bell peppers, tomatoes sauteed with virgin olive oil, garlic, white wine and a touch of cream

LINGUINE ALLE VONGOLE 13.95
Linguine with baby clams, sauteed with garlic, onions, olive oil, parsley and white wine in your choice of red or white sauce

RIGATONI CON POLLO AFFUMICATO 13.95
Rigatoni with grilled smoked chicken in a light cream sauce with parmigiano cheese

SCAMPI FRADIAVOLO 16.95
CON LENTICCHIE
Scampi braised with garlic and lentils in a spicy tomato sauce served over linguine

PAGLIA E FIENO ALLA TRASTEVERINA 17.95
Homemade spinach and egg pasta with shrimp, seabass, calamari and scallops braised with fresh tomato and mozzarella

SALMONE ALLA GRIGLIA CON CIPOLLE 17.95
ROSSE E BASILICO
Grilled salmon with sauteed Bermuda onion, basil, tomato and zucchini served over linguine

RISOTTO DEL GIORNO   Please ask your server

Dolce

A selection of desserts are prepared daily. Please ask your server.

CAFFE 1.25

ESPRESSO 2.00

CAPPUCCINO 3.00

CAPPUCCINO NAPOLETANO 4.75
Cappuccino with tuaca, sambuca, frangelico and amaretto

IRISH COFFEE 4.75
Coffee blended with Irish whiskey, topped with cream and green creme de menthe

KEOKI COFFEE 4.75
Coffee flavored with Kahlua and brandy topped with cream

Maria's When In Naples

PHONE
991-6887

HOURS
Lunch
Monday–Friday
11:30 am–2:30 pm
Dinner–Daily
5:00 pm–Close

LOCATION
7000 East Shea Blvd.
Scottsdaler, AZ 85254

CUISINE
Italian

ATTIRE
Casual

LOUNGE
Lunch
Monday–Friday
11:30 am–2:30 pm
Daily
5:00 pm–10:00 am

PATIO DINING

TAKE OUT

VEGETARIAN MEALS

RESERVATIONS
Suggested

CREDIT CARDS
MasterCard, Visa,
American Express,
Diners Club, Discover

CHECKS ACCEPTED

SMOKING
Bar Section Only

HANDICAP FACILITIES

MIRAGE GRILL
OF FOUNTAIN HILLS

Tucked away in the heart of scenic Fountain Hills is the Club Mirage. Somewhat of an desert oasis in the desert foothills, Club Mirage has the best in tennis, swimming and fitness so it is only fitting that it is also the home of the best dining in Fountain Hills.

The Mirage has upscale dining in a relaxed country club atmosphere. A varied menu offering steaks, seafood, pasta, regional favorites and salads is offered every evening starting at four. The Lunch menu consists of a create your own deli sandwich section and other Mirage favorites such as the South Western Reuben, Veggie Pita and the incredible Grilled Chicken Caesar Salad. There is always something for the kids with the children's menu available all day.

Appetizers

Crab Stuffed Mushrooms $5.50
A delectable mixture of snow crab, spices and cheese all stuffed inside a mushroom cap.

Artichoke Dip $4.95
A virtual collage of flavors! Served in an artichoke "bowl" with veggies & club crackers.

Shrimp Scampi $5.95
Garlic & Wine...the two most popular ingredients in all of Italy.

Potato Skins $4.95
Filled with cheddar and topped with bacon or green chilies and jack cheese.

Salads

Chicken Avocado $5.95
A mix of red and green leaf, cucumbers, peppers and tomato. Topped with slices of avacado and grilled chicken.

Fajitas $6.25
Sautéed peppers, onions, and your choice of beef or chicken, atop fresh salad greens.

House Salad $1.95
Red & green leaf, tossed with peppers tomatoes and cucumbers.

Pasta

Mediterranean $10.95
Sundried tomato, ripe olives, and mushrooms all sautéed with strips of chicken breast and served over spinach fettucini.

Cajun Chicken and Shrimp $11.95
A taste of Mardi Gras, at the Mirage Grill. Peppers, tomatoes, mushrooms and such, come together in a creole favorite.

Stir Fry Vegetables $8.95
A delicious mix of veggies and water chestnuts with an oriental flair. Served with rice.

Add Chicken or Beef $10.45
Add Shrimp $11.95

Seafood

Trout Almondine $12.95
Filleted, seasoned and pan fried to perfection (a house favorite).

Grilled Halibut $13.45
A charbroiled halibut loin steak, seasoned with lemon pepper.

Entrees

Filet Mignon $14.95
7oz of heaven! The tenderest cut, wrapped in bacon, and char broiled for that western flavor.

Ribeye $10.95
Cut to order. We start with an 10oz cut, where we go from there is up to you!

Order by the inch, pay by the ounce
each additional ounce .75
(1/2 inch steak= approximately 8oz. This is only an estimate as all loins vary)

St. Louis Style ribs 1/2 Rack $9.95
Full Rack $12.95
Same as the babyback ony meatier. First we bake 'em , then we charbroil 'em. All the while, basting with the chef's homemade BBQ sauce.

Fajitas Beef or chicken $9.95
Shrimp $11.95
Your choice of marinated beef, chicken or shrimp. Sautéed with peppers and onions, and served up with black beans, rice, guacamole and pico de gallo.

For The Kids

All Choices $3.99 (includes soft drink)

Pizza
Your own personal pizza, cheese or pepperoni.

Hamburger / Hot Dog
Two of Americas favorites. Served with chips.

Grilled Cheese
Just like at home. Served with chips.

Peanut Butter and Jelly Quesadilla
That old standby with a twist. Served with chips.

Spaghetti and Meatballs
Angel hair pasta, smothered with marinara and topped with two meatballs.

Dessets

Country Pie Ala Mode $5.95
Ask your server for tonight's selection. Served with vanilla ice cream.

Cheese Cake $5.95
Ask your server for tonight's selection.

Baked Bread Pudding $5.25
Just like grandma made with a little mirage magic

Mirage Bar & Grill

PHONE
837–8000

HOURS
Sunday–Thursday
11:00 am–9:00 pm
Friday & Saturday
11:00 am–10:00 pm

LOCATION
14815 North
Fountain Hills Blvd.
Fountain Hills, AZ
85268

CUISINE
Continental

ATTIRE
Casual

LOUNGE
11:00 am–11:00 pm

SUNDAY BRUNCH
10:00 am–2:00 pm

RESERVATIONS
Parties of 10 or more

CREDIT CARDS
MasterCard, Visa,
American Express

SMOKING
Section Available

HANDICAP FACILITIES

Marco Polo Supper Club

PHONE
602-483-1900

HOURS
Daily
5:00 pm–1:00 am

LOCATION
8608 East Shea
Scottsdale, AZ 85260

CUISINE
Italian/Oriental

ATTIRE
Casual

LOUNGE
5:00 pm–Closing

TERRACE DINING

AFTER THEATRE DINING

FULL SERVICE CATERING

TAKE OUT

VEGETARIAN MEALS

RESERVATIONS
Suggested

CREDIT CARDS
MasterCard, Visa,
American Express

SMOKING
Section Available

MARCO POLO
ITALIAN • ORIENTAL • CAFE

Marco Polo on Shea reunites the Italian noodle with it's Oriental origins under one roof. The result is a dynasty of dining delights—ranging from our generous selection of Italian specialties, made even more succulent by special sauces; to a variety of Oriental dishes prepared as they would have been for Marco Polo himself, by the ancient method of Wok cooking.

• APPETIZERS •

Calamari Fritte 7.25
Toasted calamari served with oriental and Italian sauce

Toasted Ravioli 5.25
Cheese ravioli, toasted and served with Italian tomato sauce

Marco Polo Pot Stickers 6.95
Homemade meat filled pasta, served crispy with a Chinese soy dip

Kung Pao Prawns 7.95
Large shrimp stir-fried in a ginger, garlic sauce with fresh peppers, pineapple, and scallions over crispy rice noodles

Cho Cho's 6.00
Tender marinated flank steak skewered and broiled in sesame seed napa cabbage slaw

• SALADS •

Insalata Valli 3.50
   with shrimp 6.75
Our special "House Salad" with sliced artichokes, pimentos, red onions, olive oil, vinegar and cheese

Caesar 4.50
Tender romaine leaves tossed with the classic original dressing recipe

Oriental Chop 4.75
Est oVest vegetables hand tossed with roasted almond slivers and sesame seed dressing presented over cellophane noodles

East Meets West Calimari 5.75
Chilled calamari tossed with Est oVest vegetables, ancient Chinese secret dressing

• NOODLES AND PASTA •

100 Almond Primavera 11.00
   with shrimp 14.00
   with chicken 12.75
Linguine noodles stir fried with an array of stir fried vegetables oriental Soya broth and lots of almonds

Pasta Cielo "Pasta Heaven" 14.00
Penne Sautéed with fresh tomatoes, onions, mushrooms, kalamalia, olives, garlic, and shrimp in marinara sauce

Angelhair Pomodora 10.95
   with Shrimp 14.00
The thinnest Italian pasta with fresh roma tomatoes, onions, mushrooms, basil, and garlic

• ENTREES •
Entrees Include Chef's Daily Side Dish

Oriental Crispy Duckling 18.95
Slow roasted till crispy. Served over stir fry oriental vegetables with a choice of szechwan or orange sauce

Hong Kong Chicken 18.95
Breast of chicken stuffed with mozzarella, shrimp, bean sprouts and spinach served over oriental seasoned linguine noodles with toasted almonds

Grilled Veal Chop 21.95
Choice of spicy Szechwan, piccata, or marsala wine sauce

Rack of New Zealand Lamb 21.95
Marinated in fresh herbs and roasted to perfection. Served with a marsala wine, mushroom sauce

Veal Piccata (Classico) 16.95
Sauteed veal in white wine, lemon and mushroom sauce

Veal Parmigiano 16.95
Rolled in homemade bread crumbs and pan sauteed with our own tomato-cheese sauce

Veal Marsala (Classico) 16.95
Sauteed veal with marsala wine and mushroom sauce

Filet Mignon Alla Mastro 18.95
Peppered prime filet mignon char-broiled, topped with mozzarella cheese and piccata mushroom sauce

Filet Mignon Broccoli Steak 18.95
Char-grilled prime filet mignon, over stir fried broccoli and Est oVest vegetables, with hoisin oyster sauce

Filet Mignon Sotto Fiammo 18.95
Peppered prime filet mignon, char-broiled with fresh garlic, white wine and fresh lemon-mushroom sauce

Lobster Spedini 22.95
Lobster tail marinated in fresh spices, skewered and lightly rolled in Italian bread crumbs, then broiled, served with lemon, butter and garlic sauce

Broiled Orange Roughy 16.75
Lightly breaded with our own homemade Italian bread crumbs served with a light tomato piccata sauce and grilled red and green bell peppers

Lobster & Shrimp Pasta 19.50
Special Alla Lo Mein
Lobster and shrimp sauteed in olive oil and a hint of fresh garlic, then added to Lo Mein noodles and stir fried in our Chinese wok with red cabbage, bok choy and a spicy Italian/Oriental marinara sauce

Sizzling Salmon 17.25
fresh fillet of salmon, grilled and presented on a bed of stir fried orzo and sweet chili vegetables, glazed in a soy sauce

Mary Elaine's
at The Phoenician

From atop the resort, Mary Elaine's offers Contemporary cuisine featuring fresh seafood from around the world, highlighting the flavors of France, Italy, North Africa and Asia. Elegant surroundings with dramatic views of the Valley, intimate patios alive with firelight and soothing jazz from the lounge combine for a memorable evening of dining.

Appetizers

✣ Roasted Sea Scallops — 11.50
with Braised Oxtail Quinoa
Pickled Beets and Pistachio Oil

Veal Sweetbread "Pot Stickers" with — 10.00
Sweet and Sour Red Cabbage and Chanterelles
Sherry Vinegar Sauce with Pine Nuts and Sultanas

Risotto of Cave Creek Escargots — 10.50
and Mushrooms
Glazed Asparagus and Aged Parmegiano Cheese

✣ Chilled Dungeness Crab — 9.00
with Toasted Cous Cous
Shaved Salad of Crisp Vegetables and Lobster-Horseradish Aïoli

✣ Gratin of Herb and Spinach Cannelloni — 9.00
Sauté of Artichokes and Wilted Greens

Applewood-Smoked Salmon and — 11.00
Potato Crisps with Spicy Tuna Tartare
Wasabi-Chile, Beluga Caviar and Celery Crème Fraîche

Cream of Lobster Soup with Morel and — 7.50
Porcini Mushroom Infusion
Lobster and Wild Mushroom Ragoût

Salads

✣ Tian of Parmegiano and Grilled Vegetables — 9.00
with Tomato Compôte
Fresh Buffalo Mozzarella with Roasted Eggplant and Pesto

Salad of Braised Artichoke and — 9.00
Goat Cheese Gratin with Chilled Ratatouille
Spiced Sumac Vinaigrette and Artichoke Coulis

Warm Salad of Lobster and Shellfish — 14.50
New Potatoes and Green Beans in Citrus-Parsley Oil

Entrées

Filet of John Dory with Basil — 31.50
and Black Truffles
"Fork-Mashed" New Potatoes and Braised Celery

Tenderloin of Veal with Roasted — 34.00
Garlic-Rosemary Jus
Tartelette of White Bean Purée and Glazed Spring Vegetables

✣ Crispy Skin Salmon — 29.00
with Gazpacho Vegetable Napoleon
Roasted-Tomatillo Sauce with Cilantro and Lime

Roasted-Muscovy Duck Breast with — 31.50
"Dolce-Forte" Sauce and Seasonal Mushrooms
Strudel of Vanilla-Spiced Peaches, Caramelized Shallots and Duck Confit

Mesquite-Grilled Tenderloin of Beef — 31.50
with Osso Bucco Cannelloni
Red Wine-Shallot Syrup and Pickled Leeks

✣ Roasted Sea Bass with Caramelized — 29.00
Red Onion Ravioli
Bouillabaisse Essence, Garlic Croûton and Whole Roasted Young Bok Choy

Garlic and Herb-Crusted Rack of Lamb — 34.00
with Tapenade
Smoked Peppers and Chiles with "Socca Niçoise"

✣ Daurade Royale with Garden Peas — 30.00
and Coconut Basmati Rice
Sweet Lobster Curry Sauce with Fried Ginger and Mango

✣ *Choices*—Superb cuisine created by Chef Alessandro Stratta with your well-being in mind.

Mary Elaine's

PHONE
602-423-2530

HOURS
Dinner
Sunday–Thursday
6:00 pm–10:00 pm
Friday & Saturday
6:00 pm–11:00 pm

LOCATION
6000 East
Camelback Road
Scottsdale, AZ 85251

CUISINE
Contemporary

ATTIRE
Seasonal attire
Jacket required

LOUNGE
6:00 pm–Closing
Jazz

PRIVATE SALONS

RESERVATIONS
Required

CREDIT CARDS
MasterCard, Visa,
American Express,
Diners Club, Discover

SMOKING
Section Available

HANDICAP FACILITIES

Molise Cucina Italiana

PHONE
423-5801

HOURS
Lunch
Tuesday–Friday
11:00am–2:00 pm
Dinner
Tuesday–Sunday
5:00 pm–10:00 pm

LOCATION
2515 North
Scottsdale Road
Scottsdale, Az 85257

CUISINE
Italian

ATTIRE
Casual

TAKE OUT CATERING

TAKE OUT VEGETARIAN MEALS

RESERVATIONS
Suggested

CREDIT CARDS
MasterCard, Visa,
American Express,
Diners Club, Discover

HANDICAP FACILITIES

Molise Cucina Italianna

Scottsdale's newest best kept secret.

Antipasto
Appetizers

Misto di Vegetali 6.50
  Eggplants, roasted peppers, and mushrooms
Cozze alla Marinara 5.00
  Mussels in garlic and lightly spiced tomato sauce
Ravioli di Lumache 5.50
  Escargot ravioli with pernod sauce
Frutti di Mare 6.50
  Seafood Salad
Antipasto Molisano 6.00
  Prosciutto, salami, provolone, anchovies, and olives
Coctail Gamberoni 6.50
  Shrimp cocktail

Pasta

Lasagna del Molise 8.25
  Homemade lasagna filled with cheese, meat sauce, and cream sauce
Crespelle alla Fiorentina 8.25
  Crepes filled with ricotta, parmigiano, and spinach in red or white sauce
Spaghetti con Salsiccia, Polpette o Bolognese 7.95
  Spaghetti with choice of sausage, meatballs, or meat sauce
Linguini alle Vongole 8.50
  Linguini with red or white clam sauce
Melanzane alla Parmigiana 8.00
  Eggplant parmigiana with pasta
Ravioli alla Casalinga 9.00
  Ravioli filled with meat or cheese with unique Molise style sauce
Gnocci alla Napoletana 8.50
  Potato dumplings with choice of tomato or creamy sauce
Cannelloni 8.00
  Pasta filled with meat, served with tomato and Bechamelle sauce

Pesce
Fish

Gamberoni Molisani 13.50
  Shrimp sauteed in garlic, butter, and lite cream sauce over fettucini
Caciucco alla Livornese 14.50
  Seafood combination of shrimp calamari, scallops, clams, and mussels

Pollo, Vitello, e Maiale
Chicken, Veal, and Pork

Filetti di Pollo Toscano 10.00
  Chicken tenders sauteed with mushrooms, artichokes in lite cream
Petti di Pollo al Marsala 10.00
  Chicken breast sauteed in marsala and mushrooms
Pollo alla Parnigiana 9.50
  Chicken breast topped with tomato, mozzarella, and parmigiano
Pollo alla Griglia 9.50
  Marinated and grilled chicken breast
Vitello al Marsala 12.00
  Veal sauteed in marsala and mushrooms
Vitello al Limone 12.00
  Veal sauteed in white wine, lemon, and capers
Saltimboca alla Romana 12.50
  Veal topped with prosciutto, mozzarella, and herbs
Vitello alla Pizzaiola 12.50
  Tender veal sauteed with garlic, tomato, and capers
Lombatine di Maiale alla Salvia 10.50
  Center cut pork chops sauteed in a white wine and sage sauce
Salsiccia Casareccia 9.00
  Grilled homemade sausage

Dolci della Casa
Dessert

Cream Caramel 13.00
Cream Broullei 3.25
Tiramisú 3.50
Spumoni 3.75
Tartufo 3.75
Hazelnut Baba 3.75

Bevande
Beverages

Soft Drinks 1.00
Mineral Water 2.00
Espresso 2.25
Cappuccino 2.50
Hot or Iced Tea 1.25
Coffee (regular or decaffeinated) 1.50

OAXACA AT PINNACLE PEAK

"An American Classic"

Nestled 1,000 feet above the valley, OAXACA at Pinnacle Peak offers a spectacular view of mystical sunsets and overlooks a blanket of twinkling city lights. Over a half million diners have enjoyed this "All American" restaurant specializing in some of the featured menu items below, complemented by an Award Winning wine list...

APPETIZERS

Oysters Rockefeller $7.95
Fresh baked oysters on the half shell, topped with seasoned creamed spinach and bacon, laced with Pernod and finished with hollandaise.

Stuffed Mushroom Caps $6.95
Dunguness crab stuffed mushroom caps baked with fresh bread crumbs and fresh fruit garnish.

Escargot $6.95
The House speciality (6) baked Escargot in garlic butter accompanied by fresh garlic bread.

Coconut Prawns $7.95
Three jumbo coconut prawns served with tangy honey mustard dipping sauce and raspberry coulis. THE CHEFS FAVORITE!

PASTA SPECIALS

Heavenly Angel Hair Pasta $12.95
Served with a Pesto Marinara Sauce.

Jodi's Angel Hair Pasta $18.95
Angel hair pasta with roasted pistachio cream sauce, three garlic sauteed prawns and marinated portobello mushrooms.

STEAKS & SUCH

Special Filet Mignon $19.95
A center cut of special aged tenderloin of beef hand cut to perfection everyday to ensure freshness and quality.

Oven Roasted Lamb Chops $24.95
Grilled double cut Australian lamb chops served with jalapeno hollandaise and mint jelly.

Oaxaca's Outrageous Steak $21.95
A perfect Steak for the adventurer. Two tenderloin medallions of beef served on grilled portobello mushrooms and topped with sauce bearnaise.

SPECIALTIES

Roast Prime Rib of Special Beef
  Lighter cut $15.95
  Regular cut $17.95
  Oaxaca cut $20.95
The house specialty! Beef slowly roasted to ensure maximum tenderness and served au jus with creamed horseradish.

BBQ Baby Back Ribs
Half slab $13.95
Full slab $17.95
Tender pork ribs cut from the loin and simmered in our Sonoran barbeque sauce.

Veal Marsala with Wild Mushrooms $18.95
Juicy medallions of veal sauteed to perfection and mantled with a Dark Forrest inspired with mushroom Marsala sauce.

Our Famous Southwestern Chicken $16.95
A tender marinated chicken breast, sauteed and topped with avocado and melted jalapeno jack cheese.

SEAFOOD

Salmon Santa Fe $18.95
A fresh filet of Atlantic Salmon, seasoned with Southwestern spices, seared and topped with red pepper-cilantro compote.

Better than Boston Style Scrod $15.95
Oven baked Boston style scrod with an alfredo herb bread crumb crust.

Filet and Coconut Prawns $21.95
Two huge coconut prawns coupled with a petite filet. THE PERFECT COMBINATION!
Extra prawns may be added for $2.50 each.

EXTRAS

Au gratin Potatoes $2.95
Extra creamy augratin potatoes a sure palate pleaser, just the way grandma makes them!

OAXACA at Pinnacle Peak

PHONE
998–2222

HOURS
Daily
4:30 pm–closing

LOCATION
8711 East
Pinnacle Peak Road
Scottsdale, AZ

CUISINE
American

ATTIRE
Appropriate Casual

TERRACE DINING

RESERVATIONS
Recommended

CREDIT CARDS
MasterCard, Visa,
American Express,
Diners Club, Discover

CHECKS ACCEPTED

SMOKING
Section Available

HANDICAP FACILITIES

Nina L'Italiana Ristorante

Best Pasta House
New Times
Best of Phoenix, 1994

"In the Valley's fiercely competitive Italian restaurant league, Nina L'Italiana looks like a sure bet to make the playoffs." —***New Times***

The aroma is strong and inviting. The instant you walk through the door you are greeted by the scent of fresh garlic and Italian herbs and spices to entice your senses. You feel as though you have happened into an authentic Italian kitchen rather than a charming restaurant in Phoenix's north valley. You're about to have an incredible dining experience, you're about to sit down to a very special meal at Nina L'Italiana.

Under the skillful guiding hand of culinary genius, chef and owner, Nina Vincenti, this family-run establishment has certainly earned its honors as "Best of Phoenix", and "Best of Arizona." But titles aside, the food at Nina L'Italiana speaks for itself.

Nina prides herself in always providing the finest quality and freshest pasta and seafood available, therefore a new menu is printed daily offering the chef's selections. And what selections they are!

The appetizer menu usually consists of seven or eight flavorful choices including such specialties as Mozzarella Caprese (fresh mozzarella on a slice of tomato with basil and olive oil), escargot in a garlic butter sauce, and Nina's own homemade ravioli. What a prelude to the meal ahead. And, now that your palate has been tempted by Nina's fine flare for the extraordinary, you should be able to completely submerge yourself in the Menu of the Day.

Chef, Nina Vincenti, and Owner, Brent Lewis are proud to present great Italian cuisine.

Since each day offers a new one of Nina's trademark recipes, you simply can't go wrong. The Mussels and Calamari Fra Diavola (fresh mussels and calamari in a light spicy tomato sauce served on a bed of spaghetti) is perfection, and the Fettuccine Mare E Monti (fettuccine in a cream sauce with shrimp and wild mushrooms), Penne Puttanesca (penne in a spicy tomato sauce with artichoke hearts, capers, black olives and anchovies), is spectacular.

And if you still have some room, take a look at the dramatic dessert tray featuring the likes of traditional Tiramisu and an assortment of cakes and tasty treats. Nina L'Italiana has it all. Its unique daily menu, warm atmosphere and superior service make it truly one of the most outstanding restaurants in the Valley.

Items shown: Napolitana Salad, Calamari Salad, Shrimp Scampi with Linguini, Fresh Homemade Mozzarella, Proscuitto e Melone, Homemade spinach and cheese ravioli, Linguine Del Marinaio and Giandoia Torte or Chocolate Hazelnut Cake

Nina L'Italiana

PHONE
482-6167

HOURS
Dinner–Daily
5:00 pm–10:00 pm

LOCATION
3625 East Bell Road
Phoenix, AZ 85032

CUISINE
Italian

ATTIRE
Casual

ENTERTAINMENT
Live Music,
Dance Floor

FULL SERVICE CATERING

TAKE OUT

VEGETARIAN MEALS

RESERVATIONS
Suggested

CREDIT CARDS
MasterCard, Visa,
American Express,
Diners Club, Discover

SMOKING
Section Available

HANDICAP FACILITIES

Menu Highlights

Appetizers

Antipasto Misto:
Mixed Appetizer with Calamari Salad,
Mozzarella Caprese, Roasted Bell Peppers
and Prociutto e Melone

Mozzarella Arcobaleno:
Homemade Mozzarella Stuffed with
Prosciutto, Tomatoes, Capers and Belgian
Endive served with Caponata

Escargot:
Escargot in a Garlic Butter Sauce

Entrees

Ravioli:
Homemade filled Ravioli Stuffed with
Spinach and Ricotta Cheese

Linguine Del Marinaio
Clams, Mussels, Shrimp,
Calamari in Light Tomato Sauce

Mare e Monti
Shrimp sauteed in Cognac served
with Wild Mushrooms

Veal Oscar
Scallopine Topped with Crab, Asparagus
and Homemade Holand Holandaise Sauce

CUISINE
Austrailian

ATTIRE
Arizona Casual

LOUNGE

TAKE OUT

RESERVATIONS
Suggested

CREDIT CARDS
MasterCard, Visa,
American Express,

CHECKS ACCEPTED

SMOKING
Section Available

HANDICAP FACILITIES

With an Aussie flair from down "Down Under" Outback Steakhouse provides high quality food & service, generous portions at moderate prices in a cheerful, comfortable & fun atmosphere.

Set yourself down amongst the boomerangs & surfboards, have an Australian beer, an Aussie-Tizer, a great steak and enjoy!

Aussie-Tizers

G'Day mate! Start your ticker off with one o' these wonders from down under!

Bloomin' Onion®
An Outback Ab-original
from Russell's Marina Bay $4.95

Grilled Shrimp On The Barbie
Seasoned and served with
Outback's own Remoulade sauce $6.45

Kookaburra Wings®
Known as Buffalo chicken wings here in the States. Mild, medium, or hot 4.95

Aussie Cheese Fries
Aussie chips topped with Monterey Jack and Cheddar cheeses, bacon and served with spicy ranch dressing $5.45

Gold Coast Coconut Shrimp
Six colossal shrimp dipped in beer batter, rolled in coconut, deep fried to a golden brown and served with marmalade sauce $6.45

Walkabout Soup®
A unique presentation of an Australian favorite. Recon!
Bowl/Cup .... $3.25/$2.25

Down Under Favorites

Heaps of hearty traditions from the shoreline to deep in the never never. Every one's a beaut. Too right!

Alice Springs Chicken®
Grilled chicken breast and bacon smothered in mushrooms, melted Monterey Jack and Cheddar cheeses, with honey mustard sauce. Served with Aussie chips $10.45

Jackeroo Chops
Two 8-ounce center cut pork chops served with cinnamon apples and a choice of potato $11.95

Veggie Pasta Pemberton
Char-grilled veggies with portabello mushrooms, sun-dried tomatoes in a unique semolina sauce flavored with garlic and herbs $8.95

Brisbane Shrimp Sauté
Seasoned and sautéed with mushrooms, over fettuccine in a light herb butter sauce $9.95

Queensland Chicken 'N Shrimp
Seasoned and grilled, over fettuccine Alfredo, topped with a light lemon sauce $11.45

House or Caesar Salad with
any Down Under Favorite $1.95

Land Rovers

Our steaks are fair dinkum-absolutely genuine-USDA cuts. It was one of these choice dishes that Mad Max was so mad about!

Victoria's Filet®
A 9-ounce tenderloin $14.95

Rockhampton Rib-Eye
A 14-ounce rib-eye steak $14.95

The Michael J. "Crocodile" Dundee
A 14-ounce New York Strip $15.95

The Melbourne
A 20-ounce porterhouse—
it's bonzer! $17.95

The Outback Special®
A 12-ounce center-cut sirloin, seasoned
and seared to perfection $11.95

Prime Minister's Prime Rib
A tempting, 8-ounce cut,
roasted slowly $11.95
12-ounce cut $13.95
16-ounce cut $15.95
Land Rover Entrees are served with a
choice of House or Caesar salad, bushman
bread and choice of jacket potato, Aussie
chips or fresh steamed vegetables.
Grilled Shrimp on the Barbie with any
Land Rover Favorite $4.95

Grilled on the Barbie
Cheers! Get a real taste of the ol' outback, seared to perfection over an open flame.

Drover's Platter®
Generous portions of ribs and chicken
breast on the barbie with Aussie
chips and cinnamon apples $11.95

Chicken On The Barbie
Seasoned and grilled breast served
with BBQ sauce and fresh veggies ... $9.45

Ribs On The Barbie
Imported baby back ribs, smoked and
grilled, with Aussie chips and
cinnamon apples $10.95

Botany Bay Fish O' The Day
Fresh catch, lightly seasoned and
grilled, with fresh veggies $12.95
House or Caesar Salad with any
grilled On The Barbie Favorite $1.95

Desserts
No worries, mate. Have a bo-peep at these treats and ava go!

Sydney's Sinful Sundae
Vanilla ice cream rolled in toasted
coconut, covered in chocolate sauce
and topped with whipped cream $2.95

Cheesecake Olivia
New York style with a choice of
raspberry or caramel sauce $3.45

Chocolate Thunder From Down Under®
Fresh-baked brownie, rich vanilla
ice cream topped with hot homemade
caramel sauce $4.45

Cinnamon Oblivion
Vanilla ice cream covered in
cinnamon apples and pecans topped
with homemade caramel sauce $4.45

Joey Menu
You'll jump with joy over this tucker
(that's food) special-like, just for you
littlies under 12!

Boomerang Burger $2.75
Kookaburra Chicken Fingers $2.75
Mac A Roo 'N Cheese $2.25
Grilled Cheese-A-Roo $2.25
Junior Ribs $3.95
Spotted Dog Sundae $1.75

Sides
Hey mates! Keep your tucker in the best
o' company with one or more of our
bonzer (terrific) accompaniments.

Sautéed 'Shrooms $2.45
Jacket Potato $1.95
Aussie Chips $1.75
Grilled Onions .... $ .95
Fresh Veggies $1.95
House or Caesar Salad $3.95

Watch For Our Paradise Valley Location Opening December 1995

Outback Steakhouse

TEMPE
PHONE
491-6064
HOURS
Monday–Thursday
4:00 pm–10:30 pm
Friday
4:00 pm–11:30 pm
Saturday
3:00 pm–11:30 pm
Sunday
3:00 pm–10:30 pm
LOCATION
1734 East
Southern Ave., #903
Tempe, AZ 85282

GLENDALE
PHONE
547-3236
HOURS
Monday–Thursday
3:00 pm–10:30 pm
Friday
3:00 pm–11:30 pm
Saturday
2:00 pm–11:30 pm
Sunday
12:00 pm–10:00 pm
LOCATION
5605 West Bell Road
Glendale, AZ 85308

Palm Court

Award Winning Cuisine...

...and special memories are served nightly in the Palm Court. This intimate gourmet dining room sets the standard for excellence evident throughout the resort...a standard which attracts top executives from around the world as well as appreciative valley residents.

PHONE
596-7700

LOCATION
7700 East
McCormick Parkway
Scottsdale, AZ 85258

CUISINE
Continental &
Contemporary
American

ATTIRE
Jackets & Ties for
Gentlemen

ENTERTAINMENT
Pianist–Nightly

SUNDAY BRUNCH

BANQUET FACILITIES

MEETING FACILITIES

RESERVATIONS
Required

CREDIT CARDS
MasterCard, Visa,
American Express,
Diners Club, Discover

SMOKING
Section Available

HANDICAP FACILITIES

Dinner Menu
Dining in the Palm Court is a leisurely experience. Our entire menu is prepared to order.

Appetizers

Traditional Shrimp Cocktail	$11.50
Pâté de Foie Gras	$9.75
Served with Sauterne gelée and toasted brioche	
Norwegian Salmon	$9.75
Mesquite smoked in our own kitchen	
Smoked Duck Breast	$9.75
With cantelope and field greens	
Prawns Provençale	$11.50
Large shrimp sautéed in garlic, butter, and pimentos with a hint of cream, herbs and spices	
Escargots Bourguignonne	$9.75
Served on toasted brioche	
Angel Hair Pasta with Wild Mushrooms	$8.75
Laced with fresh cream and parmesan	

Chef's Tureen

Soup du Jour	$4.00
Casaba Kaltschale	$4.25
A purée of fresh casaba melon enhanced with cream and a touch of Midori liqueur, served chilled	
Beef Consommé al' Italienne	$4.25
Double beef consommé with zucchini and diced tomato	
Lobster Bisque	$6.50
A golden purée of fresh lobster laced with dry sherry	

Salads

Wilted Spinach Salad	$10.00 for two
Mushrooms and bacon flambéed in a mustard raspberry vinaigrette	
Imperial Caesar Salad	$10.00 for two
With or without anchovies	
Heart of Palm Francaise	$5.25
Egyptian Heart of Palm and Romaine in a classic French dressing	
Belgian Endive Salad	$4.75
With tangerine, walnuts and Roquefort cheese tossed in a citrus-mustard vinaigrette	
California Field Salad	$4.75
Curly endive, radicchio, watercress and bibb lettuce tossed in a Pistachio vinaigrette	
Boston Bibb Lettuce Oriental	$4.75
Topped with Shitake mushrooms and cilantro in a light soy dressing	

Entrees

Steak au Poivre	$21.75
New York sirloin with three kinds of peppercorns and cognac sauce	
Veal Medallions a la Parisienne	$23.00
Sautéed escalope of veal, topped with a delicate parsley and lemon butter sauce	
Duckling Aux Framboise	$22.75
Long Island Duckling breast sautéed medium rare, complemented by crisp skinned dark meat, served in a raspberry bigarade sauce	
Prawns Provençale	$24.50
Large shrimp sautéed in garlic, butter, pimentos, herbs and spices	
Lobster Lord Randolph	$27.50
Fresh Maine Lobster, sautéed with fresh mushrooms and truffles, flamed with cognac and finished with lobster sauce and cream	
Filet of Dover Sole Amandine	$23.50
Sautéed in butter with toasted almonds and parsley	
Filet of Fresh Salmon	$21.75
Sautéed with butter sauce and herbs	
Swordfish Riviera	$22.50
Tomato, garlic and herb beurre blanc	
Beef Tenderloin	$23.75 per person
Roasted to perfection, carved tableside, with bearnaise sauce (For Two or More)	
Rack of Lamb, Diable (For Two)	$52.00
Roasted with English mustard and spices	

PANAMA REX'S BEACH BAR & GRILL

AN AUTHENTIC MEXICAN LOOK AND STYLE RESTAURANT FEATURING THE VALLEYS BEST MARGARITAS AND ZONI'S (SLIDERS)

MUNCH

1. **NACHOS SAME OLE WAY** — $4.95
   Tortilla chips, refried beans, chihuahua and jack cheese, lettuce, tomatoes, green onions, jalapenos, sour cream and homemade salsa.
2. **NOCHOS GRANDE** — $6.25
   Same as nachos same ole way, with your choice of chicken or beef. This one looks a little fancier too.
3. **QUESADILLA** — $4.95
   Fresh tortilla filled with chihuahua and jack cheese and folded over. If we left it open, it would be a cheesecrisp. Also served with our cream and salsa.
4. **QUESADILLA "MEXICANA"** — $5.95
   Same as regular quesadilla, but we add our choice of beef, chicken or bean. This is a good one.
5. **MINI BURRO SAMPLER** — $5.95
   Somewhere between 6 and 12 mini burritos filled with red and green chili and bean. This is a lot of food. Recommended for two people.
6. **PIZZA MEXICANA** — $5.95
   Open faced cheesecrisp topped with cheese, chorizo, tomatoes, jalapenos, black olives and sour cream.
7. **CANASTA DE POPPERS** — $4.95
   Basket of jalapenos filled with cream cheese and deep fried. MMMMMMMMMM Good.
8. **ZONI'S** — $5.00
   4 little burgers that will knock your socks off. These are the best. So long Chicago sliders.

STUFF

9. **SOPA Y ENSDALADA** — $3.95
   Soup of the day and house salad.
10. **ENSALADA DEL CASA** — $1.95
    In English. (house salad with dressing)
11. **PANAMA REX'S TACO SALAD GRANDE** — $5.95
    A fresh bed of greens topped with your choice of grilled chicken breast or spicy shredded beef, along with beans, cheddar cheese, guacamole, sour cream, salsa in a flour tortilla shell.
12. **ZONI BURGER** — $4.95
    A quarter pound hamburger grilled to perfection and topped with Zoni cheese, Zoni sauce (don't ask us what is in our special sauces, the cook won't tell us) lettuce and tomato and served with French fries.
13. **ZONI DOG** — $2.95
    An all beef hot dog topped with Zoni cheese, Zoni sauce and pickle, and served with French fries.
14. **ZONI CHICKEN** — $5.95
    A boneless chicken breast grilled to perfection and topped with zoni cheese, zoni sauce, lettuce and tomato, and served with French fries.

PANAMA REX'S OWN COYOTE CHILI

THE BEST SOUTHWESTERN CHILI IN THE WORLD

Coyote Chili is a chili you will not find anywhere in the world, except at Panama Rex's. We spent about 20 minutes putting the recipe together, and it cannot be duplicated. We even had a hard time duplicating it from day to day. Nobody wrote it down. All we know is that it is made with fresh ingredients and cooked for a few minutes and put in the refrigerator for a bout 20 hours to age. Someone's grandmother said it taste better the longer it sets around. You know how that story is. The Mexican cook came to us from one of those Italian restaurants that went out of business (must have been a Polish chef to hire a Mexican cook) and he had some leftover pasta, so we thought that we would try it along with our chili so we could charge a little more. Boy, did it work. You will love our chili.

16. **COYOTE CHILI** — bowl $4.95
    mesquite cooked chicken breast — dinner $6.95
17. **COYOTE BEEF** — bowl $4.95
    mesquite cooked shredded beef — dinner $6.95
18. **COYOTE BEAN** — bowl $4.50
    black beans — dinner $5.95

All dishes are served with fresh pasta, along with Mexican cheese and toasted garlic bread. The bowls are about half the size of the dinner portion. The dinner also comes with a fresh green salad and your choice of two salad dressings. This changes occasionally depending on what is on sale at the local store.

ESPECIALIDADES

The following plates are prepared with rice and beans and the freshest ingredients available and our world famous award winning salsa.

21. **BURRITOS EL CHEAPO** — $5.95
    A flour tortilla filled with your choice of chili rojo (red beef chili) of Chili Verde (green beef chili).
22. **BURRITOS EL POLLO** — $6.95
    A flour tortilla filled with fresh shredded chicken and grilled with tomatoes, onions, and cilantro.
23. **BURRITOS MOS DINARO** — $7.95
    This burro is filled with your choice of carne picado (diced beef), machaco (shredded beef) or carnita aseda (pork) along with tomatoes, onions, and celantro.
24. **ENCHILADAS ROJO** — $5.95
    Two hand rolled tortillas filled with cheese and topped with red ensalada sauce. If you want beans in these. No problem. It will cost you 50 cents more.
25. **ENCHILADAS MUCHO** — $6.95
    Two hand rolled corn tortillas filled with your choice of shredded beef or shredded chicken and topped with red chili enchilada sauce.

THIS IS JUST A SMALL SAMPLE OF THE WONDERFUL FOOD AVAILABLE AT PANAMA REXS

Panama Rex's

PHONE
994-1985

HOURS
Monday–Saturday
5:00 pm–10:00 pm

LOCATION
7164 East Stetson
Scottsdale, AZ 85251

CUISINE
Mexican

ATTIRE
Casual

LOUNGE
Monday–Saturday
4:00 pm–1:00 am

TERRACE DINNING

RESERVATIONS
Suggested

CREDIT CARDS
MasterCard, Visa, American Express

SMOKING
Section Available

HANDICAP FACILITIES

Pasta Segio's

The legend of Pasta Segio's

After arriving in New York, Papa Segio got a job and soon they started raising a family. They had nine Segios in all and each grew up fast and healthy, thanks to Mama Segios tasty Italian cooking.

The oldest of the children was Pasta. He grew up a little faster and slightly wider. He was always in the kitchen sampling Mama's cooking. In fact, he spent so much time in the kitchen that he soon learned all of Mama's secret recipes. He liked to help her with the sauces and meats, but his favorite pastime was making the pastas.

COLD APPETIZERS

ANTIPASTO ALLA INSALATA — $6.00
(ahn-tee-PAHS-toh ahl een sah-LAH-tah)
Capicollo, prosciutto, Genoa salami, mozzarella and provolone cheese surrounded by bell peppers, tomatoes, Italian olives, on a bed of lettuce topped with green onion and anchovies.

COCKTAIL DI GAMBERETTO — $6.95
(GAM-ber-etto)
Shrimp cocktail served in a chilled glass with cocktail sauce and lemon.

CALAMARI I VINAIGRETTE — $6.00
(Ca-la-Ma-ree vee-neh-GRET-aah)
Round slices of calamari, lightly tossed in a tasty combination of chopped greens and pimentos.

HOT APPETIZERS

ESCARGOT MAMA MARIA — $5.95
(es-kar-GOH MAH_MAH MAH-ree-ah)
A secret recipe given to the Sergio family by an old friend. The flavor is enhanced with lemon and garlic toast.

STUFFED MUSHROOMS — $4.00
Stuffed with crab meat in a delicately appointed sauce.

LINGUINE
Served with your choice of Soup or Salad

AGLIO E OLIO (AH-lyoheh OH-lee-oh) — 8.95
One of the basic mother sauces for pasta is garlic, olive oil and anchovies. From it has spawned a multitudinous array of sauces.

CON VONGOLE (kohn vohn-GO-leh) — 9.95
Clam sauce and pasta is a traditional Italian combination, delicately seasoned the taste is unsurpassed.

♥ **CON VONGOLE AL SUGO ROSSO** — 9.95
(kohn vohn-GO-leh ahl SOO-goROH-soo)
This red sauce is equal to the light, clear clam sauce, but takes on a spicier taste when combined with red sauce, seasonings.

CON SALSA E POLPETTINE — 8.95
(kohn SAHL-sa E pohl-pet-TEE-neh)
Cooks from Southern Italy take pride in their meatballs as we do at Pasta Segio's. we make them plump and tasty, then drench them in a robust, herby tomato gravy. What better way to cloak a steaming mound of pasta.

CON SALSA E SALSICCIA — 8.95
(kohn SAHL-sa E-sahl-SEE-che)
The hearty aroma of Italian sausage, onion and garlic simmering with a rich tomato sauce will lure anyone's appetite.

CONCHIGLIE ALLA MARINARA — 12.95
(kohn-KEEL-ee al-lah mah-ree-NAHR-ah)
Bay scallops are transformed in sautéed garlic, onions, tomatoes, parmesan cheese and spices, then lightly tossed in linguine.

FETTUCCINE
Served with your choice of Soup or Salad

ALFREDO (ahl-FRAY-doh) — 8.95
Immortalized by Alfredo's Restaurant in Rome, this is the recipe everyone thinks of when you say "fettuccine."

VERDI (VEHR-deh) — 8.95
Fettuccine Verdi combines spinach pasta and green onion with a white cream sauce for a variation on the Fettuccine Alfredo theme.

BOLOGNESE (BOH-leh-neez) — 8.95
A very rich and robust red meat sauce blended with fettuccine with a delicate nutmeg flavor that makes the sauce and fettuccine a truly culinary marriage.

PRIMAVERA (pree-mah-VEH-rah) — 9.95
Fresh Broccoli, squash, zucchini, cauliflower and carrots sautéed to perfection, then gently folded with noodles and a rich Alfredo sauce.

♥ Heart Safe, will be served in a Red Sauce.

Pasta Segio's

VERDI CON GAMBERETTI   12.95
(VEHR-deh kohn gam-be-RET-tee)
This exciting dish combines spinach pasta with flavorful shrimp, seasonings all blended together with a rich Alfredo sauce.

PESTO ALLA GENOVESE   9.95
(PEHS-to-ahl-lah JEN oh-veez)
This recipe of olive oil, basil, parsley, garlic and other spices is my attempt to recreate a favorite authentic taste.

DEL MAR TI TERRANO   14.95
(DEHL MAH-reh DEE TEHR-rahn-no)
Fresh jumbo shrimp, Ocean clams, and Bay scallops sautéed in olive oil, herbs, spices, garlic, scallions fresh tomato wedges in fettuccine noodles with a trace of red sauce then lightly topped with mozzarella cheese.

PASTA
Served with your choice of Soup or Salad

RIGATONI CON SALSA DI MELANZANE   8.95
(ree-gah-TOH-nee kohn SAHL-sa dee meh-land-ZAHN-eh)
The eggplant mixture includes tomatoes, garlic, onion, olives, pimento and anchovy paste. This excellent meatless dish is topped with grated mozzarella cheese.

RAVIOLI DI CARNE   8.95
(rah-VYOH-lee dee-KAR-neh)
In Italian, these ravioli are called Pansouti, each little pasta pillow is filled with meat, eggs and cheese, then covered with our own herby tomato sauce.

♥ **MANICOTTI CON SPINACI E RICOTTA**   8.95
(mah-ne-KOHT-tee kihn spee-NA-chee eh ree-KOHT-tah)
Ricotta and spinach, turns up in shells this time. Flavored with onion, garlic, parsley and oregano. Topped with a tomato and mushroom sauce.

LASGANE BELMONTE   8.95
(Lah-SAH-nyah bel-MON-teh)
This version is the traditional style of Southern Italy which uses a rich tomato and beef sauce and several flavorful cheeses.

TORTELLINI ALLA PANNA CON TARTUFI   9.95
(tor-teh-LEE-neh ahl-lah PAN-nah kohn tar-TOO-fee)
Indulge yourself in a trip to Italian ecstacy with this combination of special Italian meats, cheeses and spices wrapped in a pasta twist. The savory cream and cheese sauce is simple, yet enhanced with a touch of nutmeg for an excellent taste.

CANNELLONI MAIALE E SPINACHI   9.95
(kahn-nel-LOH-nee mah-Yal-eh-ehspee-NA-chee)
These zesty pork and spinach crepes are hearty but surprisingly light, with a definite accent of ricotta, romano and parmesan cheese, enhanced with nutmeg and other spices, then coated with a creamy white sauce and laced with a red sauce.

♥ **JUMBO STUFFED SHELLS**   9.95
A large pasta shell stuffed with our ricotta, mozzarella, and romano cheeses. Baked and topped with our own herby tomato sauce and a spot of Alfredo for color.

CARNE E PESCE
Served with your choice of Soup or Salad and a side of Cappellini

PIZZA DELLA NONNA   7.95
(PEE-TSAH deh-lah NOHN-NAH)
PESTO & PARMIGIANO or if you like cheese. I QUATRO FORMAGGI (the four cheeses), and MELANZANE (Eggplant. fresh tomatoes, olives, anchovies, and sweet basil.)

FILLETTO ALLA MILANESE   11.95
(fee-LEHT-toh ah-lah MEE-lahneez)
Tenderloin Medallions sautéed in fresh sliced mushrooms, spices and cognac, a flavor that is it's very own.

POLLO PICCATA (POHL-loh pee-KAHT-tah)   10.95
Chicken breasts, gently floured, sautéed with mushrooms, spices and lemon butter which creates the delectable accompanying sauce.
♥ Heart Safe, will be sautéed in lemon juice.

MELANZANE ALLA PARMIGIANA   9.95
(meh-land-ZAHN-ahl-lah par-mee-JAH-nah)
In these meatless patties, we form tasty ingredients of garlic, parsley, cheeses, spices, tomatoes and more.

VITELLO ALLA GIANNA   13.95
(vee-TEH-loh ahl-lah jah-nee-nah)
Veal sautéed in a light cream sauce with wine and brandy topped with fresh exotic mushrooms.

VITELLO ALLA PARMIGIANA   14.95
(vee-TEH-loh ahl-lah par-mee-JAH-nah)
Lightly breaded veal sautéed in a light sauce topped with fresh tomato sauce.

OSSOBUCO (OHS-soh-BOO-koh)   14.95
Italy's own stew of veal shank with marrow, the Milan garnish, gremolata, gives a colorful look.

RESCE SPADA (Peh-sheh SPAH-dah)   14.95
Swordfish sauteed in a light garlic, herb and lemon butter sauce, topped (if you choose) with tomato sauce and mozzarella cheese.
♥ Heart Safe, will be sauteed in lemon juice.

PESCE DEL GIORNO   13.95
(Peh-she dehl joh-rr-noh)
Fresh fish of the day, always a great dish regardless of the fish we catch.

DESSERTS

FRAGOLE DI SEMIFREDDO   3.95
(frah-GOH-lee dee seh-mee FRAY-doh)
Frozen dessert consists of strawberries, egg whites, orange-flavored liqueur, topped with semifreddo sauce, fresh sliced strawberries and a sprig of mint.

SPUMONI (spoo-MOO-nee)   3.25
Traditional Italian dessert combines an assortment of delicious ice cream, topped with whipped cream.

AMARETTO CHEESECAKE   3.95
Cream cheese cake, blended with a light Amaretto.

MOUSSE DI CIOCCOLATO   3.25
(moos de choh-koh LAHT-tah)
This delightfully rich dessert is topped with whipped cream and shaved chocolate.

MOUSSE DI CIOCCOLATO (BIANCO)   3.25
(moos de choh-koh LAHT-tah) White chocolate mousse topped with whipped cream and shaved chocolate.

CANOLI (KAH-noh-LEE)   3.25
Chocolate chip or amaretto almond flavored whipped ricotta cheese and cream in a tubular thin wafer.

ZUCCOTTO (zook-KOHT-toh)   3.95
This dome-shaped specialty is said to be inspired by the huge dome on the St. Croce Cathedral in Florence. Only your waiter can describe this delicious dessert.

♥ Items approved by
ARIZONA HEART INSTITUTE
Please specify to server
for some changes may have to be made to the dishes.

PHONE
277–2782

HOURS
Lunch
Monday–Friday
11:30pm–2:30pm

Dinner
Monday–Saturday
5:00pm–10:00pm
Sundays
5:00pm–9:00pm

LOCATION
1904 East
Camelback Road
Phoenix, Az 85016

CUISINE
Italian

ATTIRE
Casual

LOUNGE
5:00 pm until 1:00 am

TERRACE DINING

PATIO DINING

BANQUET FACILITIES

AFTER THEATRE DINING

FULL SERVICE CATERING

TAKE OUT

VEGETARIAN MEALS

RESERVATIONS
Suggested

CREDIT CARDS
MasterCard, Visa,
American Express,
Diners Club

SMOKING
Section Available

HANDICAP FACILITIES

Pareesa

PHONE
866–1906

HOURS
Lunch
Monday–Friday
11:30 am–2:30 pm

Dinner
Sunday–Thursday
5:00 pm–10:00 pm
Friday & Saturday
5:00 pm–10:30 pm

LOCATION
610 East
Bell Road
Phoenix, AZ 85022

CUISINE
Italian

ATTIRE
Casual

PATIO DINING

AFTER THEATRE DINING

PRIVATE PARTIES

FULL SERVICE CATERING

VEGETARIAN MEALS

TAKE OUT

RESERVATIONS
Suggested

CREDIT CARDS
MasterCard, Visa,
American Express,
Diners Club, Discover

CHECKS ACCEPTED
With Guarantee Card

SMOKING
Section Available

HANDICAP FACILITIES

"A great restaurant for the entire family! If you want fine food and service in an uplifting environment, you definitely must give them a try."
—TravelHost Magazine

"Not since I was in Italy…have I eaten such fine Italian cuisine. (It's) the best Italian food in Arizona."
—North Valley Sun

Pareesa ITALIAN RESTAURANT

APPETIZERS

ESCARGOT WITH
GARLIC BUTTER SAUCE 5.95
BAKED STUFFED CLAMS 5.95
STUFFED MUSHROOMS 5.95
STUFFED EGGPLANT 4.95
CALAMARI LUCCIANA 5.95
Sauteed in olive oil, garlic, green onions, white wine.
MUSSELS A LA TIBERIO 6.95
With spicy marinara sauce.

SOUPS & SALADS

STRACCIATELLA 3.00
Chicken broth, spinach, whisked egg, and parmigiana cheese.
TORTELLINI IN BRODO 3.00
Meat filled pasta in chicken consomme.
PASTA E FAGIOLI…PAREESA STYLE 3.00
Pasta, kidney beans, prosciutto and garlic in chicken broth with a touch of marinara.
NEOPOLITAN SALAD 3.50
Tomato, onion, artichokes, and black olives with basil dressing.
CAESAR SALAD 4.25
Romaine lettuce, garlic croutons, anti romano cheese with caesar dressing.
WARM SPINACH SALAD 4.25
Spinach, mushrooms, and onions in warm bacon dressing with hard-boiled egg.

HOMEMADE PASTA
Made to order.

BAKED PENNE 8.95
Baked with ricotta cheese and fresh tomato basil sauce.
SPAGHETTI POMODORO 8.95
With the famed tomato basil sauce.
GNOCCHI POMODORO 8.95
Potato, spinach, and ricotta cheese dumplings in tomato basil sauce.
FETTUCCINE ALFREDO 9.95
Egg pasta in cream sauce and freshly grated parmigiana cheese.
With tenderloins of chicken 12.95
MOSTACCIOLI CAPRESE 9.95
Baked with, sauteed eggplant, mozzarella cheese and marinara sauce.
LINGUINI WITH CLAM SAUCE 10.95
Sauteed in olive oil, garlic, and white wine.
CANNELLONI 10.95
Delicate crepes stuffed with, ground veal, chicken, spinach and cheese in cream sauce.
TORTELLINI PANNA 10.95
Meat filled pasta in cream sauce with parmigiana cheese.
LASAGNA NAPOLITANA 10.95
Baked pasta layered with cheeses, sausage and meat sauce.

VEGETARIAN

ANGEL HAIR PAREESA 12.95
With olive oil, garlic, sun-dried tomatoes, and broccoli.
SEASONAL VEGETABLES ITALIAN 8.95
(Grilled and brushed with herbed olive oil.

SEAFOOD SPECIALTIES
Served with garden salad and pasta of the day.

CALAMARI MARINARA 10.95
Sauteed with garlic, olive oil, and marinara sauce, over a bed of linguini.
CALAMARI BRIONES 12.95
Sauteed with lobster cream sauce, white wine, and garlic, over a bed of linguini.
SHRIMP SCAMPI 14.95
Sauteed with herbs in olive oil, garlic, and white wine.
THE GOLD OF NAPOLI 14.95
Mussels, clams, scallops, shrimp, and calamari in marinara sauce over linguini.
SHRIMP MICHELANGELO 14.95
Sauteed with mushrooms and tarragon in creamy shallot cognac sauce.

VEAL & BEEF
Served with garden salad and pasta of the day.

VEAL FIORENTINA 13.95
Sauteed scalloppine topped with spinach, melted mozzarella cheese, and creamy shallot cognac sauce.
VEAL ROLLATINI 14.95
Scalloppine stuffed with prosciutto ham anti cheeses in marsala mushroom wine sauce.
VEAL SALTIMBOCCA 14.95
Scalloppine topped with prosciutto and fresh sage in wine sauce.
NEW YORK SIRLOIN 14.95
Plain, with pizzaiola or michelangelo sauce.

POULTRY & VEGGIES
Served with garden salad and pasta of the day.

CHICKEN GENOVESE 9.95
Boneless breast sauteed with lemon butter sauce, white wine, capers and artichokes.
CHICKEN ZINGARA 11.95
Tenderloins sauteed in lemon butter sauce, white wine, garlic and mushrooms.
CHICKEN AND SAUSAGE CACCIATORE 11.95
Sauteed sausage and tenderloins of chicken in garlic, olive oil, and marinara sauce, with mushrooms, bell peppers, onions, and black olives.
EGGPLANT PARMIGIANA 8.95
Sauteed eggplant baked with marinara sauce and mozzarella cheese.

* Our chef welcomes the opportunity to prepare any of your favorite dishes that do not appear in this menu.

Pepin
restaurante español

Pepin was selected as the Best Spanish Restaurant/Tapas Bar in both the 1993 and the 1994 issues of *The Best of Arizona* and received five stars for food and service from Penelope Corcoran, the nationally acclaimed restaurant critic of the *Arizona Republic*. In addition, Pepin has received *Travel Holiday Magazine's* 1993 and 1994 Value Dining award and was featured in the October 1994 issue of *Vegetarian Times* for their exceptional vegetable paella.

Tapas • Appetizers

COLD APPETIZERS...

ENTREMESES VARIADOS	7.95
Meats, cheese, olives, asparagus	
CORDERO ASADO	5.95
Roasted lamb with sun-dried tomatoes	
MEJILLONES VINAGRETTE	4.50
Mussels in bell pepper vinaigrette	
SALMON ASTURIANO	5.95
With capers & onions	
PIMIENTOS CON QUESO DE CABRA	5.50
Roasted peppers & goat cheese on garlic roast	
SALPICON DE MARISCO	5.95
Shrimp, scallops, octopus, tomato, peppers & onions in vinaigrette	
TORTILLA ESPANOLA	3.25
Frittata of sauteed potatoes & onions	
COMBINACION PEPIN	7.50
A sampling of any three cold tapas	

HOT APPETIZERS...

GAMBAS AL AIILLO	6.50
Shrimp sauteed with garlic, olive oil, wine	
ALMEJAS TIO PEPE	5.50
Clams with Jamon Serrano & sherry	
CALAMARAS FRITOS	4.95
Fried calamari rings with garlic aioli	
MARISCO AL RIBEIRO	6.75
Shrimp, scallops, mussel & clam with tomato in a wine sauce	
COSTILLAS ASADAS	5.50
Charbroiled marinated pork ribs	
CROQUETAS DE ARROZ NEGRO	5.25
Crab & black rice croquettes with lobster sauce	
CARACOLES DEL JEREZ	6.50
Snails with garlic, wine, herbs & aioli	
ANCAS DE RANA	7.50
Frog legs with garlic and white wine	
EMPANADA GALLEGA	3.75
Baked with savory filling of meat, tomatoes, onions & peppers	
PAN CON TOMATE	3.50
Crusty bread wih pan boli sauce, Jamon Serrano & cheese	
CHAMPINONES AL JEREZ	4.95
Mushroom, sherry & pimenton	

Las Paellas
With soup of the day or salad & freshly baked peasant rolls

PAELLA DE ARROZ NEGRO	24.95
Rice lobster, shrimp, chicken, pork, chorizo, mussels, calamari	
PAELLA DE PESCADO Y MARISCO	21.95
Lobster, shrimp, mussels, clams, calamari, sea bass & salmon	
PAELLA VALENCIANA	18.95
Shrimp, chicken, pork, chorizo, mussels, clams & calamari	
PAELLA DE POLLO Y CHORIZO	11.95
Chicken & chorizo	
PAELLA JARDINERA	10.50
Saffron rice with garden vegetables	

Carnes Y Aves • Meats & Fowl

MAR Y MONTANA	19.95
Beef tenderloin & grilled shrimp	
CHULETON (14 OZ.)	16.50
Seared ribeye steak with garlic & parsley	
COSTILLAS DE CORDERO	22.50
Rock baby lamb	
TERNERA CASERA	16.95
Veal shank with red wine & mushrooms	
PATO CON ALMENDRAS	13.95
Roasted 1/2 duck; peppercorn sauce	
POLLO PEPIN	11.95
Breast of chicken, chilindron sauce, over pasta	
POLLO DON QUIXOTE	10.95
Grilled chicken, tortellini in cheese	
POLLO CAZADORA	10.50
Half chicken, herb sauce, potatoes, carrots	

Pescados y Mariscos • Fish & Seafood

ZARZUELA DE MARISCO	21.95
lobster, shrimp, scallops, mussels, clams, calamari, fish over pasta	
GAMBAS A LA PLANCHA	16.95
Grilled tiger shrimp with citrus aioli	
GAMBAS PEPIN	16.95
Tiger shrimp with chilindron sauce	
SALMON EN SALSA VERDE	15.95
Sauteed with cilantro sauce	
LUBINA A LA ONDARRESA	16.95
Bass, asparagus, clams, shrimp	
BESUGO VERACRUZ	12.95
Red snapper, tomato, peppers & onions	
PASTELES DE CANGREJO	10.95
Spanish crab cakes & citrus aioli	

Pepin

PHONE
990–9026

HOURS
Tuesday–Saturday
11:30 am–11:00 pm
Sunday
5:00 pm–11:00 pm

LOCATION
7363 Scottsdale Mall
Scottsdale AZ, 85251

CUISINE
Spanish

ATTIRE
Casual

LOUNGE
Friday & Saturday
till 1:00 am

ENTERTAINMENT
Wednesday–Saturday
Flamenco

DANCING
Friday & Saturday

BANQUET FACILITIES

FULL SERVICE CATERING

TAKE OUT

VEGETARIAN MEALS

RESERVATIONS
Suggested

CREDIT CARDS
MasterCard, Visa,
American Express,
Discover, Diners Club

SMOKING
Section Available

HANDICAP FACILITIES

PINK PEPPER
THAI CUISINE

WELCOME TO PINK PEPPER CUISINE OF THAILAND. OUR KITCHEN WILL PROVIDE YOU WITH AN EXCELLENT VARIETY OF THAI CUISINE PREPARED WITH NATURAL INGREDIENTS AND EXOTIC SPICES. WE HAVE SELECTED DISHES THAT APPEAL TO EVERYONE'S PALATE AND HOPE THAT YOUR VISIT IS A PLEASURABLE ONE.

*Peoples Choice
Best of Phoenix*

**Best Thai Food
84,86,87,89,90–95**

*Best Ambiance
85,88*

*Arizona's Best
91,92,93*

APPETIZERS, SALAD

THAI SPRING ROLL **$1.95**EA
Roll with Ground pork, bean sprouts, silver noodles and mushrooms.

THAI TOAST 91 .... **$5.50**
A combination of shrimp and chicken blended with our chefs special spices and then deep fried. Served with cucumber sauce.

CHICKEN CRAB CAKE **$5.95**
A cluster of chicken, crab, water chestnuts and onions, dipped in batter, fried to a golden brown, and served with cucumber sauce.

SOUPS

**GLASS NOODLE AND
VEGETABLE SOUP** **$2.50**
Your choice of chicken or pork.

TOM KHA GAI **$2.75**
An exotic, spicy soup with coconut milk, chicken, and lemon grass.

A LA CARTE SPECIALTIES

CHICKEN PARADISE **$8.50**
Grilled chicken filet with sweet and spicy soy sauce, served with mixed vegetables.

NUAH YANG **$9.95**
Tender beef marinated with chopped ginger garlic, and jalapeno chilies, barbecued and topped with sesame seeds. Served atop a bed of mixed vegetables.

PHRA RAM **$8.95**
Broiled Shirimp, chicken, beef and pork on a bed of vegetables topped with peanut sauce.

CRISPY CHICKEN **$8.95**
Crispy, deep-fried chicken served in a spicy plum sauce atop a bed of vegetables.

HOT SHRIMP & SCALLOP 91 .... **$12.95**
Shrimp & scallop sauteed with yellow curry sauce, baby corn, snow peas, tomato, and bamboo shoot.

CRISPY DUCK WITH PLUM SAUCE .. **$11.95**
Our famous duck marinated overnight, deep-fried until crispy, and served with plum sauce.

THAI BBQ CHICKEN '91 .... **$7.95**
Chicken pieces marinated overnight, deep-fried until crispy, and served with plum sauce.

GAI PING $8.95
Grilled chicken filets marinated with Thai spices and topped with spicy, peanut sauce.

THAI SIZZLING STEAK '91 .... $11.95
Tender steak mainated with Thai seasonings, grilled to your preference, served with sauteed mixed vegetables.

THAI ROAST DUCK '91 .... $10.95
Roasted duck with skin or without in a delicious black bean sauce served atop a bed of mixed vegetables.

GAI MA-NOW* *8.95
Sauteed chicken marinated in Thai herb and topped with fresh garlic and tasty special lemon juice sauce.

FLAMING FISH WITH
SPICY LEMON SAUCE* $11.95
Fish fillet simmered in fish broth and spicy lemon sauce.

CURRY

BEEF PANANG* $7.95
One of the masterpieces of Thai cuisine, beef, cooked in a spicy, curry mixture and coconut milk.

CHICKED RED CURRY
AND VEGETABLE* $7.95
Chicken simmered in coconut milk with homemade red curry paste and bamboo shoots.

GREEN CURRY AND VEGETABLE* $7.95
This is typical Thai specialty cooked with green curry paste, bamboo shoots, and your choice of chicken, beef or pork.

GANG PED YAANG* $9.95
Sliced, boneless roasted duck with skin or without skin simmered in coconut milk with red curry paste, tomato, and pineapple.

WOK FRIED DISHES

CASHEW NUTS AND VEGETABLES $8.50
Roasted cashews and mixed vegetables sauteed with our special black soy sauce.

GARLIC AND PEPPER $6.95
A mixture of sauteed garlic and special Thai seasonings.

PAD GRA PRAO* $7.95
A famous Thai dish with sauteed, chopped chilies, garlic, and a spicy Thai sauce.

SPICY EGG PLANT* $8.95
Egg plant sauteed with vegetables and spicy garlic sauce, choice of chicken, pork or beef.

SEAFOOD

SPICY CALAMARI 91* $8.50
A favorite delicacy in Thailand: caramali sauteed with a Thai spicy sauce and onions.

SQUID AND SHRIMP WITH CASHEWS $9.50
A mellow mild dish with sauteed, tender squid, shrimp, mixed vegetables, cashews, and black soy sauce.

SHRIMP CHU CHI* $11.95
Shrimp simmered in special curry sauce, coconut milk, mushrooms, and bellpepper.

SEAFOOD IN CRAY POT $11.95
Baked shrimp, scallops, with ginger, celery, silvernoodle with special Thai sauce.

GULF OF SIAM* $12.95
Mixed seafood stir fried with a smooth spicy chili sauce, with celantro, tomato, onion, jalapeno chili, squash.

SPICY ORANGE ROUGHY* $11.95
Deep-fried fillet of orange roughy sauteed with spicy pepper sauce and vegetables.

SPICY CATFISH WITH CHILI SAUCE* $11.95
Fillet catfish, slightly fried, sauteed with chili sauce and vegetable.

PRAWN WITH GARLIC SAUCE $12.95
Prawn sauteed in mellow garlic sauce, mushrooms and green onions.

MUSSEL WITH THAI SPICY SAUCE* ... $9.95
Mussel sauteed with Thai spicy sauce.

RICE AND NOODLES

PAD THAI '91 .... $7.95
A Thai favorite: rice noodles stir fried with shrimp, chicken, bean sprouts, green onions, and a tasty sauce topped with ground peanuts.

SPICY PASTA* $7.95
Stir-fried pasta with zucchini, bamboo shoot, water chestnut mushrooms and spicy garlic sauce. Your choice of chicken, pork, or beef.

THAI FRIED RICE $6.50
Your choice of beef, pork, or chicken pan-fried with egg and chopped green onions.

VEGGIE LOVERS

VEGGIE ROLL $2.95
Seasoned mixed vegetables wrapped with egg roll skins.

SWEET AND SOUR VEGETABLES $6.50
Assorted, mixed vegetables in our own sweet and sour sauce.

TO FU LOVERS $7.50
Pan fried To Fu, snow pea, carrot, water chestnut, Chinese mushroom with Thai special gravy sauce.

SILVER NOODLES $6.50
Noodles sauteed with egg, broccoli, bean sprouts, carrots, celery onions, and Thai seasoning.

VEGGIE CURRY* $7.50
Mixed vegetables cooked with homeade curry paste and coconut milk.

* SPICY

Pink Pepper

SCOTTSDALE LOCATION
PHONE
945-9300
LOCATION
2003 North Scottsdale Road
Scottsdale

MESA LOCATION
PHONE
839-9009
LOCATION
1941 West Guadalupe Road
Mesa

PHOENIX LOCATION
PHONE
548-1333
LOCATION
245 East Bell Road
Phoenix

CUISINE
Thai
ATTIRE
Casual

RESERVATIONS
Suggested
CREDIT CARDS
MasterCard, Visa, American Express, Diners Club
SMOKING
Section Available
HANDICAP FACILITIES

Ristorante

Pronto

Pronto Ristorante has been serving the valley fine Italian food for over 10 years. Hidden away in a quaint neighborhood at Campbell and 40th Street, Pronto Ristorante's award-winning menu is a treasure everyone can enjoy. Since its inception in 1982, Pronto has evolved to serve regional Italian cuisine. The menu combines old traditional family recipes with innovative new dishes highlighting the region specialities of Italy. Stop in and find out for yourself why the Arizona Republic wrote "a shining example of a restaurant" or why Pronto was awarded "The Best of Phoenix" for four years.

Antipasti per stuzzicare l'appetito

Antipasto della casa $6.95
Imported Italian meats and cheeses, roasted peppers, artichoke hearts, and sun dried tomatoes

Calamari fritti $6.95
Tender squid with roasted garlic and tomato

Carpaccio di Manzo $6.95
Thinly sliced beef tenderloin with shaved parmesan, olive oil, and lemon

Crostini di mozzarella $6.95
Sliced imported prosciutto on olive oil glazed bread with melted fresh mozzarella cheese

Lumache saporite ai funghi e finocchio $6.95
Escargot sauteed in butter, garlic, mushrooms, and pernod

Prosciutto e melone $5.95
Thinly sliced imported prosciutto wrapped around fresh melon

Zuppe che fanno bene

Minestra di verdure con tortellini — $3.95
Fresh seasonal vegetables in broth with cheese tortellini

Pasta e fagioli — $3.50
Cannellini beans simmered with pasta in a light tomato, garlic sauce

Insalate per la salute

Mediterranea — $4.50
Mixed greens, artichokes hearts, sun dried tomatoes, and fresh mozzarella in a lemon dijon vinaigrette

Ortolana — $3.95
Fresh mesculin mix, with arugola and radicchio, in olive oil and balsamic vinegar

Caprese — $4.95
Sliced tomatoes, fresh mozzarella and basil drizzleed with olive oil

Insalata alla Cesare — $4.95
Hearts of romaine, garlic croutons, and grated parmesan cheese

La cosa piú buona del mondo, La Pasta

Fettuccine alla bolognese — $8.95
Fettuccine pasta with chef's special meat sauce

Capellini al pomodoro — $9.95
Angel hair with fresh tomatoes, basil, and garlic

Farfalle del contadino — $11.95
Bowtie pasta with artichokes hearts, kalamata olives, and sun dried tomatoes

Capellini della casa — $9.95
Angel hair pasta in a meat sauce with vegetables and cream

Gnocchi alla romana — $10.95
Fresh homemade potato dumplings in parmesan cheese and tomato sauce

Lasagna della casa, bolognese — $10.95
Traditional oven baked lasagna with meat sauce

Linguine al pesto genovese — $10.95
Fresh basil, garlic and walnut blended with olive oil, over linguine

Linguine alle vongole — $12.95
Linguine pasta with manila clam oregano and garlic

Penne all'arrabbiata — $9.95
Penne in a spicy fresh tomato sauce with basil and garlic

Tortellini primavera alle noci — $11.95
Cheese filled tortellini with fresh vegetables, walnuts and cream

IL Gusto Di Managiare, Portate

Pollo al vino rosso ed olive — $13.95
Chicken sauteed in red wine with kalamata olives and mushrooms

Petto di pollo alla greca — $12.95
Chicken breast sauteed in white wine and olive oil with greek peperoncini, garlic and rosemary

Pollo cacciatore — $12.95
Chicken simmered with tomatoes, olives, peppers, onions and mushrooms

Scaloppine di vitello al marsala — $13.95
Veal sauteed in marsala wine with mushrooms

Involtini con fagioli — $14.95
Veal stuffed with mushrooms, pecorino cheese and pinenuts, in a bowl of cannellini beans

Cotolettine alla parmigiana — $14.95
Veal cutlet breaded and topped with tomato and mozzarella cheese

Salsicce con polenta — $11.95
Italian sausage simmered in tomato sauce with onions and peppers

Maiale alla pizzaiola — $14.95
Tender pork loin sauteed in garlic, fresh tomatoes and basil

Medaglione di bue al barolo — $15.95
Filet mignon medallion with a barolo wine sauce, shallots and rosemary

Gamberi all'anice — $15.95
Tender shrimp sauteed with mushrooms, brandy and ouzo

Capellini alla pescarese — $15.95
Shrimp, scallops, clams, mussels and calamari in tomato basil sauce, over angel hair pasta

Melanzane alla parmigiana — $8.95
Baked eggplant with tomatoes, basil and mozzarella cheese

Ristorante Pronto

PHONE
956–4049

HOURS
Lunch
Monday–Friday
11:30 am–2:30 pm
Dinner
Monday–Saturday
5:30 pm–10:30 pm

LOCATION
3950 East Campbell
Phoenix, AZ 85018

CUISINE
Italian

ATTIRE
Casual

RESERVATIONS
Suggested

CREDIT CARDS
MasterCard, Visa, American Express, Diners Club, Discover

SMOKING
Section Available

HANDICAP FACILITIES

Ristorante Pronto

Philly's Sports Bar & Grill

PHONE
860–6600

HOURS
Monday–Sunday
11:00 am–1:00 am
(9:30 am Sunday
Breakfast during
the NFL season)

LOCATION
9301 East Shea Blvd.
Scottsdale, AZ 85259
(Southeast corner of
Shea & 92nd St)

CUISINE
American & Greek

ATTIRE
Casual

LOUNGE
11:00 am–1:00 am

PATIO DINING
TV Monitor on patio

TAKE OUT

VEGETARIAN MEALS

CREDIT CARDS
MasterCard, Visa,
American Express

SMOKING
Section Available

HANDICAP FACILITIES

Philly's Sports Bar & Grill

For over five years, Philly's has been North Scottsdale's favorite neighborhood Sports Bar & Grill.

There is no better place to enjoy watching your favorite sporting events. With 5 big screen TVs & 23 monitors, every sports fan has a seat on the 50 yard line at Philly's.

Our All-Star Menu satisfies the appetite of even the most discriminating sports fan.

People travel from miles around for our famous Philly's Cheesesteak sandwiches.

STARTING LINE UPS

Buffalo Wings	$4.50
Bread Sticks	$3.50
Southwest Spinach Dip	$5.75
Chicken Quesadilla	$5.50
Super Nachos	$5.25
Fresh Veggie Platter	$4.75
Tater Skins	$5.25
Onion Strings	$3.75
Fresh Zucchini	$4.50
Clam Strips	$4.75
Chicken Strips	$4.75
Cajun Curly Fries	$2.95
Steak Fries	$2.95

ON THE GREEN

Caesar Salad	$5.25
Cajun Chicken Caesar Salad	$7.25
Aztec Chicken Salad	$7.25
Cobb Salad	$6.50
Chef Salad	$6.50
Albacore Tuna Salad	$6.50

SOUPer BOWLS

Homemade Chili	Bowl $2.95	Cup $2.50
Soup of the Day	Bowl $2.25	Cup $2.00

HAMBURGER HALL OF FAME

495er Burger	$4.95
Bacon Cheese Burger	$5.75
Ben Franklin Burger	$5.75
Quaker Burger	$5.75
Southwest Burger	$5.75

BALL PARK BIG HITTERS

Hot Dog, Brat or Polish Sausage	Single $3.75
(Your choice of any 2 of the above)	Double $6.25

ALL SANDWICHES SERVED WITH YOUR CHOICE OF CAJUN CURLY FRIES, STEAK FRIES, POTATO SALAD, COLE SLAW OR GARDEN SALAD.

SANDWedges

Famous Philly Cheesesteak	from $5.25
Chicken Cheesesteak	from $6.25
Toppings (grilled onions, grilled bell pepper, mushrooms, cherry peppers, jalapeno peppers)	30¢ ea
Philly Club Sandwich	$6.25
Deli-Style Sandwich	$6.25
Italian Sausage	$5.95
BBQ Turkey	$5.95
Beef Cheddar Dip	$6.25
California Chicken	$6.25
Western Chicken	$6.25
Santa Fe Chicken	$6.25
Terriyaki Chicken	$6.25
Cajun Chicken	$6.25
Reuben On Rye	$6.25
Veggie Sandwich	$5.75
Albacore Tuna Melt	$5.95
Bacon, Lettuce and Tomato	$4.95
Albacore Tuna Salad Croissant	$6.50
Hot Ham And Swiss Croissant	$6.50
Grilled Turkey, Bacon & Cheese Croissant	$6.50

GREEK-STYLE OLYMPIC GOLDS

Gyro Sandwich	$6.25
Grecian Chicken	$7.25
Greek Village Salad (Horiatiki)	$6.75

FORWARD PASSta

Fettucini Alfredo	$6.50
Spaghetti Marinara	$5.95
Bow Tie Pasta	$6.95
(artichokes, mushrooms, sundried tomatoes)	

LITTLE LEAGUERS

(For the Philly's fan 12 years of age and under)

Chicken Strips	$3.25
Cheeseburger	$2.75
Hot Dog	$2.75
Grilled Cheese Sandwich	$2.75
Triple Decker Peanut Butter & Jelly	$2.75
Cheese Crisp	$2.75

4TH-QUARTER FINISHES

Apple Pie	$2.95	A La Mode	$3.95
French Vanilla Ice Cream			$2.00
Toppings			$ .75
(strawberries, amaretto, or chocolate)			

Raffaele's
ITALIAN CUISINE

We are honored to have you with us and pleased to prepare for you the finest in Italian food. We appreciate your confidence and will always do our utmost to deserve your friendship and patronage. If our menu does not include what your appetite craves, please let us know... we might suprise you!

Buon Appetito! Raffaele Contacessi

Antipasti Freddi • Cold Appetizer

Carpaccio Di Bresaula Valtelina — 8.95
Dried cure filet mignon, with arugula and grana, extra virgin olive oil

Carpacclo Con Rugola & Parmigiano Grana — 0.95
Very thin sliced raw filet mignon with arugula and grana. extra virgin olive oil and lemon

Piatto Rustico — 9.95
Fresh homemade buffalo mozzarella stuffed with imported prosciutto. Served wtth roasted red bell pepper, basil and sun dried tomato

Antipasti Caldi • Hot Appetizer

Agilo Al Forno — 4.95
Baked garlic with extra virgin olive oil and spices.

Bocconcini Con Prosciutto É Spinaci Fresci — 7.50
Buffalo mozzarella wrapped in imported prosciutto ham and baked with fresh spinach.

Lumache Alla Raffaele — 7.95
Tender snail sauteed wtth garlic butter and brandy

Antipasto Misto for Two — 12.95
Combination af clams casino, shrimp scampi, stuffed eggplant, escargot, and arschoke hearts

Pasta of the day—ask server — 6.95

Minestre • Soup

Stracciatella Alla Fioentina — 4.50
Chicken broth with parmigiano. spinach and whisked egg.

Pasta E Faggioli — 4.50
Canelli beans with pasta.

Insalate • Salad

Panzanella — 5.95
Grilled country style bread topped with marinated fresh diced tomatoes, diced bermuda onions, fresh basil, diced cucumber and baby artichoke hearts

Insalata Alla Cesare — 4.95
The traditional caesar salad

Insalata Alla Moda — 4.95
Hearts of romaine, bermuda onion, tomato, olives and extra virgin olive oil.

Insalata Di Spinaci, Con Mandorie É Mandarino — 6.95
Spinach salad with almonds, and mandarin oranges in lite balsamlic vinegar

Farinacei • Pasta
Served with a fresh garden salad and soup of the day.

Fettuccine Alfredo — 10.95
The original from Alfredo in Rome. Corrected by us

Gnocchi Alla Veneziana — 11.95
Potato dumplings tossed with fresh mushrooms and peas, with cream and a touch of tomato sauce

Tortellini Alla Principessa — 12.95
Meat filled pasta topped with cream, parmesan, fresh spinach & walnuts

This is just a small selection of menu items available at Raffaele's

Le Specialita Del Maestro
Specialities of the Master Chef
Served with a fresh garden salad, soup of the day and side of pasta

Linguine Del Vaticano (Vatican Style) — 14.95
Grilled chicken breast cut jullienne style, sauteed with fresh garlic, extra virgin olive oil, white wine, fresh herbs, and diced tomato over linguine.

Risotto Alla Milanese Con Safferano — 15.95
Asborio rice sauteed with shitake and oyster mushrooms with saffron.

Risotto Del Marinaio — 16.95
Arborio rice sauteed with shrimp, scallops, mussels and calamari.

Risotto Del Ortolano — 15.95
Asparagus tips and baby artichoke hearts, sauteed with fresh garlic, olive oil and white wine, over Italian rice.

Vitello & Manzo • Veal & Beef
Served with a fresh garden salad, soup of the day and side of pasta

Vitello Alla Marsala — 16.95
Veal scallopine sauteed with marsala wine and mushrooms

Vitello Con Carciofi — 17.95
Sauteed veal scallopine with baby artichoke hearts, capers, white wine and lemon butter sauce.

Filetto Di Manzo Al Funghi O Al Gorgonzola — 19.95
Fillet mignon with mushrooms or gorgonzola sauce

Pollami & Specialita • Poultry & Specialities
Served with a fresh garden salad, soup of the day and side of pasta

Melanzane Parmigiana — 13.95
Layered sliced eggplant with cheese, baked in marinara sauce.

Melanzane Ripiene — 13.95
Rolled eggplant stuffed with ricotta, baked with marinara topped with mozzarella

Pollo Alla Calabrese Con Polenta — 15.95
Chicken breast and homemade sausage braised in white wine, bell peppers, mushrooms, onion and garlic. served with a light tomato sauce, with polenta.

Molluschi & Crostacei • Seafood
Served wtfh a fresh garden salad, soup of the day and side of pasta.

Catch at the day — Ask you server

Tortelli (Ripieni Di Pesce) Fatti In Casa — 16.95
Homemade pasta stuffed with seafood, topped with scallops, shrimp, capers, with a very light brandy cream sauce.

Linguini Con Calamari — 13.95
Calamari sauteed with garilc, basil and fresh tomato sauce. served on a bed of linguini

Capelli Di Angelo Del Marinaio — 15.95
Shrimp, scallops and clams braised with garlic, fresh tomato sauce and basil on a bed of angel hair pasta.

Salmone Di Al Capone — 19.95
King salmon, shrimp, and scallops, sauteed with gariic, olive oil, red and green bell peppers, mushrooms, with a light cream tomato sauce over fettucine.

Gamberi Fradiavolo Or Marinara — 19.95
Shrimp braised with garlic, basil and spicy marinara sauce over llnguine.

Gamberi Alla Barese — 19.95
Shrimp, artichoke hearts, mushrooms and sun dried tomato sauteed with fresh garlic, herbs, and white wine sauce over linguine

Cioppino — 23.95
A combination ofshell fish sauteed in zesty marinara over linguine

---

Raffaele's

PHOENIX LOCATION

PHONE
952–0063

LOCATION
2999 North
44th Street
Phoenix, AZ 85018

MESA LOCATION

PHONE
838–0090

LOCATION
2909 South
Dobson Road
Mesa, AZ 85224

HOURS
Lunch
Monday–Friday
11:30 am–2:30 pm

Dinner
Monday–Thursday
5:00 pm–10:00 pm
Friday & Saturday
5:00 pm–11:00 pm

CUISINE
Italian

ATTIRE
Casual

LOUNGE
5:30–Closing

TERRACE DINING

PATIO DINING

TAKE OUT

VEGETARIAN MEALS

RESERVATIONS
Suggested

CREDIT CARDS
MasterCard, Visa,
American Express,
Discover, Diners Club

SMOKING
Section Available

HANDICAP FACILITIES

Riazzi's Italian Garden

Since 1947, The Riazzi Family has been serving homemade Italian food to generations of Valley residents and Out-Of-Towners alike. The menu has changed somewhat in that time, but most items are still prepared by hand as they were back then. Now located in Tempe the atmosphere is still casual and friendly, appealing to a wide variety of clientele.

The Riazzi family

Riazzi's
A Family Tradition Since 1947

Riazzi's

Appetizers

Zucchini Breaded & Fried	4.00
Eggplant Breaded & Fried	4.00
Meat Ravioli Fried (5)	7.25
Ricotta Ravioli Fried (3)	7.25
Meat (3) Ricotta (2) Ravioli Fried	8.75
Calamari Breaded & Fried	6.25
Mushrooms Breaded & Fried	4.00
Shrimp Cocktail	7.25
Fried Cheese	5.00

Salad & Soup

Italian Salad	2.50

Lettuce, tomato, pepperocine, olive & beets.

Antipasto Salad For One	3.00

Lettuce, tomato, pepperocine, olive, celery, pickle, salami, cheese, onion & beets.

Caesar Salad	5.00
Fresh sliced tomatoes with olive oil	5.25

herbs and spices, topped with thinly sliced mozzarella cheese.

Large Antipasto Salads Include:
Lettuce, tomato, pepperocine, olive, celery, salami, cheese, onion, tuna, sardines, pickles & beets. Anchovies available on request.

for two - 5.50	for four - 6.75	for six - 8.00	
Minestrone Soup (Bowl)			2.50
Scarpel Soup			3.00

Italian crepes rolled up with grated romano cheese, served with homemade chicken soup.

Pasta Entrees

Spaghetti or Linguine (Imported Pasta) with:

Meat Balls & Tomato Sauce	7.25
Meat Sauce	7.25
Meat Sauce & Meat Balls	9.00
Sausage (2) & Tomato Sauce	9.25
Mushrooms & Tomato Sauce	7.50
Bell Peppers & Tomato Sauce	7.50
Shrimp & Tomato Sauce	9.50
Clams, White or Red	9.25
Calamari & Tomato Sauce	9.25
Garlic & Oil	7.25
Marinara Sauce (no meat)	7.25

Steaks & Ribs

New York Cut	13.95
New York Ala Pizzaiola	15.95

Steak broiled to your taste, topped with tomato sauce, cheese, mushrooms then sizzled on the broiler to fully enhance the taste.

Steak & Scampi	18.50
Steak Sandwich	8.50
Baby Back Ribs	13.50

Rack of Baby Back Ribs topped with spicy barbecue sauce & served with French fries or mostaccioli.

House Specialities

Lasagne Imbottite	9.25

Layered homemade noodles, ricotta cheese, homemade sausage topped with mozzarella cheese, baked in tomato sauce.

Manicotti	9.25

Ricotta Cheese with ham wrapped in Egg Crepe, topped with tomato sauce and cheese.

Cannolloni	10.25

Beef & turkey wrapped in Egg Crepe baked in special sauce, topped with cheese.

Baked Mastaccioli	8.75

Mostaccioli, sausage and cheese baked in tomato sauce.

Eggplant Parmigiana with Fettuccine Riazzi	8.75

Eggplant breaded, baked with tomato sauce and cheese.

Sausage & Bell Peppers	9.25

Homemade sausage sliced and fried with bell peppers, served with mostaccioli.

Cavatelli (Gnocchi)	7.75

Homemade pasta made with potatoes served with meat balls or meat sauce.

Stuffed Eggplant	10.95

With seasoned Ricotta, diced ham, fresh herbs and spices in a Red Sauce topped with melted Provolone served with Fettuccine.

Homeade Ravioli Stuffed With:

Meat & Spinach with Meat Balls or Meat Sauce	9.75
Meat & Spinach with Sausage & Tomato Sauce	10.75
Meat & Spinach with Mushrooms or Bell Peppers	9.75
Ricotta Cheese with Meat Balls or Meat Sauce	10.00
Ricotta Cheese with sausage	11.00

Tortellini Riazzi	9.75

Pasta stuffed with turkey, chicken & mortadella served in a cream & cheese sauce.

Fettuccine Riazzi	8.75

Noodles in cream & cheese sauce.

Half & Half	9.00

Spaghetti & meat ravioli with meat balls or meat sauce.

PHONE
731-9464

HOURS
Monday–Thursday
11:00 am–10:00 pm
Friday
11:00 am–11:00 pm
Saturday
5:00 pm–11:00 pm
Sunday
4:00 pm–10:00 pm

LOCATION
2700 South Mill Ave
Tempe, AZ 85282

CUISINE
Italian

ATTIRE
Casual

RESERVATIONS
Suggested

CREDIT CARDS
MasterCard, Visa, American Express, Discover, Diners Club

SMOKING
Section Available

HANDICAP FACILITIES

ROXSAND Restaurant & Bar

PHONE
381–0444

HOURS
Lunch
Monday–Saturday
11:00 am–4:00 pm
Sunday
12:00 pm–4:00 pm

Dinner
Monday–Thursday
5:00 pm–10:00 pm
Friday & Saturday
5:00 pm–10:30 pm
Sunday
5:00 pm–9:30 pm

LOCATION
2594 East
Camelback Road
Phoenix, AZ 85016

CUISINE
New American

ATTIRE
Resort Casual

FULL SERVICE BAR

PATIO DINING

TAKE OUT

VEGETARIAN MEALS

BANQUET FACILITIES

RESERVATIONS
Suggested

CREDIT CARDS
MasterCard, Visa,
American Express,
Diners Club

CHECKS
With Guarantee Card
(in state only)

SMOKING
Area In Bar

HANDICAP FACILITIES

R O X S A N D
(R e s t a u r a n t & B a r)

1990	Arizona Republic One of Arizona's Top Ten Restaurants	1994	Di RoNA Award
1991	Rising Chef Series James Beard House	1995	Di RoNA Award
1991	Best New Restaurant Esquire Magazine	1995	James Beard Foundation Nominated "Best Chef of the Southwest"

*"Transcontinental Divide: Is there a more interesting restaurant in this city than **RoxSand**? After a recent return visit, I'd have to say no.*

By any standard, it's a sophisticated, snazzy-looking place. You can pass several enjoyable minutes staring at the offbeat, attention-getting art. I get a kick gazing at the huge, metal pineapple suspended from the ceiling by the entrance. People-watching never fails. And neither, it seems, does the food."

Howard Seftel, *New Times*, August-94

Owners, Roxsand Suarez Scocos and Spyro Scocos, offer a unique atmosphere and dining experience.

Recognied by **Gourmet Magazine, U.S.A. Today, Esquire Magazine, and Food and Wine Magazine** as one of America's most unique restaurants, RoxSand stands alone in the Phoenix market offering adventuresome new American food with Asian and Southwestern influences. Roxsand offers vegetarian and healthy alternatives for your special dining needs.

RoxSand's specialties include, but are not limited to:

Air Dried Duck, Sizzling Sea Scallop Salad, Rice Tamales, Chilean Sea Bass, Grilled Ahi and Roast Rack of Lamb, Roxsand offers the valley's largest daily dessert pastry selection and more than 60 wines by the glass.

Join us for Lunch, Dinner, Cocktails or Dessert.

Rustler's Rooste

Mountaintop at the Pointe Hilton Resort on South Mountain, Rustler's Rooste offers beef and brew with a view. Horny the Bull will greet you at the entrance to an old mine, before you take the old tin slide to the good times and good grub that have made this eatery a long time favorite. Cookie's specialties include mesquite-broiled steak, pork chops, swordfish, Indian fry bread and cowboy beans. Known for its Western fare, friendly service, breathtaking view and live country-western music, don't miss this Valley landmark.

Beginnings

The Roundup — $4.95
A tasty combination of our mushrooms, buffalo wings and nachos.

Mushrooms — $4.25
Plump mushrooms, deep-fried.

Zucchini — $4.25
Italian squash, breaded and deep-fried.
All above served with a side of ranch dressing.

Shrimp Cocktail — $8.95
Served with tangy cocktail sauce.

Buffalo Wings — $4.25
Braised, spicy chicken wings, served with either mild (2 alarm) or hot (5 alarm), also can be made with barbecue sauce for the tenderfoot, and served with scallions and bleu cheese.

Tater Skins — $5.25
Deep-fried and filled with cheddar cheese and bacon. Served with salsa and sour cream.

Rattlesnake (seasonal)

Deep-fried without the rattles, and served with cucumber dressing — $8.95

I ate rattlesnake T-shirt — $12.95

The Chuckwagon

Trail Boss — $21.95
Dern near 2 pounds of porterhouse steak.

Trail Hand — $15.95
One-pound T-bone steak.

BBQ Beef Ribs — $11.95
More, if you can eat them. (each) $1.95

Pork Chops — $13.95
Extra thick and juicy. Served with barbecue sauce.

Wagonmaster — $15.95
Ten ounces of choice New York steak. No bones about it.

Boneless Prime Rib of Beef
Cowboy size — $15.95
Cowgirl size — $13.95

Rustler's cut — $13.95
Ten ounces of top-sirloin steak served piping hot, right off the coals.

Tenderfoot — $17.95
Choice center-cut ten-oz. filet.

Cattleman's — $10.95
A tender beefsteak battered, breaded and fried like a chicken! Mashed potatoes and country gravy.

Mixed Grill

Some a This and Some a That — $11.95
BBQ beef ribs with BBQ chicken. (Pork Ribs, add $2.00)

Top-Sirloin Steak with Shrimp or Swordfish. — $14.95

The Fishin' Hole

All our fishin' hole meals come with salad, choice of dressing, corn on the cob, blended wild rice, biscuits and Indian fry bread.

Marinated Broiled Swordfish — $14.95
En Guarde, Cowboy.

Jumbo Shrimp — $15.95
Served sautéed or battered and deep-fried.

Mesquite Grilled Catfish — $10.95
Dewhiskered, declawed and mesquite-grilled.

The Hen House

Barbecued Chicken — $10.95
Half a hen, right down the middle.

Southern Fried Chicken — $10.95
It'll make you think of Grandma.

Hey Grazers!
(Vegetarian)

Ask your server to have Cookie whip you up something vegetarian (without any meat in it). — $8.95

The Menu Above is Just a Small Samplin' of Items Available at Rustler's Rooste.

Rustler's Rooste

PHONE
431-6474

HOURS
Sunday–Thursday
5:00 pm–10:00 pm
Friday & Saturday
5:00 pm–11:00 pm

LOCATION
7777 South
Pointe Parkway
Phoenix, AZ 85044
The Pointe
Hilton Resort on
South Mountain

CUISINE
Western

ATTIRE
Casual

LOUNGE
4:00 pm–Midnight
Appetizers only

ENTERTAINMENT
Live Music &
Dancing nightly

TERRACE DINING

AFTER-THEATER DINING

BANQUET FACILITIES

FULL-SERVICE CATERING

TAKE OUT

VEGETARIAN MEALS

RESERVATIONS
Suggested

CREDIT CARDS
MasterCard, Visa,
American Express,
Diners Club, Discover

SMOKING
Section Available

HANDICAP FACILITIES

Royal Barge
Thai Cuisine

For anyone who remembers seeing the play The King and I and wonders what Anna really saw in Siam, maybe it was the food. Siam of course is Thailand located in the Indo-China penninsula and thus finds itself at cultural and culinary crossroads. To have a wonderful Thai food experience make sure to visit the Royal Barge, truly one of the valley's finest.

About the Royal Barge
It has Been Noted

"Royal Barge continually strives to keep it's cuisine current with the trends of today's lifestyle and succeeds admirably."

—Scottsdale Magazine

"Superb... Yes, superb. That's the word that I use to describe our dinning experience."

—Donald Downes
Scottsdale Progress

"We recommend dining at the Royal Barge not because the food is delicious, but because the food is healthy and delicious."

—Dr. and Mrs. Stewart Mann
Scottsdale Internist

Appetizers

Crispy Chicken Wings	$3.95
marinated and deep fried	
Royal Spring Roll	$3.50
Thai egg roll stuffed with crab, pork, shrimp, sprouts and mushroom stuffed with seasonal vegetables	
Mee Krob	$4.95
crispy sweet noodles with shrimp and chicken	
Satay	$5.95
marinated, grilled beef or chicken served with peanut sauce	
Royal Barge Paddle	$6.95
whole shrimp tucked in minced pork, chicken and vegetables wrapped in noodles and crisp fried	

Salad and Soups

Thai Salad	$5.95
greens, bean sprouts, chicken, hard boiled egg topped with peanut dressing	
Royal Chef Salad	$6.95
greens, carrot, onion, shrimp, chicken and pork tossed in spicy dressing and topped with chopped peanuts	

Calamari Salad	$6.95

thinly sliced squid on onion, lemon grass, red chile sauce and lemon juice on greens

Won Ton Soup	for two $4.50
	for four $6.50

chicken stuffed wontons in broth

Chicken Coconut Soup	for two $4.95
	for four $6.95

with mushrooms, lemon grass, lime juice and chiles

Royal Fisherman's Soup	for two $6.95
	for four $8.95

Shrimp, scallops, squid & red snapper with ginger

Chicken and Duck

Barbecued Chicken	$7.95

marinated in ginger, coriander and garlic and grilled

Pad Prig Pao	$7.95

chicken stir fried with bell pepper, carrot and onion in roasted red chile sauce

Cashew Chicken	$7.95

sautéed with vegetables

Musamun Curried Chicken	$7.50

simmered with potatoes and roasted peanuts in a mild, sweet curry sauce

Green Curried Chicken	$7.50

with bamboo shoots, peas and bell pepper

Cashew Duck	$10.95

sautéed with vegetables

Curried Roasted Duck	$10.95

simmered with pineapple in red chile paste with coconut milk

Beef and Pork

Black and White Beef	$7.95

stir fried with black mushrooms and white ginger

Red Curried Beef	$7.95

with bamboo shoots

Sizzling New York Steak	$12.95

brushed with Thai marinade, grilled to order and served with sautéed vegetables

Garlic and Pepper Pork	$7.95

sautéed with seasonal vegetables

Sweet and Sour Pork	$7.95

sautéed with pineapple, green pepper and onion

Seafood

Spicy Calamari	$8.95

hand cut and sautéed with vegetables in roasted chile sauce

Spicy Catfish	$9.95

fillets sautéed with vegetables in roasted chile sauce

Dancing Fish	$10.95

marinated orange roughy fillet deep fried and combined with sautéed vegetables in sweet spicy sauce

Ginger Catfish	$12.95

steamed fillet with mushrooms (takes extra time to prepare)

Yellow Curried Lobster	$13.95

with onion, bamboo shoots and mushrooms

Pra Ram	$9.95

sautéed shrimp with chicken, pork and beef on a bed of greens topped with peanut sauce

Royal Curried Seafood	$12.95

snapper, scallops, shrimp, squid, onion and mushrooms simmered in a red chile paste with coconut milk

Vegetarian

Curried Eggplant	$7.25

simmered in green sauce with coconut milk

Sauteed Tofu	$6.95

with bean sprouts in garlic sauce

Noodles and Rice

Royal Thai Sukiyaki	$10.95

Shrimp, chicken, squid, egg, vegetables and glass noodles

Pad Thai	$7.95

rice noodles stir fried with shrimp, chicken, sprouts, green onion and egg sprinkled with ground peanuts

Silver Noodles	$6.95

glass noodles stir fried with egg, vegetables and pork

Thai Fried Rice	$6.95

with chicken, egg and vegetables

Basil Fried Rice	$6.95

with beef, onion, bell pepper and chiles

Royal Barge

PHONE
443-1953

HOURS
Lunch
Monday–Friday
11:00 am–2:00 pm

Dinner
Sunday–Thursday
5:00pm–9:30pm

Friday & Saturday
5:00–10:30

LOCATION
8140 North
Hayden Road
Suite H-115
Scottsdale, AZ 85258

CUISINE
Thai

ATTIRE
Casual

RESERVATIONS
Suggested

CREDIT CARDS
MasterCard, Visa,
American Express,
Diners Club, Discover

CHECKS ACCEPTED
with guarantee card

SMOKING
Section Available

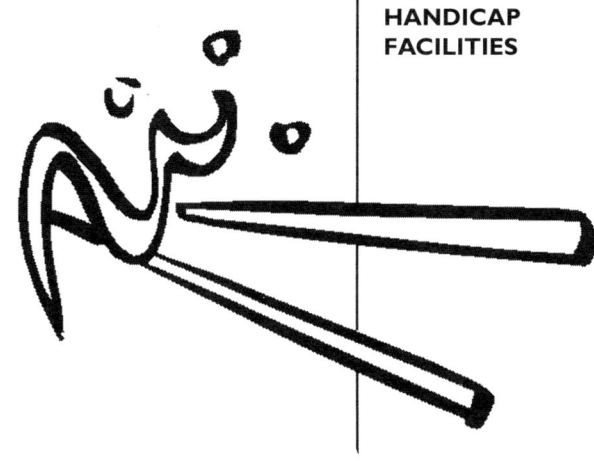

HANDICAP FACILITIES

Ristorante Sandolo

PHONE
991-3388

HOURS
Daily
6:00 pm–10:30 pm

LOCATION
7500 East
Doubletree Ranch Rd.
Scottsdale, AZ 85258

CUISINE
Italian

ATTIRE
Casual

ENTERTAINMENT

OUTSIDE TERRACE DINING

VEGETARIAN MEALS

RESERVATIONS
Suggested

CREDIT CARDS
MasterCard, Visa,
American Express,
Diners Club, Discover

SMOKING
Outside Terrace Only

HANDICAP FACILITIES

SANDOLO

Ristorante Sandolo brings a touch of Venice to the desert. Here the accent is on Venetian inspired fare served in a fun and relaxing setting complete with singing servers and a complimentary Sandolo ride through the resort's waterways.

Antipasta

Calamari Fritti	4.25
Fried squid with a squash-vinaigrette relish	
Bocconcini Di Bufola	5.25
Fresh mozzarella with plum tomatoes	
Mozzarella e Pane	4.25
Stuffed mozzarella with prosciutto in tomato basil sauce	

Zuppe

Pasta e Fagioli	2.50
White bean soup with ham and pasta	
Minestrone	2.50
Traditional country vegetable soup	

Insalata

Caesar Salad	4.00
With garlic croutons	
Antipasta Salad	4.25
On field greens	
Fresh Spinach Salad	4.00
With fried mozzarella	

Pizza

Shrimp and Scallops With Fresh Herbs and Plum Tomatoes	10.95
Honey Baked Ham, Smoked Pineapple, Fresh Basil and Three Cheeses	10.75
Roasted Chicken, Sundried Tomatoes and Goat Cheese	10.95

Primi Piatti

Spaghettini Marinara*	10.25
Fresh Herbs in Tomato Sauce	
Ravioli Rosa*	10.75
Veal Stuffed Pasta Shells with Tomato Cream Sauce	
Farfalle Alla Salmone	11.50
Bowtie Pasta With Smoked Salmon and Garden Vegetables	
Fettucini Alfredo*	10.50
Cream Sauce With Reggiano Parmesan Cheese	
Mostaccioli Bolognese*	10.25
Traditional Tomato Meat Sauce	
Vermicelli Primavera*	10.25
Vegetables With Herbs and Fresh Tomato Sauce	
Lasagne Ferrara	11.25
Baked With Prosciutto, Parmesan and Tomato	
Scaloppina Sugo Di Carne	13.75
Veal Medallions With Pasta and Tomato	
Spaghetti Con Sugo Di Pollo	10.75
Roasted Chicken Sauteed With Cream Sauce	
Petto Di Pollo Alla Riviera	12.25
Sauteed Chicken Breast With Lemon Butter and Artichokes	
Vitello Al Limone	13.75
Marinated Veal Loin Grilled With Lemon Butter	
Pane Con Aglio	2.00
Grilled Fresh Garlic Bread	

Dolci

Tiramisù	3.00
Torte De Chocolaté	3.50
Gelati	2.75
Cassata Napoletana	3.50
Espresso	2.50
Cappuccino	2.75
San Pellegrino	5.25
Cappuccino Sandolo	5.25

*Items Available In Appetizer Portions   6.25

Pass the Ciao!

Big, steaming platters of the freshest Italian recipes served family style are our specialty. Our Pass the Ciao! Platters are so big, in fact, that you've just got to share. You may not be able to take the whole gang to Italy, but you can bring them to Spageddies. So put your heads-and forks together, and pick a platter to pass around the table. The hard part is deciding which one...or two...or three... Pass the Ciao! And enjoy.

Starters

	SOLO	CIAO!
Pepperoni Bread	4.65	
Fried Calamari	5.95	9.95

Salads

	SOLO	CIAO!
Garden Salad	3.95	5.95

Crisp mixed greens, roma tomatoes, cucumbers, red onions, Italian vinaigrette, croutons & parmesan cheese

	SOLO	CIAO!
ᵥ Chopped Chicken & Pasta Salad	5.95	8.95

Oak grilled chicken tossed with fresh greens and pasta shells, Italian vinaigrette & parmesan cheese

	SOLO	CIAO!
Shrimp Caesar Salad	6.95	10.95

Our Caesar Salad topped with succulent shrimp

Oak-Fired Pizza

	SOLO	CIAO!
Pizza Bianca	5.95	

Rotisserie chicken, garlic & asiago cheese on alfredo sauce

Pizza Margherita	4.95	

Sliced roma tomato, mozzarella cheese & fresh basil

BBQ Chicken Pizza	5.65	

Roasted chicken with spicy BBQ sauce and red onion

Pizza Supreme	5.95	

Bacon, ham mushrooms, peppers & black olives

Pasta

	SOLO	CIAO!

All Solo dinners are served with your choice of soup or house salad.

	SOLO	CIAO!
ᵥ Spaghetti Marina	6.45	9.45

Spaghetti tossed with a spicy marinara sauce

Penne Rustica	7.50	10.50

Penne pasta tossed with oregano & pancetta in a hearty tomato sauce

	SOLO	CIAO!
Shrimp & Penne Alfredo	9.95	14.95

Penne pasta in creamy alfredo sauce with bacon, fresh mushrooms, tomatoes, peas & topped with succulent shrimp

Chicken Fettuccine	8.75	12.50

Fettuccine in a pesto cream sauce topped with oak grilled chicken

Specialties

	SOLO	CIAO!

All Solo dinners are served with your choice of soup or house salad.

	SOLO	CIAO!
Chicken Scaloppini	8.95	13.95

Chicken medallions sautéed in a lemon butter sauce with bacon, tomatoes & mushrooms

Tuna Carino	9.95	

Oak grilled tuna steak with a zesty Sicilian relish, rosemary potatoes & fresh vegetables

Sizzlelini	7.95	14.95

Sizzling skillet of chicken, sausage or both with spaghetti, grilled peppers & onions

ᵥ Chicken Diavolo	7.25	10.25

Oak grilled chicken breast with spicy marina sauce

Veal Parmigiana		16.95

Italian breaded cutlets topped with tomato sauce & mozzarella cheese

Desserts

Cappuccino Cheese Cake		2.95

Light cappuccino flavor

Tiramisu		2.95

Lady fingers and a light sponge cake filled with an espresso custard

ᵥ *Spageddies Light—*
These dishes are low in fat and big on taste.

Spageddies Italian Kitchen

SCOTTSDALE
661-5511

HOURS
Daily
11:00 am–10:00 pm

LOCATION
10520 North
90th Street
Scottsdale, AZ 85258

PHOENIX
953-0100

HOURS
Daily
11:00 am–10:00 pm

LOCATION
12031 North
Tatum Blvd.
Phoenix, AZ 850281

CUISINE
Classic
Homestyle Italian

ATTIRE
Casual

RESERVATIONS
Suggested

CREDIT CARDS
MasterCard, Visa,
American Express,
Diners Club, Discover

HANDICAP FACILITIES

6th Avenue Bistrot
Chez François

It's easy to see why 6th Avenue Bistrot in Scottsdale earned food critic Penelope Corcoran's "Best French Restaurant" honors in this year's AZ Best special section. Owner Francois Simorte combines thoughtfully prepared meals with impeccable service and warm atmosphere to create one of the most memorable dining experiences found in the valley.

Fans of French food must visit 6th Avenue Bistrot. Dinner entrees start at $15.50, lunch $6.25.

Soup

Vegetable soup du jour 3.95

Appetizers

Mussels sauce poulette 6.95

Frog legs provençale 6.75

Sautéed escargot with garlic butter 6.25

Sautéed mushroom feuillette 5.95

Country paté 5.75

Pastas

Penne rigatte with tomato, basil, ... 11.50
garlic, and olives

Orzo with smoked salmon and 11.95
Chardonnay Sauce

Steamed Mussels with linguini 12.50
sauce poulette

Entrees

Traditional Coq au vin 16.25

Filet of beef 17.95
with bleu cheese sauce

Our "cassoulet" toulousain 16.50

Lamb shank au jus 16.50

Seared salmon 16.50
with pistou crust

Peppered Ahi tuna fillet 17.95
with balsamic vinegar sauce

Tenderloin of pork with 17.25
port wine sauce

Sautéed jumbo shrimp 17.50
with provençale sauce

Salads

Traditional Ceasar salad 4.50

Seasonal mixed greens with balsamic 4.50
vinaigrette and goat cheese croutons

Duck confit seasonal salad 4.50

Desserts

Crème caramel 4.50

Mousse au chocolat 4.50

Tarte Tatin 4.50

Traditional bread pudding 4.50

6th Avenue Bistrot

PHONE
947–6022

HOURS
Lunch
Tuesday–Friday
11:30 am–2:00 pm
Dinner
Daily
5:30 pm–10:00 pm

LOCATION
7150 East
6th Avenue
Scottsdale, AZ

CUISINE
Country French

ATTIRE
Casual

RESERVATIONS
Recommended

CREDIT CARDS
MasterCard, Visa, American Express

HANDICAP FACILITIES

Sushi on Shea

Veteran Valley sushi chef Fred Yamada and restaurant entrepreneur Michael McDermott recently opened Sushi on Shea at 7000 East Shea Boulevard. The 3,000 square foot restaurant features a Japanese dining atmosphere. Diners at the sushi bar can watch the chef prepare the meal and view two large salt water aquariums. Besides sushi, the menu features authentic items such as tempura, Nabemono, terriaki and a variety of other dishes.

Appetizers

YAKITORI **$3.95**
Two skewers of chicken and green onion with teriyaki sauce.

TEMPURA **$4.95**
Shrimp and vegetables lightly battered and deep fried.

SOFT SHELL CRAB **$6.95**
Blue crab deep fried served with ponzu sauce.

BEEF NEGIMA **$6.00**
Rolled beef with green onion grilled with authentic sauce.

AGE DASHI TOFU **$4.50**
Deep fried bean curd with house special sauce.

YAKKO TOFU **$3.50**
Chilled cold bean curd.

CHICKEN WINGS **$4.50**
Deep fried ginger flavor chicken wings.

MOTOYAKI **$6.50**
Baked green mussel with motoyaki sauce.

Soups

TOFU AND WAKAME MISOSHIRU **$2.50**
Miso soup with bean curd, seaweed and green onion.

NAMEKO AKADASHI **$3.00**
Red miso soup with nameko mushroom.

SUIMONO **$3.50**
Clear broth soup with chicken and vegetable.

CHAWAN MUSHI **$5.50**
A light custard soup with chicken, shrimp and mushroom. Preparation takes up to 30 minutes. Thank You.

Salads

GREEN SALAD **$2.50**
Garden fresh vegetables with house special soy dressing.

SUNOMONO **$3.50**
Sliced cucumber, seaweed, kanikama and octopus with Japanese dressing.

SASHIMI SALAD **$8.50**
Sliced fresh tuna slightly grilled and garden vegetable with special dressing.

GOMA-AE **$3.00**
Steamed spinach or broccoli served cold with sesame soy dressing.

CHICKEN SALAD **$6.50**
Tender chicken with garden fresh vegetables and steamed rice.

CRAB SALAD **$7.95**
Fresh crab tossed with vegetables in special creamy sauce and steamed rice.

Side Orders

BOWL OF RICE **$1.00**

SAUCE **$1.00**

GARI OR WASABI **$1.00**

TSUKEMONO **$3.95**
A variety of pickled vegetable.

Entrees
Served with green salad, miso soup and steamed rice

CHICKEN TERIYAKI **$9.50**
Half chicken charbroiled with teriyaki sauce.

BEEF TERIYAKI **$14.00**
New York steak charbroiled with our authentic teriyaki sauce.

SALMON TERIYAKI **$14.50**
OR SHIOYAKI
Filet charbroiled with teriyaki sauce or salted.

VEGETABLE TEMPURA **$7.50**
A variety of garden fresh vegetables lightly battered.

SHRIMP TEMPURA **$12.00**
Shrimp lightly battered.

SHRIMP AND **$15.50**
VEGETABLE TEMPURA
Shrimp and vegetables lightly battered.

FISH TEMPURA **$9.50**
Codfish lightly battered.

SEAFOOD AND **$13.50**
VEGETABLE TEMPURA
Fish, shrimp and vegetable lightly battered.

PORK FILET KATSU **$10.50**
Filet of pork in seasoned egg and bread crumbs.

CHICKEN KATSU **$9.95**
Tender chicken in seasoned egg and bread crumbs.

EBI FRI **$12.50**
Large shrimp in seasoned egg and bread crumbs.

CHICKEN TERIYAKI **$12.95**
AND TEMPURA
Chicken teriyaki with shrimp and vegetable tempura. Nabemono. Served with sunomono or green salad and steamed rice.

SUKIYAKI $15.50
Thinly sliced beef and vegetables with sukiyaki sauce.
MIZUTAKI $13.95
Tender chicken and vegetables with ponzu sauce.
SHABU-SHABU $16.00
Thinly sliced beef and vegetables with goma sauce and ponzu sauce.
YOSENABE $15.00
Chicken and selected fresh seafood and vegetable with ponzu sauce.
KAISEN NABE $21.00

Children's Meal
(Under 10 years old)

Choice of one:
CHICKEN TERIYAKI, CHICKEN KATSU, SHRIMP AND VEGETABLE TEMPURA OR TERIYAKI BEEF PATTY $5.95
With Miso Soup, Salad and Ice Cream.

From the Sushi Bar
Served with green salad and miso soup

ASSORTMENT SASHIMI $24.00
A variety of fresh fish exquisitely sliced.
ALL TUNA SASHIMI $21.00
Tuna lover special exquisitely sliced.
ASSORTMENT SUSHI $15.95
A variety of fresh fish fashioned into bite-size morsels with seasoned rice.
ASSORTMENT JO SUSHI $21.00
A variety of prime sushi.
CHIRASHI SUSHI $15.95
A variety of fresh fish over the seasoned rice.
UNA-JU $16.00
Broiled freshwater eel on steamed rice with special sauce.
SASHIMI AND TEMPURA $14.00
Sashimi with shrimp and vegetable tempura.
SUSHI AND TEMPURA $14.00
Sushi with shrimp and vegetable tempura.

Noodles

TEMPURA SOBA $8.95
Buckwheat noodles with Shrimp Tempura or Zaru Soba served cold.
TEMPURA UDON $8.95
Thick noodles with Shrimp Tempura.
YAKI SOBA $8.95
Soba noodles with stir fry vegetables and shrimp or pork.
CURRY UDON $8.95
Sliced New York beef and vegetables with thick noodles and hot curry sauce.

Desserts

GREEN TEA ICE CREAM $2.00
CHOCOLATE CHIP COOKIE DOUGH ICE CREAM $2.00
LEMON SHERBET $1.50
WAGASHI $2.50
CHEESECAKE $2.50
FRESH FRUIT IN SEASON $3.50

Lunch
11:30 am–2:30 pm
Served with green salad, miso soup and steamed rice.

CHICKEN TERIYAKI $5.50
Charbroiled with our authentic teriyaki sauce.
BEEF TERIYAKI $8.95
Rib eye steak charbroiled with our authentic teriyaki sauce.
SALMON TERIYAKI $8.50
OR SHIOYAKI
Filet charbroiled with teriyaki sauce or salted.
VEGETABLE TEMPURA $4.50
A variety of garden fresh vegetables lightly battered.
SHRIMP AND $9.50
VEGETABLES TEMPURA
Shrimp and vegetables lightly battered.
SHRIMP TEMPURA $7.50
Shrimp lightly battered.
SEAFOOD AND $8.50
VEGETABLE TEMPURA
Fish, shrimp and vegetables lightly battered.
PORK FILET KATSU $6.95
Filet of pork in seasoned egg and bread crumbs.
CHICKEN KATSU $6.00
Tender chicken in seasoned egg and bread crumbs.
EBI FRY $8.00
Large shrimp in seasoned egg and bread crumbs.
CHICKEN TERIYAKI $7.50
AND TEMPURA
Chicken teriyaki with vegetable tempura.

Sushi on Shea

PHONE
483-7799

HOURS
Lunch
Monday–Saturday
11:30 am–2:30 pm

Dinner
Sunday–Thursday
5:30 pm–10:00 pm
Friday & Saturday
5:30 pm–11:00 pm

LOCATION
7000 East
Shea Blvd.
Scottsdale, AZ 85254

CUISINE
Japanese

ATTIRE
Casual

RESERVATIONS
Suggested

CREDIT CARDS
MasterCard, Visa, American Express, Diners Club, Discover

HANDICAP FACILITIES

Steve Stone's Chicago Grill

PHONE
844-8448

HOURS
Daily
11:30 am–11:30 pm

LOCATION
161 North
Centennial Way
Mesa, AZ 85201

CUISINE
American

ATTIRE
Casual

HAPPY HOUR

TERRACE DINING

RESERVATIONS
Suggested

CREDIT CARDS
MasterCard, Visa,
American Express

CHECKS ACCEPTED

SMOKING
Section Available

HANDICAP FACILITIES

Certainly one of the premier sports bar restaurants in the Valley. Steve Stone's Chicago Grill is the perfect place for burgers, fries, salads, and sandwiches. The service is excellent and the prices are reasonable. Relax over lunch or dinner or enjoy a drink at the bar.

APPETIZERS

CALAMARI	$4.95

Lightly fried, served with cocktail sauce

CHICKEN TENDERS	$4.50

Breaded chicken breast, hot honey mustard sauce

POTATO SKINS	$3.95

Cheddar, bacon & sour cream

GOLDEN FRIED ONION RINGS	$3.25

A Chicago favorite

NACHOS WITH THE WORKS	$5.95

Chili, jalapenos, tomatoes, sour cream, guacamole, black olives and cheddar cheese

MUSHROOM & ZUCCHINI COMBO	$4.95

Served with ranch & honey mustard

JALAPENO POPPERS	$4.25

Jalapenos stuffed with cream cheese, served with ranch

HOT OR BBQ WINGS	$4.25
CHICKEN QUESADILLA	$5.50

Breast of chicken, cheese, served with salsa

HEALTHY SPECIALTIES

STUFFED TOMATO	$4.50

Tuna salad served with cottage cheese, egg, roll and butter

BROILED COD FILLET	$4.95

Broiled in lemon & water, served with cottage cheese. (low Cholesterol)

SOUPS & SALADS

LITE LUNCH	$4.95

Garden salad and a bowl of soup

TACO SALAD	$5.95

Breast of chicken, iceberg, guacamole, sour cream, tomato and olives, served in a tortilla bowl with salsa

CAESAR SALAD	$5.95

Romaine, caesar, croutons & parmesan

WRIGLEY CHOP SALAD	$5.95

Turkey spinach, tomato, lentils, mozzarella & creamy Italian

GRILLED CHICKEN SALAD	$5.95

Warm cajun chicken breast, iceberg, orange slices & tomato

CAJUN CHICKEN CAESAR SALAD	$5.95

Romaine, caesar, croutons & parmesan

CHEESE TORTELLINI SALAD	$5.95

Iceberg, feta cheese, cucumbers, olives, tomatoes, peppers, red onion, florentine dressing

BURGERS

Served with cajun french fries and garnish

SOUTH OF THE BORDER	$5.95

Cheddar Jalapenos and guacamole

BLEU BURGER	$5.95

Bleu cheese and bacon

CHILI BURGER	$5.95

Smothered in chili & cheese and topped with onions

WESTERN BURGER	$5.95

BBQ sauce, cheddar and bacon

1003 BURGER	$5.95

3 cheeses and 1000 island dressing

TURKEY BURGER	$5.95

Swiss and sauteed mushrooms

SOURDOUGH BURGER	$5.95

Cheddar cheese, grilled onions, mustard relish on sourdough

TERIYAKI BURGER	$5.95

Teriyaki mushrooms, swiss, topped with pineapple & chives

SANDWICHES

Served with cajun french fries and garnish

GRAND SLAM CHICKEN	$5.95

Grilled breast of chicken, mozzarella, bacon, mushroom and pesto mayo

FRENCH DIP	$5.95

Sliced beef on a hoagie with au jus and horseradish sour cream

MILWAUKEE BRATWURST	$4.95

Grilled and served with sauerkraut

BBQ BEEF	$5.95

Shredded beef served on a hoagie

PORK TENDERLOIN SANDWICH	$5.95

Grilled, topped with mozzarella, sauteed onions, tomato and pesto mayo

GRILLED TURKEY MELT	$5.95

Grilled turkey with cheddar, tomatoes and bacon sourdough

CHICAGO CLUB	$5.95

Ham or turkey on wheat, with lettuce, tomato, mozzarella, bacon and mayo

TURKEY SANDWICH [LOW CALORIE]	$4.95

Lettuce, tomato on whole wheat with cranberry, mayo and cottage cheese

HOUSE SPECIALTIES

CAJUN CHICKEN ALFREDO	$6.25

Spirelli pasta, chicken breast served alfredo style with garlic bread

NEW YORK STEAK SANDWICH	$6.95

Topped with onions and mushrooms

SHRIMP JAMMERS	$6.95

Stuffed shrimp with jack cheese, hushpuppies, fries and cole slaw

ENTREES

Served with rice

TERIYAKI CHICKEN	$7.95

Served with vegetables, garnished with pineapple

HALIBUT STEAK	$8.95

Topped with lemon reduction sauce and steamed vegetables

CHICKEN FINGER PLATE	$7.25

Served with french fries and honey mustard

CHICKEN FAJITAS	$7.95

Served with warm flour tortillas, sour cream and guacamole

PORK TENDERLOIN	$8.95

Marinated and grilled, topped with a peppercorn reduction sauce, and steamed vegetables

BATTERED COD FISH	$6.95

French fries & cole slaw

The Terrace
DINING ROOM

A tradition for 65 years at the Wigwam Resort…true Southwest hospitality.

Familiar American fare by former White House Chef during the Reagan Administration, Chef Jon Hill.

Enjoy the beautiful surroundings and the magnificent southwestern art and sculptures.

THE WIGWAM RESORT
Authentic Arizona

Terrace Dining Room Entrees
- USDA Prime Midwestern Corn-Fed Beef and Steaks
- Filet Mignon, Ribeye, New York Strip
- Pan Roasted Pacific Northwest Salmon
- Dijon Herb Crusted Rack of Lamb
- Coconut Beer Shrimp Tempura

Sunday Brunch:
Served 11:30 am–2:30 pm

A traditional highlight, with weekly changing entrees, omelettes made to order, bountiful selection of seafoods and salads, and of course—lavish desserts

For restaurants call 935–3811 ext. 1140

The Terrace Dining Room

PHONE
935–3811, ext. 1140

HOURS
Lunch–Daily
11:30 am–2:00 pm
Dinner–Daily
5:30 pm–10:00 pm
Twilight Dinner
5:30 pm–6:30 pm

LOCATION
The Wigwam Resort
Litchfield Park
AZ 83540

CUISINE
American

ATTIRE
Jackets Required
Nov–May

ENTERTAINMENT
Bill Wise Orchestra

TERRACE DINING

SUNDAY BRUNCH

BANQUET FACILITIES

VEGETARIAN MEALS

RESERVATIONS
Suggested

CREDIT CARDS
MasterCard, Visa,
American Express,
Discover

SMOKING
Not Permitted

HANDICAP FACILITIES

The Terrace Dining Room

PHONE
602-423-2530

HOURS
Breakfast
Monday–Saturday
6:00 am–11:00 am
Sunday
6:00 am–10:00 am
Lunch
Monday–Saturday
11:30 am–4:00 pm
Dinner
Monday–Thursday
4:00 pm–10:00 pm
Friday & Saturday
4:00 pm–11:00 pm
Sunday
6:00 pm–10:00 pm

LOCATION
6000 East
Camelback Road
Scottsdale, AZ 85251

CUISINE
Italian

ATTIRE
Semi Casual

LOUNGE
11:00 am–Closing

TERRACE DINING
SUNDAY BRUNCH
11:00 am–3:00 pm

PRIVATE SALONS

CHILDRENS MENU

RESERVATIONS
Recommended

CREDIT CARDS
MasterCard, Visa,
American Express,
Diners Club, Discover

SMOKING
Section Available

HANDICAP FACILITIES

The Terrace Dining Room
at The Phoenician

Elegant surroundings and gracious service, with live music and dancing during dinner and Sunday brunch. Imaginative Italian dishes served indoors or out, overlooking the pool gardens.

Antipasti

✿ Seasonal Oysters on the Half Shell	Half Dozen	10.00
	Dozen	17.00
Sampling of Antipasti	(per person)	7.50
Grilled Eggplant, Tomato and Fresh Mozzarella with Basil		8.75
✿ House-Smoked Salmon with Lemon Aïoli and Grilled Country Bread		9.75
✿ Carpaccio of Beef with Arugula and Black Pepper		10.00
Hearts of Romaine with Creamy Garlic-Parmegiano Dressing		7.50
✿ Mixed Greens with Roasted Garlic, Sun-Dried Tomato and Bell Peppers		8.25
Grilled Polenta with Portobello Mushrooms and Cambozola Cheese		11.00
Pasta e Fagioli Soup		6.00

Pasta

Risotto with Artichokes and Pancetta	8.50/15.00
Bowtie Pasta with Spinach, Bell Peppers and Cream	8.00/14.50
Potato Gnocchi with Tomato Sauce, Mozzarella and Pesto	8.50/15.00
Roasted Maine Lobster with Spaghetti and Tomatoes	15.50/28.00
Pappardelle with Meat Sauce	9.50/16.00
✿ Angel Hair with Prosciutto and Peas	7.75/12.50
✿ Penne with Grilled Chicken, Roasted Peppers, Eggplant and Parsley	9.50/16.00

Entrées

Osso Bucco with Vegetable Sauce and Saffron Risotto	23.00
✿ Grilled Swordfish with Lemon and Oregano	25.00
Grilled Rib Eye of Beef with Spinach Wild Mushrooms and Shredded Potatoes	26.00
Roasted Maine Lobster Spaghetti with Tomatoes and Basil	28.00
b Filet of Salmon "A La Planca" Balsamic and Tomatoes	24.00
Fresh Water Striped Bass with Fennel and Black Olives	23.00
Pan-Seared Chicken with Lemon, Parsley and Garlic	22.00
"Scampi Style" Shrimp Borlotto Beans and Roasted Cauliflower	24.00

✿ *Choices*—Superb cuisine created by Chef Jeffrey Gosselin with your well-being in mind.

Tucchetti

A neighborhood restaurant featuring homemade Italian specialities. With it's warm and comfortable atmosphere and adjoining cocktail lounge, this "Lettuce Entertain You"® restaurant is perfect for both social gatherings and intimate dinners.

The signature Baked Spaghetti is a Tucchetti favorite. Featuring house specialities such as lasagna, Chicken Vesuvio, Thin Crust Pizzas, Pastas, Veal and Freshly prepared salads.

Starting Off

Fried Zucchini	3.95
Toasted Ravioli	3.95
Stuffed Mushrooms With Spinach Stuffing	3.95
Fried Calamari With Spicy Marinara Sauce	5.25
Baked Clams (6 of them)	5.50

Salads 'n' Such—Big 'n' Small

The Three Caesars: .... Small ...... Large

Caesar Salad with
Genuine Homemade Croutons	2.95	6.50
Caesar Salad with Roasted Chicken	3.95	7.95
Caesar Salad with Garlic Shrimp	4.95	8.95
Famous Chopped Pasta & Chicken Salad with Bacon & Blue Cheese	3.95	7.95

Italian Sandwich of the day 6.95

Cheese Ravioli Dishes

with Marinara Sauce, Meat Sauce, Alfredo Sauce ... 8.95
   With Meatball or .... add 1.00
   Italian Sausage on above

Eggplant Parmesan Dishes

Marinara Sauce, Meat Sauce, ... $8.95
Tomato & Mushroom Sauce
   With Meatball or .... add 1.00
   Italian Sausage on above

Stuffed Shells

with Cheese & Alfredo Sauce, with Cheese 8.95
& Marinara Sauce, Cheese & Spicy Tomato Sauce
   With Meatball or .... add 1.00
   Italian Sausage on above

Famous Baked Spaghetti

with Marinara Sauce, Meat Sauce, ... 9.95
Tomato & Mushroom Sauce, or Spicy Tomato Sauce
   With Meatball or .... add 1.00
   Italian Sausage on above

Special Recipe Lasagna Dishes

with Marinara Sauce, Meat Sauce, ... $9.95
Tomato & Mushroom Sauce, Spicy Tomato Sauce
   With Meatball or .... add 1.00
   Italian Sausage on above

Thin Crust Pizza Pies *As they often serve in Naples, Italy!*

Prosciutto, Artichokes & Mushrooms	8.95	13.95
Goat Cheese, Sun-Dried Tomatoes & Olives	8.95	13.95
Bacon, Spinach & Red Onion	8.95	13.95
Grilled Vegetables, Lightly Smoked Mozzarella	8.95	13.95
Roast Chicken, Alfredo Sauce, Peppers & Provolone	8.95	13.95

Old Fashioned Spaghetti or Mostaccoli or Linguine or Fettuccine or Angel Hair

with your choice of these .... $7.95–$9.50
fine sauces: Marinara Sauce, Low Fat Marinara Sauce, Rich Meat Sauce, Clam Sauce, Spicy Tomato Sauce, Tomato & Mushroom Sauce, Garlic & Oil, Alfredo Sauce, Pesto Sauce

Large Pasta Dishes— Served in a Big Bowl

Tortellini with Alfredo
Prosciutto, Peas 12.95
Mostaccoli with Chicken
Fresh Mozzarella & Spicy Tomato Cream 12.95
Angel Hair Pasta with Shrimp
Fresh Tomato, Basil, Garlic Oil 13.95

Old World Chicken & Veal Specialties

Chicken Vesuvio With Sausage 'n' Peppers	11.95
Chicken Milanese With Side of Fettuccine Alfredo	11.95
Chicken Siciliano With Side of Angel Hair	11.95
Veal Parmesan With Side O'Pasta	13.95
Veal Picatta With Side O'Pasta	13.95

The menu listed above is just a small sample of the excellent cuisine offered at Tucchetti.

Tucchetti

PHONE
957-0222

HOURS
Monday–Thursday
11:15 am–10:00 pm
Friday
11:15 am–11:00 pm
Saturday
12:00 pm–11:00 pm
Sunday
4:30 pm–9:00 pm

LOCATION
2135 East
Camelback Road
Phoenix, AZ
(In the Town and Country Shopping Center)

CUISINE
Italian

ATTIRE
Casual

PATIO DINING
Seasonal

LOUNGE

TAKE OUT

VEGETARIAN MEALS

RESERVATIONS
Accepted

CREDIT CARDS
MasterCard, Visa, American Express, Diners Club, Discover

SMOKING
In Bar Area Only

HANDICAP FACILITIES

TIMOTHY'S

An abundance of delicious appetizers and an eclectic menu of entrees are served in the ambiance of intimate vine-covered cottage. Pan-seared Ahi with Three Sauces, Rack of Lamb with Rosemary/Garlic Spiked Au Jus, and Chicken with Prosciutto and Spinach on Mostaccioli are just a few of the dinners elegantly served every night from 5 pm until midnight at this long time Valley favorite. The cool sounds of live jazz are delivered nightly from 8:30 until 12:30 am. Top entertainers often stop by for dining and/or an impromptu set with the group.

Appetizers

Served from 11:00 am until Midnight Every Night

Focaccia $4.95
Italian flatbread with:
  Grilled chicken, jack cheese and cilantro pesto.
  Goat cheese, sun dried tomatoes and black olive tepenade.

Smoked Salmon Mousse Cheesecake $3.95
A creamy combination of smoked salmon, cream cheese and smoked provolone on a parmesan and bread crumb crust with tomato concasse and chive aioli.

Gulf Stream Crab Cakes $5.25
Served in a cream sauce with jack cheese and green chilies.

Escargot $7.95
Fresh Petite Gris snails, bleu cheese and garlic baked in phyllo dough, served on Pernod cream sauce.

Duck Spring Rolls with Voodoo Sauce $4.95
Gingered duck, vegetables and sesame noodles in spicy red pepper ginger sauce with wasabi.

Baked Goat Cheese and Blue Corn Chips $5.95
Served with tomatillo salsa.

Pate Maison au Poivre $3.95
Chicken liver blended with cognac and peppercorns.

Pot Stickers $5.95
Pork and goat cheese pouches with tomatillo salsa for dipping.

Baked Brie $6.95
Topped with toasted almonds, served with apple slices and bread.

Calamari $4.95
Deep fried, served with remoulade sauce.

Jambalaya $5.25
A complex rich blend of shrimp, sausage, catfish, ham, tomatoes, bell peppers, onions, celery, herbs and spices on saffron rice.

Angel Hair Pasta al Fresca $4.95
Tomatoes, mushrooms, homemade sausage, fresh basil and garlic.

Chilled Stuffed Chile $3.95
Roasted and peeled Anaheim chile, stuffed with goat cheese, feta cheese, and fresh oregano.

Greek Salad $4.95
Garden greens, feta cheese, cucumbers, tomatoes, olives, red onions and artichoke hearts.

Rumaki $4.95
Chicken livers and sliced water chestnuts, wrapped in bacon and deep fried.

Timothy's has received awards for "Best Jazz Club" and "Most Romantic Restaurant." You'll have to pinch yourself to remember that you're still in Phoenix.

Timothy's

Dinner
Served from 5:00 until Midnight Every Night
All dinners are served with a bowl of our homemade soup, our acclaimed mixed greens salad tossed in a white wine, lemon, Dijon mustard dressing topped with bleu cheese, walnuts, and apple slices, and bread and butter.

Jambalaya — $19.95
A complex rich blend of shrimp, sausage, catfish, ham, tomatoes, bell peppers, onions, celery, herbs and spices on saffron rice.
Wine Suggestion: Chardonnay, White Burgundy.

Blue Corn Encrusted Seabass — $20.95
Baked seabass with bluecorn tortilla crust on a spicy tomatilla salsa with black bean toastada and roast corn relish.
Wine seggestion: Sauvignon Blanc, Semillion.

Pan Roasted Veal Chop Carne Seca — $24.95
Served in hickory spiked demi-glnce with roast peppers, grilled onions and hominy with roast corn and garlic mashed potatoes.
Wine suggestion: Pinot Noir, Soave

Ropa Vieja — $18.95
Spiced rum and citrus marinaded roasted pork tenderloin in pan gravy with saffron rice, black beans and fried plantain.
Wine suggestion: Gewurztraminer, Pinot Noir.

Pan Seared Ahi with Three Sauces — $21.95
Served rare with sesame mustard, wasabi and ginger sauces, with curried noodles and sauteed baby vegetables.
Wine suggestion: Savignon Blanc, Beaujolais Village.

Shrimp Ixtapa — $25.95
Shrimp in cilantro pesto and goat cheese on fetuccine with red chile alfredo.
Wine suggestion: Chardonnay, Semillion

Seared Catfish with Louisianna Shrimp Sauce — $18.95
Boneless skinless fillet seared with herbs and spices, served in a spicy shrimp sauce with black bean tostada and corn relish.
Wine suggestion: Chenin Blanc, Chardonnay, Sauvignon Blanc.

Hickory Smoked Duck Breast — $23.95
Served in a port, ginger and sage sauce with sauteed kale and garlic mashed potatoes.
Wine suggestion: Shiraz, Merlot

Citrus Marinated Swordfish — $21.95
Broiled and served with three melon pico de gallo on vermicelli cake with sauteed baby vegetables.
Wine suggestion: Chenin Blanc, Vouvray.

Herb and Horseradish Encrusted Prime Rib — $22.95
Roasted and served in pan gravy with sauteed kale and garlic mashed potatoes.
Wine suggestion: Cabernet, Red Bordeaux.

Mostaccioli with Chicken and Prosciutto — $18.95
Grilled chicken sauteed with prosciutto, spinach, mushrooms, fresh herbs and garlic.
Wine suggestion: Pinot Grigio, Brouilly.

Grilled Rack of Lamb in Drunken Chile Sauce — $26.95
Pepper crusted rack of lamb in ancho chili tequila sauce with margarita salsa and feta cheese. Served with black bean tostada and roast corn.
Wine suggestion: Red Burgundy, Pinot Noir.

New York Steak Au Poivre — $25.95
Coated in crushed peppercorns, flambeed in brandy, served with sauteed kale and garlic mashed potatoes.
Wine suggestion: Zinfandel, Petite Sirah

Two Way Salmon Tamale — $20.95
Fillet of salmon wrapped in phyllo dough with corn salsa, spinach, tomatoes, cilantro, red bell pepper and green chilies, served on red pepper and green chile sauces with black bean tostada.
Wine suggestion: Chardonnay, Plesporter Goldtropfchen.

Seafood Newburg — $26.95
Shrimp, scallops and lobster with roast peppers in a cream sauce with angel hair tumble weed and corn cakes.
Wine suggestion: White Bordeaux, Sauvignon Blanc.

Garlic and Herb Roasted Breast of Chicken — $19.95
Served with pan drippings on saffron risotto with sauteed baby vegetables.
Wine suggestion: Chardonnay, White Burgundy.

Braised Salmon Roulade in Saffron Fume — $22.95
Basil pesto stuffed braised salmon in saffron chardonnay sauce on vermicelli cake with tomato mint vinaigrette and sauteed baby vegetables.
Wine suggestion: Sauvignon Blanc, White Meritage.
Additional plate charge $3.00

Vegetarian Specialties
Served with soup and salad

Baked Penne — $16.95
Pasta with eggplant, spinach, cauliflower, mushrooms, pine nuts and smoked mozzarella.

Paella — $20.95
Pan roasted baby vegetables with artichoke hearts, roast corn, eggplant and mushrooms in saffron risotto.

Eggplant Ixtapa — $1795
Eggplant in cilantro pesto and goat cheese on fettucine with red chile alfredo.

Steamed Vegetables with Sesame Noodles — $15.95
Julienne vegetables, spinach and mushrooms in sesame noodles with ginger and wasabi sauces.

Fettucine Caribe — $14.95
Fettucine with black beans, roast corn, and roast pepper relish with goat cheese.

Timothy's Twilight Delight
Available 5:00 pm - 7:00 pm Sunday - Thursday
Served with your choice of soup or salad

Pan Seared Shrimp and Scallops — $16.95
Served in tomatillo salsa with roast corn and corn cakes.

Roast Pork Tenderloin — $14.95
Served with spiced apple chutney and red potato hash.

Baked Penne — $11.95
Pasta, Italian sausage, mushrooms, and kale, topped with smoked mozzarella.

Pollo Masconi — $12.95
Breast of chicken sauteed with tomatoes, spinach, artichoke hearts, mushrooms, red and green bell peppers, and pine nuts, on an herbed vermicelli cake.

Baked Salmon — $13.95
Served on an herbed vermicelli cake with herb lemon caper vinaigrette.

Drunken BBQ'd Ahi Tuna — $15.95
Seared rare ahi served on an herbed vermicelli cake with beer barbecue sauce.

PHONE
277-7634

HOURS
Monday–Friday
11:00 am–1:00 am
Saturday & Sunday
5:00 pm–1:00 am

LOCATION
6335 North
16th Street
Phoenix, AZ

CUISINE
American

ATTIRE
Casual to dressy

LIVE JAZZ
Nightly
8:30 pm–12:30 pm

TERRACE DINING

AFTER THEATER DINING

VEGETARIAN MEALS

RESERVATIONS
Suggested

CREDIT CARDS
MasterCard, Visa, American Express, Diners Club, Discover

SMOKING
Section Available

HANDICAP FACILITIES

Uncle Sal's
Italian Ristorante

For many years Uncle Sal's has served the Valley outstanding traditional and contemporary Italian food. Warm hospitality, casual atmosphere, and extensive menu create the setting for a truly pleasurable lunch or dinner. Join us in our comfortable cocktail lounge.

PHONE
990–2533

HOURS
Monday–Saturday
11:00 am–10:00 pm
Sunday Dinner
4:00 pm–9:30 pm

LOCATION
3370 North
Hayden Road
Scottsdale, AZ 85251

CUISINE
Italian

ATTIRE
Casual

LOUNGE
11:00 am until closing

HAPPY HOUR
3:30 pm–6:30 pm

FULL SERVICE CATERING

TAKE OUT

VEGETARIAN MEALS

RESERVATIONS
Suggested

CREDIT CARDS
MasterCard, Visa,
American Express,
Diners Club

SMOKING
Section Available

HANDICAP FACILITIES

Appetizers

Antipasto Misto	6.00
Shrimp Cocktail	6.25
Escargots	6.25
Steamed Clams	Market Price
Calamari-Marinara or Fra Diavlo	6.25
Baked Clams	6.25
Stuffed Mushrooms	4.50

Pasta Specialties
Choice of Soup or Salad

Tortellini Alla Panna	9.25
Prosciutto, mushrooms, peas in Alfredo Sauce	
Canneloni	9.95
Stuffed with veal, chicken, spinach, cheese	
Pasta Amatriciana	8.95
Bacon, ham, onion in a fresh tomato & basil sauce	
Fettuccine Alfredo	8.25
Fettuccine Alfredo with Chicken & Broccoli	9.95
Spaghetti or Linguine Carbonara	9.95
Bacon, onion, peas, & cheese	
Gnocchi	8.95
Homemade pasta with red, white or bolognese	
Pasta with Pesto	8.95
Linguine and Clams	9.95
Red or white	
Lasagna	8.75
Baked Ziti	8.25
Manicotti	8.25
Ravioli	8.25
Meat or cheese	
Tortellini	8.25
Red or white sauce	
Eggplant Parmigiana with Spaghetti	9.50
Sausage & Pepper with Spaghetti	9.95

Spaghetti

Tomato Sauce	7.75
Meat Sauce	8.25
Meatballs or Sausage	8.50
Mushrooms with Red or White Sauce	8.25
Aglio Olio (Garlic and Olive Oil)	7.75

Chicken
All Entrees Served with Pasta and Choice of Soup or Salad

Chicken Cacciatore	12.95
Onion, green pepper, mushrooms, black olives in a marinara sauce	
Chicken Francese	12.95
Delicately egg dipped and sauteed in butter, lemon, white wine sauce	
Chicken Parmigiana	12.95
Lightly breaded topped with marinara and baked with cheese	
Chicken Piccata	12.95
Lemon, butter, white wine, artichoke and capers	
Chicken Marsala	12.95
Marsala wine and fresh mushrooms	
Chicken Saltimbocca	13.95
Spinach, prosciutto, mushrooms, cheese in a white wine sage sauce	

Veal & Pork
All Entrees Served with Pasta and Choice of Soup or Salad

Veal Parmigiana	13.95
Lightly breaded, topped with marinara and baked with cheese	
Veal Marsala	13.95
Marsala wine and fresh mushrooms	
Veal Piccata	13.95
Lemon, butter, white wine, artichoke and capers	
Veal Francese	13.95
Delicately egg dipped and sauteed in butter, lemon, white wine	
Veal and Peppers	13.95
Served in a delicious red sauce	
Veal Saltimbocca	14.95
Spinach, prosciutto, mushrooms, cheese in a white wine sage sauce	
New York Strip Steak (12 oz)	13.95

Seafood
All Entrees served with Pasta and choice of Soup or Salad

Shrimp Scampi	14.75
Garlic, lemon, butter, and white wine	
Shrimp Fra Diavolo	14.75
Spicy hot marinara	
Shrimp Marinara	14.75
Sauteed in our marinara sauce	
Hot Seafood Combo Platter	15.95
Clams, shrimp, mussels, scallops in a red or white sauce	
Cioppino	18.95
Shrimp, scallops, clams, mussels, calamari and fresh fish of the day in a delicious marinara	
Calamari Marinara	12.95
Fresh tomato sauce	
Calamari Fra Diavolo	12.95
Spicy hot marinara	

VAGARA BISTRO

Having studied and worked with some of the world's most acclaimed master chefs, Vagara Bistro Chef/Owner Peter Houfler has perfected what he calls "Cross-Cultural Cuisine"—the blending of European, Far Eastern and American cooking to create extraordinary taste sensations. Drawing rave reviews, the ingenious and flavorful dishes offered at Vagara Bistro stretch the boundaries of culture and imagination to create a memorable and unique dining experience.

Appetizers and Salads

Pan Seared Dungeness Crab Cake — 7.95
roasted corn relish and sun dried tomato remoulade

Fried Calamari Salad — 8.25
mushrooms, bell peppers, and carrots on lettuce chiffonade

Fire Cracker Shrimp Roll — 8.45
black sesame seeds and citrus ponzu sauce

Bruchetta Grilled Country Bread — 5.75
with garlic basil, tomatoes and balsamic vinegar

Caesar Salad — 4.50
romaine lettuce, herb garlic croutons, parmesan cheese, crisp beet chips and caesar dressing

Assorted Mesclum Greens — 4.25
julienne carrot, red onion and tomato, tarragon vinaigrette

Main Courses

Basil Crusted Chilean Sea Bass — 17.25
Mediterranean vegetable stir fry, sweet and sour red pepper coulis

Oven Baked Halibut — 16.75
toasted Nori seaweed and scallion cous cous with orange ginger sauce

Five Spice Coated Black Tiger Prawns — 17.95
barley, spinach and corn risotto with parsley infused olive oil

Oriental Barbecued Salmon — 15.25
sauteed spinach, plum wine marinated black bean sauce and vegetable spring roll

Grilled Jamaican Jerked Pork Chop — 14.95
apple thyme, mashed potatoes, spicy banana relish plantain chips

Grilled Calves Liver — 13.95
caramelized onions and aged sherry vinegar

Oven Roasted Rack Of Lamb — 18.95
dried shitake mushrooms and walnut crust with black olive sauce

Chile Seared Beef Tenderloin Napoleon — 17.95
sauteed wild mushrooms, roasted shallots, natural pan jus

Oven Roasted Half Chicken Stuffed With Black Olives — 12.95
marinated with lemon garlic and rosemary, mashed potatoes, and baba ganoush

Pasta

Linguini Noodles — 9.95
plum tomatoes, basil, garlic, snow peas, olives and parmesan

Singapore Noodles — 12.95
stir fried chicken, bell peppers, julienne carrots, green onions and toasted sesame seeds (mild, medium or hot)

Angel Hair Pasta With Salmon — 13.95
pan seared chinook salmon, carrots, artichokes and tomatoes with dill vodka cream

Penne Pasta — 11.95
grilled chicken, mushrooms, tomatoes and broccoli with pine nut pesto sauce

Angel Hair Pasta With Mussels — 12.50
New Zealand mussels, concasse tomatoes with lemon saffron sauce

Desserts

Caramelized Warm Apple Tart — 3.95
with vanilla bean sauce

Strawberry Phillo Tower — 4.25
with strawberry brandy and whipped cream

Watermelon Vodka Sorbet — 4.50
with almond fruit rattatouille and coconut crisp

Raspberry Chocolate Creme Brulee — 4.95

Warm Chocolate Tart — 5.25
with bitter orange compote

Vagara Bistro

PHONE
948-9928

HOURS
Monday–Saturday
11:30 am–2:30 pm
Daily
5:30 pm–10:00 pm

LOCATION
6137 North
Scottsdale Road
Scottsdale, AZ 85253

CUISINE
Cross Cultural

ATTIRE
Casual

TERRACE DINING

RESERVATIONS
Suggested

CREDIT CARDS
MasterCard, Visa, American Express, Diniers Club, Discover

CHECKS ACCEPTED

SMOKING
Section Available

HANDICAP FACILITIES

Ventura Grill

By the name alone you get the feeling of an establishment that is nostalgic, but at the same time "Hip."

Ventura Grill is a comfortable, casual yet sophisticated, and fun, adult gathering spot with great libations, fare and entertainment, suited to lunch, dinner, happy hour, or a post theater stop off to enjoy a cocktail or cappuccino, some piano, and conversation before bed.

Prices

Entrées: Lunch $5–$10
Dinner $10–$25

Appetizers

Marinated Asparagus, Cambonzola Cheese, and a Sweet Red Onion Relish with a Lemon Vinaigrette Dressing. Garnished with Sweet Plum Tomatoes.

Eastern Shore Blue Crab Cakes grilled, served with Roasted Corn Salsa over Tender Mixed Greens and Sweet Chili Sauce.

Peasant Bread, Slow Baked with Olive Oil, Warmed Goat Cheese, Fire Roasted Peppers and Rosemary, served atop Fresh Spinach and Balsamic Vinegar.

Jumbo Prawns in a Roasted Garlic Lemon Grass Sauce, Crisp Asparagus Spears, and Beefsteak Tomato.

Portabello Mushroom marinated, sliced, and grilled with Granny Smith Apples served over a warmed Herb Bread Salad.

Soups

Lobster Bisque

Roasted Corn Chowder

Caroles Minestrone

Soup Du Jour

Salads

Ventura
Tender Mixed Greens, Portabello Mushroom, Sweet Onion, Plum Tomatoes, and our House Dijon.

Beefsteak Tomato
With Fresh Basil, Sweet Onion Relish, and Virgin Olive Oil over Mixed Greens.

Caesar Salad
Tossed with only the Hearts of Romaine, Regiano Parmesan, Homemade Croutons and Roma Tomatoes.

Pan-Fried Lobster
Tender Mixed Greens, Lemon Grass, Fire Roasted Peppers, and Red Onion, with a Sweet Chili Dressing.

Entrees

Two Pound Lobster split, grilled then basted in Lemon Butter and Fresh Herbs, served with Grilled Corn on the Cob, Twice Baked Sweet Potato and a Russian Sea Salt Rye Bread.

Grilled Marinated Portabello Mushroom, Smoked Salmon and Red Caviar served with a Dollop of Sour Cream, Asparagus and Plum Tomato Risotto.

9 oz Filet of Beef Tenderloin served Medium Rare, with a Potato Chive Pancake, Homemade Applesauce, and a Sunflower Seed Bread.

7 oz Filet of Beef Tenderloin served medium rare with an Apple-Sherry Demi Glaze, Twice Baked Potato, and a Sourdough Walnut Bread.

Sea Scallops with lightly grilled Red Peppers, and Fresh Basil in a Creamy Coconut Milk Sauce over Lemon Pepper Linguini with a Wild Rice Oatmeal Bread.

Grilled Sea Bass in a Lemon Caper Ale Sauce served with Pan Seared Red Potatoes, Grilled Corn on the Cob and a Pistachio Honey Oat Bread.

22 oz Porterhouse Grilled Medium Rare, served with Sweet Potato Hashbrowns, Grilled Vegetables, and a Buttermilk Cornbread.

Grilled Lake Michigan White Fish, seasoned with Fresh Herbs and Lemon Butter, accompanied by Grilled Plum Tomatoes and Asparagus. Garnished with a Warm Cucumber Salad in a Raspberry Vinaigrette. Butter and Creamed Red Potatoes.

Half a Chicken marinated and grilled, served with Smashed Sweet Potatoes, Grilled Vegetables, and a Rosemary, Red Pepper, and Chevre Bread.

Steamed Mussels served in a Natural Broth, Roasted Garlic-Tomato Linguini, with Fresh Plum Tomatoes, Sweet Onion, and Basil with Homemade Garlic Bread for sopping.

Boneless Chicken Breast sautééd in a Roasted Shallot-Tarragon Sauce, Pan Seared Red Potatoes, and Pistachio Apricot Bread.

Surf and Turf
6 oz Filet of Beef Tenderloin grilled Medium Rare in a Sundried Cherry BBQ Sauce and three Giant Prawns in a Roasted Garlic Lemon Grass Sauce served with Buttered and Creamed Red Potatoes and an Apricot Pumpernickel Bread.

Ventura Grill

PHONE
(602) 922-1500

HOURS
Monday–Saturday
11:00 am–1:00 am
Food Service
11:00– 10:00 pm
Sunday
5:00–Midnight
Food Service
5:00–10:00 pm

LOCATION
8380 East
Via de Ventura,
Building G
Scottsdale, AZ

CUISINE
American

ATTIRE
Casual

ENTERTAINMENT
Live Piano
4 Nights Weekly

PATIO DINING

RESERVATIONS
Suggested

CREDIT CARDS
MasterCard, Visa, American Express, Diners Club, Discover

SMOKING
Section Available

HANDICAP FACILITIES

Voltaire

FRENCH RESAURANT

PHONE
948-1005

HOURS
Monday–Saturday
5:30 pm–10:00 pm
Open for Mothers day

LOCATION
8340 East
McDonald Drive
Scottsdale, AZ 85250

CUISINE
French Provincial

ATTIRE
Sem-Casual

MEETING FACILITIES
Small Groups (15–20)

VEGETARIAN MEALS
Upon Request

RESERVATIONS
Suggested

CREDIT CARDS
MasterCard, Visa, American Express

SMOKING
Section Available

HANDICAP FACILITIES

Food prepared with pride by two French chef owners and served in a friendly, quiet atmosphere. All reservations honored on time.

Dis moi ce que to manges et je te dirai qui tu es.

HORS D'OEUVRES

ESCARGOTS DE BOURGOGNE
$7.00

CHAMPIGNONS FARCIS BOHEMIENNE
$7.00

SHRIMP COCKTAIL
$8.50

PATE MAISON
$7.00

SMOKED SALMON WITH GARNISH
$8.50

POTAGES

COLD VICHYSSOISE
$3.50

SOUPE A'LOIGNON PARISIENNE
$4.50

SOUP DU JOUR
$2.50

SALADS

TOMATO SALAD WITH HEART OF PALM
$4.50

CAESAR MAISON
$4.50

SALAD VERTE
$2.50

DESSERTS

LES PATISSERIES DU CHEF
$4.50

MOUSSE AU CHOCOLAT
$4.50

PROFITEROLLES AU CHOCOLAT
$4.50

CHERRIES JUBILEE (FOR 2)
$12.00

CREPES SUZETTE (FOR 2)
$12.00

(This is just a sample of the special desserts we have to offer.)

ENTREES

LE SANDAB SAUTE VERONIQUE
Sandab Sauted in lemon butter, with white grapes.
$18.00

BAKED LOBSTER TAILS
With lemon butter
MARKET PRICE

LE POULET A LA NORMANDE
Boned breast of chicken with apples.
$16.00

LE CANARD A'LORANGE
Long Island duckling with orange sauce.
$18.00

LES GRENADINES DE VEAU SAUTE GRENOBLOISE
Veal saute with lemon butter and capers.
$19.50

LES MEDAILLONS DE VEAU MARSALA
Veal saute with mushrooms and marsala sauce.
$19.50

LES RIS DE VEAU VOLTAIRE
Calf sweetbreads sauted in lemon butter with capers.
$18.50

LE TOURNEDOS BEARNAISE
Tenderloin of beef with mushrrom caps.
$19.50

LE STEAK AU POIVRE SAUTE RICHELIEU
New York steak with cracked pepper.
$19.50

LE STEAK GAULOIS
New York steak with fresh garlic butter.
$19.50

LE CARRE D'AGNEAU A L'ESTRAGON
$20.50
Spring rack of lamb roasted with tarragon.
All entrees include soup de jour or salad verte, vegetable and dauphine potatoes.

Windows on the Green
at The Phoenician

Aptly named for its sweeping views of the resort's championship golf course, Windows on the Green serves Southwestern cuisine with an artistic flair. The ambiance is light and airy by day, dramatic by night.

Appetizers

Grilled Striped Bass Tostado, Steamed Carrot Salsa *Organic Salad of Mizuna, Arugula and Pea Shoots*	7.50
Venison Braised in Red Wine and Sage, Spinach Pasta *Salad of Fresh Organic Herbs and Endive*	8.00
Lobster in a Cracked Corn Custard with Wild Mushrooms *Dried Monterey Jack Cheese*	9.00
✪ Barbecued Chicken and Sweet Onions in a Blue Corn Crêpe *Sweet Corn and Pickled Onion Relish*	7.00
✪ Grilled Flatbread with Rock Shrimp and Poblano Chiles *Salsa of Papaya, Avocado and Red Onion*	8.00
Pan-Fried Dallas Mozzarella Cheese on a Black Bean Cake *Tomatillo Salsa, Roasted Tomato-Chipotle Sauce*	7.00

Soups and Salads

✪ Tortilla Soup with Wood-Roasted Chicken and Avocado	6.00
Rustic Chowder of Red Snapper and Salt Cod *New Potatoes, Leeks and Mexican Oregano*	6.00
Young Red Romaine Lettuce, and Watercress Lime Dressing *Garlic Croûtons and Dried Jack Cheese*	5.50
✪ Organic Lettuces Wrapped in a Jícama Tortilla *Sun-Dried Tomato Vinaigrette*	5.00

Entrées

Filet of Salmon "Campfire-Style" on Chipotle Vinaigrette *Salad of Fingerling Potatoes and Vegetables*	19.50
Roasted Half Chicken with Avocado and Orange Salsa *Cornbread Chorizo Stuffing, Red Honey Glaze*	17.50
✪ Barbecued Striped Bass on a Mango Lime Sauce *Brown Coconut Rice and "Jerk" Spice Vegetables*	18.00
Tenderloin of Beef on Blueberry Barbecue Sauce *Roasted Garlic-Green Chile Mashed Potatoes*	23.50
✪ Grilled Rum-Glazed Florida Dorado, Cucumber Relish *Steamed Lobster Dumplings, Mushroom Noodles*	19.00
Pork Tenderloin with a Sweet Potato-Poblano Gratin *Balsamic Vinegar, Maple Syrup and Hatch Chiles*	20.00
✪ Yellowtail Snapper, Black Bean-Yogurt Sauce, "KonK" Chile *Spinach Sautéed with Lemon and Kafir Lime Leaves*	20.50
Grilled Colorado Lamb Loin with Green Corn Sauce *White Bean Purée with Mint Marigold and Chile Aji*	26.00
Pan-Roasted Black Grouper in Gumbo, Shrimp Remoulade *Skillet-Roasted Parsley Potatoes and Onion Shoots*	20.50
✪ Sugar and Chile-Cured Venison Chop, Logan's Farm Grits *Fire-Roasted Red Onion Sauce*	25.00

✪ *Choices*—Superb cuisine created by Chef Robert McGrath with your well-being in mind.

Windows on the Green

PHONE
(602) 423–2530

HOURS
Lunch
Monday–Friday
11:00 am–3:00 pm

Dinner
Tuesday–Saturday
6:00 pm–10:00 pm
Closed
Sunday & Monday

LOCATION
6000 East
Camelback Road
Scottsdale, AZ 85251

CUISINE
Southwestern

ATTIRE
Casual to Business

LOUNGE
11:00 am–Closing

PRIVATE DINING

SATURDAY & SUNDAY BRUNCH
A la Carte Brunch
10:00 am–3:00 pm

RESERVATIONS
Recommended

CREDIT CARDS
MasterCard, Visa,
American Express,
Diners Club, Discover

SMOKING
Section Available

HANDICAP FACILITIES

WRIGHT'S

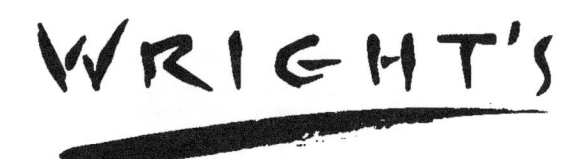

Formerly the Orangerie, Wright's is the result of the Arizona Biltmore's recent $35 million renovation. Though still under the talented hands of Chef de Cuisine Denny Hillin (named "Rising Star Chef," Esquire Magazine, 1993) the revamped dining room boasts a less formal atmosphere, and the still gourmet menu boasts creative fare with an emphasis on the freshest local ingredients and flavor "punches" from South America, the Mediterranean and Asia. An award winning wine cellar and fine service complete the experience.

PHONE
954-2507

HOURS
Monday–Saturday
Breakfast
7:00 am–11:30 am
Lunch
11:30 am–2:30 pm
Dinner
6:00 pm–10:00 pm

LOCATION
24th Street & Missouri
Phoenix, AZ 85016

CUISINE
Contemporary American

ATTIRE
Casual

LOUNGE
Monday–Saturday
11:30 am–1:00 am
Sunday
10:00 am–1:00 am

PATIO DINING

SUNDAY BRUNCH
10:00 am–2:30 pm

RESERVATIONS
Suggested

CREDIT CARDS
MasterCard, Visa, American Express, Discover

CHECKS ACCEPTED

SMOKING
Patio only

HANDICAP FACILITIES

SOUPS AND SALADS

Onion Broth, Napa Cabbage and Pancetta   5.25

Shellfish Vegetable Soup   7.25

Regional Farm Greens, Hearts of Palm, Citrus Vinaigrette   7.75

Baby Red and Green Romaine, Rosemary Caesar Dressing   6.00

Lolla Rossa Salad, Cambozola Flan, Walnut Vinaigrette   7.75

APPETIZERS

Sashimi of Smoked Salmon and Marinated Tuna   12.50

Tiger Prawns with Prosciutto and Chick Pea Puree   12.00

Angel Hair with Dungeness Crab, Asparagus and Tomato   10.75

Escargot with Portabellos and Roasted Garlic   7.75

Pesto Risotto with Seared Chicken Livers   7.00

Grilled Vegetables with Herbed Boursin Cheese   6.25

Golden Tomato and Goat Cheese Tart, Black Olive Oil   6.00

MAIN COURSES

Spinach Linguini, Roasted Roma Tomato, Pepper Mushroom Cream   17.75

Penne with Shrimp and Oven Dried Tomatoes   22.00

Salmon Scaloppine, Red Chard and New Potato Mash   23.00

Sesame Seared Ahi Tuna, Ginger Sticky Rice   27.00

Poached Maine Lobster, Wilted Leeks, Corn Dumplings   33.00

Striped Sea Bass, Saffron Potatoes, Julienned Vegetables   26.75

Poached Alaskan Halibut, Steamed Baby Vegetables, Black Mussel Broth   26.00

Grilled Breast of Chicken, Wild Mushrooms and Roasted Garlic Fettuccine   21.50

Braised Muscovy Duck, Spiced Beets, Wild Rice Pancake   24.00

Pepper Crusted Tenderloin of Beef, Brie Potato Puree, Grilled Spring Onion   27.00

Grilled Lamb Chops, Scalloped Blue Potato, Mint Sauce   26.50

Smoked Venison Loin, Herb Spaetzle, Garlic Spinach   28.50

Roasted Veal Chop, Glazed Root Vegetables, Black Trumpet Mushrooms   27.50

RECIPES

PHOENIX CUISINE '96

5th Anniversary Issue

Recipes

Appetizers

Black Rose Irish Skins *Black Rose*	127
Shrimp and Scallion in Mixed Herb Cream *Different Pointe of View*	127
Portobello & Salmon Canape with Saffron Cream *OAXACA*	127

Soups

Yellow Bell Pepper Soup *Arizona Cafe & Grill*	127
Smoked Corn Chowder *The Arizona Kitchen*	128
Brandied Onion Bisque *The Impeccable Pig*	128
Tortilla Soup *The Terrace Dining Room*	128

Salads

Marinated Cucumber *Roxsand*	128
Italian Chopped Salad *Ristorante Sandolo*	128
Piccolini Raviolini *Ristorante Sandolo*	129
Pasta e Fagioli *Ristorante Sandolo*	129
Italian Cactus Garden with Baja Shrimp-Yellow Pepper Vinaigrette *Ristorante Sandolo*	129

Sauces

Lunguini Paradiso *Carolinas Paradiso*	129
Espresso Sauce *Christophers Bistro*	130
Chamomile Orange Sauce *Different Pointe of View*	130
Sauce Alfredo *The Impeccable Pig*	130
Pesto Basil Sauce *Pronto*	131

Vegetables

Roasted Creamed Sweet Sauce *Aunt Chilada's*	131
Southern Caramelized Onion Bisque *Aunt Chilada's*	131
Onion Tart *Christopher's*	131

Side Dishes

Dirty Rice *Baby Kay's*	132
Anaheim Chili-Pocketed with Cilantro Goat Cheese Tomato Salsa *Golden Swan*	132
Pineapple Fried Rice *Royal Barge*	132
Cowboy Beans *Rustler's Rooste*	132

Pasta

Ravioli *Ambrosino's*	132
Fettuccine Verdi Con Porcini and Truffle Oil *Franco's Trattoria*	132
Paglia e Fieno *Gianni*	133
Southwestern Shrimp Pasta *Goldies*	133
Cavatelli Con Broccoli *Guido's*	134
Puttanesea *Hops!*	134
Gratin of Herbed Cannellonni Saute Artichokes and Wilted Greens *Mary Elaine's*	134
Pasta with Pesto Sauce *Pasta Segio's*	134
Spin Cold Soba Noodles *Roxsand*	135
Potato Gnocchi "Quatro Formagi" with Toasted Walnuts *The Terrace Dining Room*	135
Spaghetti All Amataiciana *Uncle Sal's*	135

Main Meat/Poultry

Chicken Pillard *Avanti*	135
Citrus Veloute' Roasted Duck *Backstage*	136
Black Rose Shepherd Pie *Black Rose*	136
Chicken Chardonnay *Chances Are*	136
Faux Filet *Christopher's*	137
Duck Cakes with Chamomile Orange Sauce *Different Pointe of View*	138
Country Style Baby Back Ribs *Hole-In-The-Wall*	138
Chicken Fantasia *Lo Cascio*	138
Sonora Enchiladas *Los Olivos*	139
"Choucroute" with Champagne *Marché Gourmet*	139
Tenderloin of Veal with Garlic-Rosemary Jus Tartelette of White Bean Puree and Glazed Spring Vegetable *Mary Elaine's*	139
Grilled Quali Breast in Phyllo with Caper Herb Lemon Butter *Palm Court*	140
Pad Prig Pao Beef *Royal Barge*	140
Drunken Formula Chicken *Royal Barge*	141
Radicchio Risotto with Roasted Quail *The Terrace Dining Room*	141
Pepper Encrusted Rack of Lamb *Timothy's*	141
Veal Black Forestier *Voltaire*	141
Tenderloin of Beef on a Blueberry Barbeque Sauce *Windows on the Green*	141

Main Seafood

Chili Seared Giant Sea Scallops *Aunt Chilada's*	142
Shrimp Gabrielle *Chances Are*	142
Salmone *Gianni*	142
Orange Honey Barbecued Salmon with Baby Greens in Painted Cilantro Dressing *Golden Swan*	142
Soy Ginger Shrimp *Hops!*	143
Pescatore Linguine *Il Forno*	143
Sautée of Daurade with Garden Pea Coconut Rice Sweet Lobster Sauce *Mary Elaine's*	143
Broiled Ahi Tuna & Mango Kiwi Compote *OAXACA*	143
Lobster Mousse and Spinach Roulade with Holland Pepper Chive Coulis *Palm Court*	144
Paella *Pepin*	144
Salmon En Salsa Verde *Pepin*	144
Roasted Swordfish with Warm Tomato and Arugala Salad and Basil Orzo *The Terrace Dining Room*	144
Lobster in Cracked Corn Custard with Wild Mushrooms Dried Monterey Jack Cheese *Windows on the Green*	145
Pan-Roasted Black Grouper in Gumbo, Shrimp Remoulade Parsley Potatoes, Onion Shoots and Celery Leaves *Windows on the Green*	145

Bread

Pepper Jack Polenta Sticks *Aunt Chilada's*	146
Taco Shells *Aunt Chilada's*	146

Dessert

Black Irish Pie *Coyote Springs*	146
Bourbon Fruit *Baby Kay's*	146
Apple Tart *Christopher's*	146
Parnassienne De Mousse Au Chocolat *Christophers Bistro*	147
White & Dark Chocolat Amaretto *OAXACA*	147

Recipes

Appetizers

Black Rose Irish Skins
(6 persons as an appetizer)

    12 Red Medium Potatoes
cut in half, scoop out center, boil 10 minutes, set aside.

Stuffing:
- 1/2 lb Diced fine cooked corned beef
- 1 lb Cooked cabbage - diced fine
- 1 lb Vermont white cheddar

Mix all ingredients together. Stuff potatoes. Bake in oven for 5 minutes.

Sauce:
- 1 cup Sour Cream
- 1 cup Dijon Grained mustard

The Pointe Hilton Resort at Tapatio Cliffs

Shrimp and Scallion in Mixed Herb Cream

Makes 4 appetizer servings
- 8 Medium scallops
- 8 Medium shrimp, peeled and de-veined
- 3 TB. Clarified butter
- 1 1/2 cups Heavy cream
- 2 TB. Shallots, chopped
- 1/2 cup Fresh mushrooms, sliced
- Juice from 1 1/2 limes
- 1/4 cup Spinach, chopped
- 2 TB. Mixed herbs: chives, tarragon, parsley, cilantro, summer savory
- Salt & pepper to taste

- Saute shrimp and scallops in butter. Remove from pan and set aside. In the same pan, add shallots and sliced mushrooms. Saute until shallots are golden. Add cream and reduce by half, or to desired consistency. Add lime juice. Season with salt and pepper to taste. Add spinach and mixed herbs. Return shrimp and scallops to pan.
- Serve immediately.

OAXACA AT PINNACLE PEAK

Portobello & Salmon Canape with Saffron Cream
by Executive Chef Travis Vierthaler

Serves 4
- 4 Firm Portobello mushrooms with stems removed
- 12 Asparagus
- 4 3 oz. Salmon Filets, cut into round medallions

Saffron Cream:
- 4 cups Heavy cream
- 1/4 cup Fresh grated Parmesan
- 1 pinch Saffron
- Salt & white pepper to taste

- Reduce heavy cream by 1/4. Add other ingredients and reduce that by 1/4. Strain sauce through fine mesh to remove saffron strands. Grill Salmon and Portobello mushrooms. Poach asparagus. Place Saffron sauce on 4 plates and put one grilled Portobello in the center of each plate. Top each mushroom with Salmon medallions and fan asparagus out on the plate. Enjoy!...
- And come and see us soon at AT PINNACLE PEAK.

Soup

Yellow Bell Pepper Soup
Christopher Gross

Servings: 6
- 4 TB. Olive oil
- 7 Medium yellow bell peppers
- 3 Leeks (white part only), chopped
- 2 Medium carrots, peeled and chopped
- 2 Medium onions, chopped
- 7 cups Chicken stock, rich
- 2 Potatoes, peeled and chopped
- 2 Sprigs thyme
- 1 Bay leaf
- 1 1/2 qt. Heavy cream
- Salt and white pepper, freshly ground
- 1/4 lb. Butter

- Saute vegetables with one tablespoon olive oil in heavy medium saucepan over medium heat until softened, about 10 minutes.
- Add chicken stock and potatoes.
- Increase heat and simmer until reduced by 1/3, about 30 minutes.
- Puree in blender in batches.
- Strain soup back into saucepan until desired consistency.
- Remove from heat and stir in remaining olive oil.
- Finish with butter.
- Season with salt and white pepper and serve.

Suggested wine: Mumm Cuvee Napa, Blanc de Noirs

Recipes

The Arizona Kitchen

Smoked Corn Chowder

Yield - 1 Gallon - (16 servings)

- 1/2 cup Onion
- 1/2 cup Celery
- 1/2 cup Leeks
- 1/2 cup Carrots
- 1/4 cup Red bell pepper
- 4 cloves Garlic
- 8 ears Corn on the cob
- 1 cup Diced potatoes
- 1/2 TB. Thyme
- 1/2 TB. Oregano (fresh)
- 1/2 tsp. Cinnamon
- 2 quarts Chicken stock
- 8 oz. Roux (4oz. butter and 4oz. flour)
- 1 gallon Heavy cream
- Salt and black pepper to taste
- 1/4 cup Olive oil
- dash Tobasco sauce

Preparation and procedure:

- Clean ears of corn, place in smoker and smoke for 30 minutes. Remove kernels from cob, add cobs to boiling chicken stock pot.
- In a large bowl, cover kernels with water, and break apart with hands - skim off excess pulp from top. Set aside.
- In a large very hot sauce pot, add olive oil and saute vegetables except corn and potatoes - add thyme, oregano, basil, garlic cinnamon, chili powder, and cumin.
- While the vegetables are cooking, add Roux to chicken stock to make veloute - remove from heat.
- Add corn, potatoes, and half of the water (no more than 2 cups) to the vegetables, and strain veloute through a china cup.
- Heat heavy cream to a boil and reduce by 1/4 and add to vegetables. Stir in and let simmer for about 20 minutes, stirring frequently.
- Season with salt and pepper and a dash of tobasco.

The Impeccable Pig
Scottsdale

Brandied Onion Bisque

(Makes 8 cups)

- 2 Medium onions
- 1/2 lb Butter
- 4 cups Beef stock
- 3 cups Heavy cream
- 4 cup Brandy
- 1/4 cup Sherry
- 2 tsp. Garlic salt
- 4 cup Red wine
- Salt & Pepper to taste

- In a one gallon pot, melt butter on medium heat. Add onions and sautee until onions start to brown and are translucent. Add brandy & sherry. Sautee for approximately 5 minutes. Add beef stock and bring to a boil stirring occasionally. Turn soup off and cool down. Once cooled off, add cream bring back up to boil, then simmer for 15 minutes. Salt and pepper to taste Serve hot and garnish with chopped green onions.

The Terrace
DINING ROOM

Tortilla Soup

Jon Hill, Exec. Chef

Servings: 6 portions

- 1/2 gallon Chicken stock
- 3 each Corn tortillas (cut into strips)
- 1 cup Celery
- 1 cup Red onion (diced)
- 1 cup Carrot
- 1/4 cup Butter
- 1/4 cup Corn meal
- 1/8 cup Green chiles (diced)
- 1/2 TB. Chipotle Chile
- Salt and pepper to taste

- Saute carrots, onions, and celery in butter.
- Add corn meal to make a roux.
- Cook roux for approximately 15 minutes.
- Add chicken stock and bring to boil.
- Add diced green chiles and Chipotle chile.
- Add corn tortillas.
- Puree.
- Season to taste.

Salad

ROXSAND
(Restaurant & Bar)

Marinated Cucumber

- 1 English cucumber, thinly sliced
- 1 clove Garlic, minced
- 3 tbsp Ginger, minced
- 3/4 cup Sugar
- 3 1/4 Cup Cider Vinegar

- Marinate the above ingredients for 1 hour. Then add 3 1/4 cups Cider Vinegar, continue marinating for up to 3 hours.

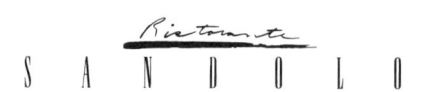

Ristorante SANDOLO

Italian Chopped Salad

Serves 1

- 1/8 head Iceberg lettuce
- 1 oz. Prosciutto, chopped
- 1 oz. Artichoke hearts, chopped
- 1 oz. Vinaigrette
- Dash of parsley
- Parmigianna mixture

- Dice lettuce into 1/2"x1/2" pieces. Add all ingredients excepting parmgianna mixture.
- Toss well and serve chilled on 7" salad plate.
- Sprinkle mixture in center of salad.

Recipes

Ristorante SANDOLO

Piccolini Raviolini
Serves 9

- 4 oz.   Veal Ravioli
- 6 oz.   Heavy cream
- 2 oz.   Parmesan cheese, grated
- 2 oz.   Whole butter
-         Salt and pepper to taste
-         Nutmeg to taste
-         Fresh parsley, chopped

- Boil ravioli in salted water for 4-6 minutes or until firm, drain and set aside.
- Heat cream, salt and pepper in a saute pan. Let it simmer over medium heat for 2-3 minutes.
- Add ravioli and simmer for another 2 minutes.
- Add nutmeg, whole butter and Parmesan cheese.
- Fold until creamy consistency forms, approximately 1-2 minutes.
- Serve with a garnish of chopped, fresh parsley.

Ristorante SANDOLO

Pasta e Fagioli
Serves 4-6

- 2 cups   Small pasta
- 2 TB.   Olive oil
- 1/2 cup   Onion, chopped
- 1/4 cup   Red bell pepper, diced
- 1/4 cup   Green bell pepper, diced
- 2   Garlic cloves, minced
- 2 cups   Degreased chicken stock
- 1 16 oz. can Whole tomatoes
- 1 cup   Frozen baby lima beans
- 2 TB.   Parsley, chopped
- 1 1/2 cup   Canned Cannellini beans
- 5 oz.   Fresh spinach, trimmed
- 2   Green onion tops, cut into pieces
-             Freshly grated Parmesan cheese
-             Freshly ground pepper to taste
-             Salt to taste

- Dice red and green peppers into 1/4" pieces. Remove whole tomatoes from their can (along with the liquid), and press through a food mill or sieve.
- Drain and rinse the cannellini beans, and trim the fresh spinach leaves into 1' widths.
- In a same pan, heat olive oil. Saute garlic until golden brown, then add red and green bell peppers, onions, pasta and cannellini beans.
- Saute this mixture until golden brown.
- Pour saute mixture into a large soup pot.
- Add tomatoes, chicken stock, lima beans, and onion tops. Simmer until the ingredients are soft.
- Finally, add the spinach, Parmesan cheese, pepper, salt and parsley.

*If desired, bacon can be used instead of salt.

Ristorante SANDOLO

Italian Cactus Garden with Baja Shrimp-Yellow Pepper Vinaigrette
Serves 4

- 8   Cactus leaves
- 4   Radiccio leaves
- 8   Belgian endive leaves
- 1 head   Bibb lettuce
- 1   Red bell pepper
- 1 bunch Oak leaf lettuce
- 8   Large sized prawns

Dressing:

- 1 cup   Olive oil
- 1/3 cup   White vinegar
- 1 tsp.   Salt
- 3/4 cup   Diced yellow pepper (roasted)
- 1 tsp.   Cilantro
- 1 tsp.   Tarragon
- 1 TB.   Anaheim chili (diced)

- Whisk vinegar, herbs and chili together, adding olive oil slowly. Then add bell pepper and salt to taste.

Sauce

Carolina's PARADISO
CUCINA ITALIANA

Linguini Paradiso
Serves 4 to 6

- 2 TB.   Olive oil
- 2   Cloves diced garlic
- 1   Red onion, diced
- 1/2 lb.   Cleaved shrimp
- 1/4 lb.   Bay scallops
- 8   Quartered lg. mushrooms
- 16   Broccoli; florettes blanched
- 1 1/2 cups Heavy cream
- 2 TB.   Capers
- 1 cup   Fish boullion
- 1   Tomato, diced
- 1/4 cup   Brandy
-            Salt and pepper to taste
- 1 1/2 cup Romano cheese

- Place olive oil, garlic, diced onion in medium sauce pan. Cook until tender.
- Add mushrooms, shrimp, scallops, capers and increase heat. Cook quickly.
- Add brandy, flame and reduce.
- Add cream, boullion, broccoli, and tomato. Cook quickly until slightly thickened.
- Add to cooked linguini Romano cheese, and butter.
- Toss and serve. Bon Appetit

Recipes

Christopher's Bistro

Espresso Sauce
Chef Christopher Gross

(For Chocolate Tower, see desserts p. 136)

8	Egg Yolks
3 1/2 oz.	Sugar
2 cups	Half & Half
1/2 cup	Vanilla Bean
1/2 tbls	Vanilla Extract
3 oz.	Espresso Beans

For Garnish: with fruit & mint

Preparation:

- For the espresso sauce, with a hand held mixer, cream the yolks and sugar in a medium bowl. At the same time bring the half and half with the vanilla bean to a simmer in a medium sauce pot. when half and half is hot, temper the egg yolk and sugar mixture by adding 1/4 cup hot half and half Stir well. Pour the egg and sugar mixture into the rest of the half and half with the espresso beans and cook gently over low heat stirring constantly. W]ien sauce is thick enough to coat the back of a spoon, strain and let cool.
- To present dessert, ladle sauce onto 8 plates. Place mousse tower in the center of the plate and garnish the top with fruit and mint sprig. Allow to defrost.

Different Pointe of View

Chamomile Orange Sauce

1 1/2 cup	Sugar
8 tbsp	Chamomile flowers
3/4 cup	Double strength chamomile infusion
2	Oranges, juiced
2 oz	Currant jelly
1	Cinnamon stick
2	Whole cloves
2	Whole Allspice
1 tbsp	Whole black peppercorn
1 1/2 oz	Corn starch
1 cup	Orange juice
3 tbsp	Red wine vinegar

- Dissolve sugar into vinegar. Add cinnamon, cloves, allspice, peppercorns and bring to a boil stirring until caramelized. Add juice of orange, currant jelly and orange juice. Continue to simmer for several minutes, add chamomile and infusion and simmer for 10 minutes. In separate pan dissolve the cornstarch in cold water. Stir into sauce to thicken and strun. Serve over hot duck cakes.

Hole in the Wall

Milk Gravy

16 oz	Flour
1 1/2 gal	Milk
16 oz	Pork sausage
8 oz	Butter

- In a sauce pan, melt butter, then slowly add flour while stirring continuously. Allow roux mixture to thicken. In a separate pan, cook the pork sausage. When sausage is cooked, pour into roux mixture. In a double-broiler, heat milk until a thin covering forms. Once covering has formed, stir in roux mixture, and turn heat down to a simmer. Stir occasionally, allowing the mixture to thicken. Once gravy has thickened, add salt and pepper to taste.

the Impeccable Pig
Scottsdale

Sauce Alfredo

(Makes about 40 oz.)

1/2 lb.	Butter
1 1/2 lb	Cream cheese
1 pint	Heavy cream
1 clove	Garlic (fresh chopped)
	Onion salt & white pepper to taste
	Optional: (1/4 cup Parmesan)

- In a medium saucepan, melt butter on medium heat. Add garlic and saute for a couple of seconds and whip in cream cheese. Once the cheese has melted add 1/2 the pint of heavy cream, garlic salt, and white pepper. Keep on low heat, stirring occasionally. Right before serving add Parmesan and top your favorite pasta.
- Note: Even if sauce Alfredo is basic, use your imagination to create an Italian Delight. Items you may add to obtain this are sherry, romano cheese, smoked ham, sauteed vegetables, or your favorite foods.

Recipes

Pesto Basil Sauce

Enough sauce for 1 lb. of pasta

- 2 cups solidly packed fresh basil leaves
- 3 garlic cloves, cut into pieces
- 1/3 cup pine nuts, very lightly toasted
- 1/2 tsp. salt
- 1-2 twists freshly milled black pepper
- 1/2 cup freshly grated Parmigiano cheese
- 1/4 cup freshly grated romano cheese
- 1/2 cup Extra Virgin olive oil
- 2 TB. sweet butter, softened to room temperature

- Put the basil leaves, garlic, pine nuts, salt, pepper, and oil into a blender or food processor. Blend to a smooth purée, stopping the machine once or twice to scrape the sides of the container with a rubber spatula so that all of the ingredients are equally ground.
- Add the grated cheeses and the butter and whirl for about 15 seconds. Scrape the sides again and turn on the processor for another few seconds. Do not overdo the grinding in the food processor or your pesto will have very little texture.
- Cook one pound of Italian Linguini pasta in salted boiling water until al dente.
- Drain pasta and mix with pesto sauce and serve.

Vegetable

Roasted Creamed Sweet Corn

Served with Chili seared sea scallops on pg ???

- 3 ears Fresh sweet corn with husk off
- 1 pint Heavy cream
- 3 TB. Corn oil

- Preheat oven to 500. Brush corn with corn oil. Place on sheet pan and roast in oven 10 minutes. Remove and let cool.
- Cut corn from cob using a sharp knife. Reserve for later use.
- Using a cheese grater, scrape cob's to remove remaining pulp and liquid.
- Add to heavy cream in a sauce pan. Over medium high heat bring to a boil and reduce by 1/4. Add reserved corn and season with salt and pepper. Keep warm

Southwestern Caramelized Onion Bisque

- 2 oz. Dive oil
- 2 oz. Butter
- 3 cups Diced onion
- 1 cup Diced carrot
- 1/2 cup Diced green chili
- 1/2 cup Diced celery
- 2 cups Bbeef stock
- 2 cups Chicken stock
- 1/2 cup Chili paste
- 2 cups Heavy cream

Roux to thicken

- Preheat a stock pot over medium high heat, add oil and butter. When butter has melted add onion, stirring often until onion is deep brown without burning. Add celery and carrot. Saute' an additional 5 minutes.
- Add beef stock, chicken stock, diced green chilies and chili paste. Simmer uncovered 30-45 minutes until stock is reduced by 1/4. Thicken slightly with roux.
- In batches, puree bisque in a blender and strain back into stock pot, return to medium heat Add heavy cream and simmer 15 minutes.

Onion Tart

- 1 Onion
- 1 tbsp. Butter
- 4 oz. Cream
- 1 Egg yolk
- Salt
- Pepper
- Nutmeg

Preparations

- Finely dice onion and saute in butter until soft. Add cream, and seasoning. Finish with one egg yolk. Pour mixture into puff pastry strip o or round, and bake at 350 degrees for 10 minutes, or until golden brown. Serve with a dollop of creme fraiche.

Continued On Next Page ▶

Recipes

Side Dishes

Dirty Rice
Chef Baby Kay

- 5 lbs Ground Beef
- 1 lb Spicy pork sausage
- 3 diced Onion
- 2 diced Green bell peppers
- 2 stalks Celery (diced)

- Season with red pepper, black pepper, salt to taste. Simmer ground beef and sausage - add onion, pepper, celery and seasoning. Allow to sweat, mix half and half with long grain white rice.

Anaheim Chili-Pocketed with Cilantro Goat Cheese Tomato Salsa
Serves 6

- 6 Anaheim Chiles, roasted and peeled
- 8 oz. Goat cheese
- 1 Small bunch cilantro
- 1/4 tsp. Salt
- dash cayenne pepper

- Roast, peel and seed chiles splitting down back (leaving stem intact).
- Bring goat cheese to room temperature.
- Add chopped cilantro, cayenne and salt.
- Form to shape of pepper.
- Place in center seam, side down.

Tomato Salsa:
- 2 cups Diced tomato, seeded
- 1 TB. Fresh chives, chopped
- 1 TB. Fresh cilantro, chopped
- 1/4 cup Olive oil
- Juice from 1/2 of lemon
- 1/8 cup White vinegar
- Salt
- Dash of cayenne pepper
- 1 Bunch watercress

- Peel and seed tomatoes.
- Add remaining ingredients.
- Season and garnish with watercress.

Pineapple Fried Rice
Yield: 2 servings

- 2 TB. Vegetable oil, divided
- 2 TB. Dried shrimp
- 1/2 cup Diced pork
- 2 TB. Finely diced onion
- 1/2 cup Diced bread
- 1 T. Oyster sauce
- 1 T. Maggie sauce*
- 3 cups Cooked cold rice
- 1/2 cup Diced pineapple
- 1 Red pepper julienned
- Cilantro sprigs for garnish

- Heat 1 TB. of oil in a wok or large nonstick skillet over medium-high heat. Add dried shrimp and stir-fry until lightly browned. Remove shrimp to a plate.
- Add remaining oil to wok. Add pork and stir-fry for 1 to 2 minutes. Add onion and bread and stir-fry until bread is golden and onion is translucent. Stir in oyster and Maggie sauces. Add cooked cold rice and stir-fry to coat the rice. Add pineapple and cook until heated through. Spoon fried rice on serving plate(s) and garnish with reserved fried shrimp, red pepper julienne and cilantro sprigs.

Cowboy Beans
Chef J. Watson

- 5 lbs. Pinto beans, soaked
- 2 pcs. Celery, diced (stcks not stalks.)
- 1 med. Onion, diced
- 1 lb. Bacon
- 2 med. Tomatoes, diced (cut into pieces.)
- 2 gal. Chicken stock
- 8 oz. Flour
- 1 tbsp. Garlic, granulated
- 1 tsp. Cumin
- Salt to taste

- Sauté onions, celery and bacon.
- Add seasonings and flour to make roux.
- Add chicken stock, blend mixture into beans.
- Cook beans until tender.
- Add diced tomatoes, remove and serve
- Enjoy

Pasta

Ravioli
Chef Louis Ambrosino
Yield: 24 Ravioli

Ravioli Dough
- 1 1/2 tsp Melted shortening or oil
- 1/2 tsp Salt
- 1 egg Yolk, slightly beaten
- 1/2 cup Lukewarm water
- 2 cup Sifted all purpose flour (or enough to form medium dough that does not stick.

Continued On Next Page ▶

Recipes

- Melt shortening and combine with salt, beaten egg yolk and lukewarm water. Beat in about 2 cups sifted flour, a little at a time, to form medium dough. Turn out onto well floured board and knead gently for a few minutes until smooth. Cover with warm bowl and allow to stand at room temperature for about 30 minutes until smooth. This ripens dough, making it easier to roll. Roll into 2 rectangles about 16 x 18 inches. Brush half of dough with well beaten egg white. Arrange about 1 teaspoon of filling over dough, leaving about 1 inch space between each section and cover with other half of dough. Press dough, starting in center and around each section, to press out air. Cut into squares with ravioli wheel, and with fingers pinch around ends, if open. Keep on lightly floured wax paper and turn over occasionally so that filling does not settle to bottom. It is better to let stand about 1 hour before boiling.
- When ravioli are ready to be cooked, lower gently into rapidly boiling salted water cover with wet towel and cook gently for about 20 to 25 minutes, more or less depending on size and thickness of dough.
- When done, pour a little cold water into utensil to cool water slightly, remove with perforated ladle, and drain thoroughly.

Meat and Spinach Filling

1/2 lb	Freshly ground beef, veal, lamb or pork, or left over roasted meat
1/4 cup	Cooked spinach, chopped very fine
1/4 cup	Chopped parsley
1/2 tsp	Salt
1/8 tsp	Nutmeg (a little hot pepper may also be used)
1/8 tsp	Pepper
1 small	Clove garlic, finely chopped
1 tbsp	Parmesan cheese
1 small	Egg

- If using fresh ground meat, fry slowly in 2 tbsp of butter or olive oil about 10 minutes. Add finely chopped spinach and other ingredients, except egg to the meat. Cook together over low flame for several minutes until thoroughly blended. Add egg and beat quickly. Turn off heat

Ricotta filling:

1 lb	Fresh ricotta
1	Egg yolk
1/4 cup	Chopped parsley
1 tsp	Salt
1/8 tsp	Pepper
2 tbsp	Grated Italian parmesan cheese

- Drain the ricotta (may be purchased in Italian Grocery store) and beat until creamy. Add the egg yolk and parsley; salt and pepper and grated cheese. Do not have the filling too soft.

FRANCO'S TRATTORIA
CUCINA TOSCANA

Fettuccine Verdi Con Porcini and Truffle Oil

Chef Franco Fazzuloi

4 oz.	Pasta
1/2 cup	Cream
1 Spoon	Butter
1/4 Cup	Porcini mushrooms (dry or fresh)
1 tsp.	Truffle Oil
1 tsp	Chopped Italian Parsley

- Take spoon of butter, melt it in a sautée pan.
- Add 1/2 cup of salsa.
- Heat it for a couple of minutes.
- Add chopped porcini, cook for 3-4 minutes
- Add cooked & strained fettuccine
- Add truffle oil mix up and serve
- Color with chopped parsley

Gianni

Paglia e Fieno (Straw of Italy)
(Serves 4)

1/2	Green tagliatelle
1/2	White tagliatelle
1 cup	Diced cooked ham
1 cup	Peas (fresh or frozen)
2 cups	Heavy cream
1/2 cup	Parmigiano cheese

- Boil the pasta al dente
- Pour cream into pan, add a pinch of salt and pepper, add parmigiana cheese, when cream boils add diced ham and peas. Then just add the pasta and saute for a couple of minutes. Bon Appetito!

Goldie's neighborhood SPORTS CAFE

Southwestern Shrimp Pasta

Chef Michael Goldman

Southwestern Sauce:

Prepare in order of ingredients:
Start with Hot Skillet

2 tbsp	Olive oil (e::tra virgin)
2 tbsp	Butter or margarine
4 tbsp	Minced shallot
4 tbsp	Minced red onion
1 tsp	Tabasco sauce
1/4 cup + 2 tbsp	Worsteshire sauce
4 tbsp	Cajun Dust™ (available at Smith Meat Dept.)
4 tbsp	Honey
1 lb	Peeled deveined shrimp

- Saute until shrimp are opaque. Add 1 tsp fresh garlic and stir well.

Pasta:

- In separate pot bring 2 quarts of water to rapid boil. Add 1 to 1 1/2 pounds of your favorite pasta and cook al dente. We prefer spinach linguini. Pour sauce over pasta and serve.
- Preparation time 10 - 15 minutes.

Recipes

Guido's Chicago Meat & Deli Ristorante

Cavatelli Con Broccoli
Serves 2-4
- 1 lb. Caeser's Cavatelli
- Boil cavatelli for 10 to 12 minutes
- 1 lb. broccoli florets
- Steam separately with chicken broth

Basic Marinara Sauce:
- Fry 1/2 finely chopped large onion in pan with light olive oil.
- Add fresh garlic and basil.
- Add 2 cans of imported peeled tomatoes
- Black pepper and red pepper to taste.
- Bring to simmer.
- Now put everything together: pasta, broccoli with the chicken broth and marinara.
- Add Romano cheese while serving. Enjoy!

Hops! Bistro and Brewery

Puttanesea
- 2 oz   Olive oil
- 1/2 oz Fresh garlic chopped
- 1/2 oz Fresh shallots chopped
- 2 oz   Red onion sliced
- 2 oz   Sun dried tomato julienne
- 1 oz   Calamata olives pitted and sliced
- 1 oz   Capers
- 4 oz   Red cooking wine
- 12 oz Crushed tomatoes (canned)
- 1/2 lb Fresh Ahi
- 18 ea Large shrimp
- To taste Salt & Pepper
- To taste Cajun Seasoning
- 2 lbs Linguini (cooked)

- In a large skillet, heat the olive oil and then add the garlic, shallots and red onions. Cook until red onions are soft stirring constantly. Then add the sun-dried tomatoes, calamata olives, capers, shrimp and ahi. Continue to saute for one minute, and then deglaze with the red wine. Add the tomatoes and season with the salt, pepper and Cajun seasoning to taste, simmering until the seafood is cooked through. Toss with the linguini and serve.

Mary Elaine's

Gratin of Herbed Cannellonni Saute Artichokes and Wilted Greens
Chef Alessandro Stratta, Executive Chef
Serves 4

Cannelloni Filling
- 1 1/2 cup Spinach puree, squeezed dry
- 2 TB. Extra virgin olive oil
- 2 TB. Parmegiano reggiano
- 1 TB. Basil
- 1 TB. Chives
-       Salt to taste
-       White pepper to taste
- 8   Small won ton wraps; cut in half lengthwise
- 1 TB. melted whole butter

Garnish
- 4 cups Mixed greens
- 2 Artichokes, 48 count hearts, sliced as thinly as possible
- 1 tsp Oive oil
- 1 clove Garlic
-        Reduced Brown Chicken Sauce

- Make filling with spinach puree, oil, cheese, herbs and seasoning.
- Blanch pasta in boiling water and dry. Place oil on a sheet sprinkled liberally with parmegiano. Roll cannelloni (3 per order); brush with melted butter and sprinkle with more cheese. Refrigerate.
- mixed greens. Garnish with reduced brown chicken stock and chervil

Chicken Stock—5 Gallons
- 12 1/2 pounds chicken bones
- 2 cups Onions
- 2 cups Celery
- 2 cups Carrots
- 2 cups Fennel
- 10 heads Garlic, cut in half
- 6 Bay leaves
- 4 TB. Thyme
- 2 TB. White peppercorns
- 5 gallons Water

- Roast bones at 350 degrees, until golden brown. Add vegetables until wilted. Add herbs. Add water: cook
- 8 hours at a slow simmer. Strain and reduce to desired consistentcy.

Pasta Sergio's

Pasta with Pesto Sauce
Chef Tony Caputo
(Serves 4 to 6)
- Fragrant fresh sweet basil leaves, garlic, walnuts or pine nuts and olive oil make a delicious sauce for homemade pasta

- 1 lb   Fresh pasta or 12 oz. dried pasta
- 2 cups Fresh basil leaves
- 3 large Cloves garlic
- 3/4 cup Chopped walnuts or pine nuts
- 3/4 cup Fruity olive oil
- 3/4 cup Freshly grated Parmesan cheese
- 1/2 tsp Salt, or to taste
-         Freshly ground pepper

- While pasta is cooking, place fresh basil leaves, garlic nuts and olive oil in food processor bowl or blender container. Process until ingredients are well mixed, scraping down sides of container once or twice. Process until mixture is fairly smooth. Pour into bowl, and stir in cheese, salt, and pepper. Toss with hot, well-drained pasta in warm bowl.

Continued On Next Page ▶

Recipes

- Variation: Cook 1 cup Kizo or other rice-shaped pasta according to package directions. Stir in 1/3 cup Pesto Sauce. Fill 4 hollowed out, medium size tomatoes with mixture. Top with Parmesan cheese and bake in 375° F oven 15 minutes. Serve hot with barbequed lamb or steaks.

ROXSAND
(Restaurant & Bar)

Spin Cold Soba Noodles
Chef Roxsand

1/3 cup	Soy Sauce
1 tbsp	Molasses
1/4 cup	Sesame oil
1/4 cup	Tahini
1/4 cup	Brown sugar
1/4 cup	Chili oil
3 tbsp	Balsanic or red wine vinegar
1/2 bunch	Scallions, white or green parts, thinly sliced
	Salt to taste
1/2 lb	Soba or Japanese buckwheat Noodles

- Place soy sauce in a pan over high heat and reduce by half. Turn heat to low. Stir in molasses and warm briefly. Transfer to a mixing bowl. Add sesame oil, tahini, brown sugar, chili oil, vinegar and scallions and whisk to combine. Season to taste with salt, if desired.
- Bring a large pot of salted water to rapid boil. Add noodles, bring back to a boil and cook stirring occasionally, until they just begin to soften, about 3 minutes. (Soba noodles can overcook very quickly, so stay nearby).
- Have ready a large bowl of iced water. Drain noodles, plunge in iced water and drain again. Place in a colander and rinse well under cold running water. Combine noodles and sauce, toss well and chill.

The Terrace Dining Room

Potato Gnocchi "Quatro Formagi" with Toasted Walnuts
Chef Alessandro Stratta, Executive Chef
Serves 4

4 cups	Potato dumplings (gnocchi)

Sauce:

1/2 cup	Cream
1/4 cup	Gorgonzola cheese
1/4 cup	Asiago cheese
1/4 cup	Parmegiano cheese
1/4 cup	Provolone cheese
	Salt and pepper
1/4 cup	Toasted walnuts
2 TB.	Chives

To prepare the & Gnocchi:
- Cook gnochi in salted simmering water until they float for approximately 1 minute.

To prepare the sauce:
- In a heavy sauce pan, reduce cream with mix of finely grated cheese until thick, season and finish with toasted walnuts and chives. Glaze gnocchi in sauce and serve in a hot bowl.

Presentation:
- Garnish top with walnuts and chives.

Uncle Sal's
ITALIAN RISTORANTE

Spaghetti all Amataiciana

1 1/2 lb.	Spaghetti
2 1/2 TB.	Oil
5oz.	Panchetta of Bacon
1	Diced or thin sliced onion
1/2 cup	Dry white wine
1 lb.	Ripe or canned tomatoes
1/2 cup	Frozen green peas
	Salt and pepper
1 cup	Grated Parmesan, Pecorino or mixed

- Heat the oil and sauté onion over low heat until soft.
- Add the Panchetta or bacon and fry slowly for a few minutes.
- Add white wine and cook until it reduces a little.
- Peel, chop, and seed tomatoes, and add to pan.
- Season to taste with salt and pepper.
- Cook over medium high heat until desired consistency, but not more than 12 minutes.
- Add frozen peas 3 or 4 minutes before completion.

Main Meat/Poultry

Avanti

Chicken Pillard
Executive Chef: Ted Reiley

2, 8oz.	Chicken breasts (boneless, skinless)
1/4 cup	Olive oil
2 cloves	Garlic minced
1	Lemon—sliced thin
2 tbsp	Rosemary—fresh, chopped coarse
1/4 tsp	Black pepper—fresh ground
pinch	Salt
2 tbsp	White wine

- move all bones and skin from chicken breasts. Pound them thin with meat mallet. Combine remaining ingredients together in a small mixing bowl. Add chicken and marinate for at least 6 hours or overnight. Cook over a hot grill on each side for 45 minutes or till done. Remove from heat and squeeze lightly with more fresh lemon.

135

Recipes

Citrus Veloute' Roasted Duck

- ONE (1)5/6 lb Duck de-boned except for drumstick

To make Citrus Veloute' Duck Sauce:

- Stuff duck carcass with chopped carrots, celery, onions, oranges, fresh herbs.
- Roast Duck carcass until brown and crispy
- Deglace pan with raspberry liquor and brandy.
- Scrape all deposits from pan and place in stock pot with duck carcass.
- Cover with water and boil until reduced by half.
- Strain and allow to cool. When cool remove fat layer.
- Put two (2) cups Chardonnay into sauce pan with chopped garlic, shallots, mixed herbs, Two (2) cups oz. heavy cream, six (6) oz. orange juice concentrate. Mix well. Reduce by half.
- Add duck stock, cook for one (1) hour. Stir frequently.
- Add corn starch or arrow root that has been mixed with water to sauce. Using wire whip, mix well.
- Add fresh chopped oregano, basil, parsley, rosemary. Cook gently.
- Sauce should thicken slightly and coat a spoon.
- Sprinkle Duck pieces with pepper and salt and broil until skin is lightly browned.
- Place duck pieces in oven and roast until internal temperature of duck pieces is at 170 degrees, then remove from oven.
- While duck is roasting boil four (4) peeled sweet potatoes. When done, add chopped basil, parsley, oregano, with melted butter, 1 TB. brown sugar,, sprinkle a pinch of salt and pepper and whip well.
- Steam broccoli florets until al dente.
- Heat duck sauce.
- To plate put sweet potatoes in center of plate. Set broccoli around the sweet potatoes.
- Place duck drumstick and thigh slightly into the sweet potatoes.
- Fan the duck breast out in front of the drumstick and thigh.
- Drizzle drumstick and thigh with citrus velouté and lightly coat the duck breast.
- With raspberry paint lightly decorate the duck breast.
- Sprinkle with fresh herb mix and place tortilla fan and fresh sprig of rosemary into sweet potatoes behind drumstick and thigh....Serve.

Black Rose Shepherd Pie

(For 8 people)

3 lbs	Shoulder clod - 1 inch cubes
2 cups	1 inch diced Onion
2 cups	1 inch diced Celery
2 cups	1 inch diced Carrots
3 tbsp	Garlic (finely diced)
1/2 cup	Tomato paste
2 tbsp	Fresh basil
1 tbsp	Thyme
8	Bay leaves
1 qt	Beef stock
1 tbsp	Black pepper
2 cups	Burgundy

- Sautee meat in 1/2 cup of vegetable oil for 15 minutes, add vegetables, spices tomato sauce. Add wine and beef stock. Simmer for 30 minutes.
- Mix cup of corn starch with 2 1/2 cups of cold water, add to the stew. Served with mashed potatoes and top with Vermont white cheddar.

Chicken Cardonnay

Mel Rosales Executive Chef
Serves 6

6 - 6 oz.	Boneless Skinless chicken breasts
2 oz.	Melted butter
1	Clove of garlic
1/2 tsp.	Black pepper
1 cup	Heavy cream
2 oz.	Chardonnay wine
1	Medium shallot
6	Artichoke hearts
1/4 tsp.	Seasoning salt
1 cup	Flour

- Dredge chicken with flour. Sautée in butter until golden brown. Add mushrooms, artichoke hearts to the wine and the rest of the ingredients
- Simmer for about 8 minutes.
- Serve with Rice Pilaf or Pasta.

Sautéed Lamb with Curry

Chef Christopher Gross

1	Lamb Loin

Mirpoix

2 Oz	Carrots
2 Oz	Celery
2 oz	Onions
1 clove	Garlic
	Sprig of Thyme

ForSauce:

1/2 oz	Curry powder
2 oz.	Olive oil
2 oz	Butter

Continued On Next Page ▶

Garnish:
- 1 pk. Katafi
- 1/2 lb Cleaned bok choy
- 2 Basil leaves

Preparation:
- Bone and cut lamb in cubes about 1/2 inch squares. Take all meat trimmings, defatted and brown. Add Mirpoix sliced thinly. Cook a couple of minutes, then add enough water to cover meat trimmings. Cook one hour then strain and reduce consomme by half Wisk in 2 oz. butter and curry. Season to taste.

Cooking of Lamb:
- In a very hot pan, add olive oil. Dust lamb with curry and salt and pepper. Add lamb and brown very quickly and cook until medium rare about 3 minutes. Place lamb in a colander to let oil drain.
- Cooking of Bok Choy: Add 1 oz. olive oil to a large saute pan. Add Bok Choy and cook until wilted. Add salt and pepper to taste.
- Cooking Katafi: Spread Katafi out on cooking sheet. Dust with curry and olive oil. Bake until golden brown.
- Cooking Basil: Heat pan of olive oil reaching 375 degrees. Place basil in oil. Leave in oil for approximately 20 seconds. Take out, place on absorbent towel and season.
- Cooking Potatoes: Use same pan as step three. Place potatoes in oil until golden brown in color, take out and place on towel season.

Preparation of Potatoes (For Lamb)
- 2 Potatoes
- 1 cup Potato flakes
- 2 Eggs
- 1 cup Flour
- 1/2 oz Curry powder

- Cube potatoes into 1/4 inch squares. Cook and Shock potatoes. Season potatoes with salt, pepper and curry. Place flour, egg and potato flakes into three separate bowls. Place potatoes into flour, secondly into eggs, and thirdly into potato flakes. repeat into eggs and potato flakes for a tasty breading.

To Serve
- Place Bok Choy in center of the plate.
- Place lamb and potato cubes on top of Bok Choy and ladle sauce on top of lamb. Top with Katafi and fried basil.

Christopher's

Faux Filet
Chef Christopher Gross
Yeilds 4 Servings

- 1 1/2 puond Sirloin (Faux Filet)
- 23 tbsp. Truffle oil
- 2 cups Alderwood sawdust
- 4 Shallots, medium sized
- 1/2 tbsp Unsalted butter
- 2 branch Fresh thyme

Preparations:
- Marinate sirloin in truffle oil for 24 hours.
- using a pan on top of the stove, place the sawdust in the bottom in a small mound.
- elevating the sirloin cover the top with foil and slowly smoke on low heat for 15 minutes.
- Take 4 shallots and dice very fine. sweat in 1/2 tablespoon of butter until tender then add chopped leaves of thyme.

White Sauce
- 8 Shallots
- 1 oz. Butter
- 3 Cups Chicken stock
- 1 Cup Heavy Cream
- 3 tbsp. Butter

Preparations
- Take the other 8 shallots and 1 ounce of butter. Add to 3 cups of chicken stock in a small pan and cover. Cook slowly until shallots are tender. When shallots are finished, remove from stock; these will be your garnish.
- Reduce the remainder of the stock then add cream. Reduce then wisk in 3 tablespoons butter then strain.

Red Wine Sauce
- 4 Cups Red wine
- 3 Shallots (chopped)
- Black Pepper
- 3 Cups Veal stock
- Salt and Pepper
- 1/2 lb. Butter

Preperation
- Reduce red wine with shallots, thyme and black pepper. Add stock, salt and pepper to taste. Add butter, strain and blend.

Fareki
- 3/4 lb. Fareki (cleaned)
- 3 Cups Garlic sauce
- 1 tbsp. Harrissa
- 5 tbsp. Shallots (diced)
- 5 tbsp. Chives (Diced)
- 1 tbsp. Butter

Cooking Fareki
- Wash then strain
- place in hot pan on oven and heat stirring briskly.
- Add garlic sauce, cook till tender stirring often
- When cooked, saute the shallots in another pan til tender. Add chives
- Add this to your Fareki along with your harissa, salt and papper to taste.

Garlic Sauce
- 1 qt. Veal stock
- 3 Cloves Garlic
- 2 oz. Basil leaves
- 1/4 pound unsalted butter

Preparation
- Reduce the veal stock by 1/2 with garlic cloves and basil. Blend in the butter and strain.

Harissa
- 5 Red peppers, roasted in a very hot oven and peeled
- 3 Cloves garlic
- 1 pinch Cayenne
- 1/4 Minced onion
- 1 pinch Red dried chilies
- 3 drops Sate oil

Continued On Next Page ▶

Recipes

- When peppers are clean, put in a blender and purée with all ingredients.

Plating the Faux Filet with Fareki

- Sauté the sirloin to preferred temperature.
- Quenelle the fareki a little above center of plate.
- Place the whole shallot at 3:00 and 9:00.
- Sliced the sirloin and place on the bottom of plate. Top with dices shallots and thyme
- Put the red wine sauce on bottom of plate.
- Then the white sauce over the whole shallots.
- Lastly, place the potato tuile in the Fareki

Note: Garnish with potato thyme wafer

Duck Cakes with Chamomile Orange Sauce

14 1/2 lb	Fresh or frozen (thawed) duckling
1 tsp	Salt
1 tsp	Pepper
1 medium	Yellow onion, halved lengthwise and sliced thin
1 medium	Red Onion, halved lengthwise and sliced thin
3 large	Leeks, cut into fine julienne
3 large	Shallots, cut into fine julienne
3	Eggs
3 tbsp	Clarified butter

- Prick skin of duckling with fork in several places. Rub duckling with salt and pepper. Place duckling, breast side up, on rack in open roasting pan. Roast duckling in 350°F oven for about 2 1/2 hours or until meat pulls from the leg bone with ease. Remove from oven and let cool. Remove and reserve the skin. Shred the meat from the duckling into a large mixing bowl. Add your eggs, vegetables and finely chopped skin. Mix well. Form into 20–24 patties and pan fry over medium high heat in clarified butter until crisp.

The Pointe Hilton Resort at Squaw Peak

Country Style Baby Back Ribs

Makes 6 servings

1 cup	Catsup
1	Large lemon
1 cup	Water
1	Clove garlic, minced
1 cup	Apple cider vinegar
2 tbsp	Butter or margarine
1/4 cup	Worcestershire sauce
4 lbs.	Lean country-style baby back pork ribs
1	Medium onion

Procedure

- In a 2 to 3 quart pan, combine catsup, water, vinegar, worcestershire, onion, lemon, garlic and butter. Bring to a boil over high heat; reduce heat and simmer, uncovered, stirring occasionally for 30 minutes. Brush ribs with sauce.
- Place ribs, fat side up on grill. Cook ribs brushing occasionally with sauce until meat near the bone is no longer pink (about 1 to 4 hours).
- To serve, heat remaining sauce and spoon over ribs.

Chicken Fantasia

Chef Giovanni

Serves 2

4	4 oz. Chicken breasts (Boneless/Skinless)
3	Cloves minced garlic
3 TB.	Butter
1 cup	Sliced mushrooms
1/2 cup	Sliced black olives
2	Artichoke hearts (cut in halves)
1/2 cup	Dry white wine
1/4 tsp.	Lemon juice
2 cups	Chicken broth
1/4 cup	Flour
1/4 tsp.	Salt (Sicilian salt)
1/4 tsp.	White pepper
2	Full slices of Prosciutto (ham) 1/2 cut
4	Slices of Provolone (cheese)
4	Toothpicks

- Lightly pound chicken breast with meat mallet, sprinkle with salt and white pepper and flour both sides.
- In a large skillet combine butter, garlic, mushrooms, olives, and artichoke hearts. Cook on a high heat.
- Shake excessive flour from chicken breasts and add to the ingredients in the skillet. Sautée breasts on both sides.
- Add chicken broth, white wine, lemon juice, and one pinch of flour. Bring to a boil, reduce heat, and let simmer until juice is reduced to less than half.
- Take chicken and artichoke hearts out.
- Layer chicken breast, 1/2 slice Prosciutto, one slice Provolone, chicken breast, 1/2 slice Prosciutto, one slice Provolone, 2 1/2 artochoke hearts and hold together with 2 toothpicks.
- Repeat for the 2 chicken breasts that are left.
- Return prepared chicken to skillet until juice thickens.
- Serve each chicken breast on a plate with the toothpick intact.

Recipes

Los Olivos

Sonora Enchiladas

Red Chili Sauce:

- 10 Dried red chilies
- 3/4 lb Cheddar or monterrey cheese
- 4 tbsp Shortening
- 1 tbsp Salt
- 2 1/2 tbsp Flour
- 2 cloves Garlic

- Garlic Boil red chilies in enough water to cover. Cook for about 15 minutes or until tender. Place in blender and puree.
- Heat shortening on medium-high and melt, add garlic and cook until light brown. Then add flour and brown, stirring constantly. Add salt and chili puree. Simmer until thickened. If too thick, add water to desired consistency and more salt if needed.

Masa:

- 2 lbs Corn masa (may be bought at local supermarket)
- 1/2 lb Cheddar cheese
- 1 1/2 tbsp Salt
- 1 tbsp Baking powder
- Oil
- Deep fryer set at 450°
- 1 cup Instant mashed potatoes
- 2 cups Water

- Mix all the ingredients together. It's a rough dough, so a little kneading may be required. When well mixed, make 3 inch balls. Flatten balls to about 1/2 inch patties. Place in oil one at a time until golden brown.

Prepare Enchiladas:

Garnishes:
- Cheese
- Chopped green onion
- Shredded lettuce
- Chopped tomato
- Olives

- Place fried patty on plate and pour enough red chili sauce to cover, then put cheese and onion (if desired) on top and put in oven until melted. Top with shredded lettuce, tomatoes and olives.
- You may vary enchiladas

Marché Gourmet

"Choucroute" with Champagne

Chef Jean-Marie Rigoliet
(Serves two)

- Sautee 1 medium size onion in 2 oz of duck fat until golden, then add one clove of fresh garlic, chopped, stir one minute; add 2 cups of good dry white wine, 1 medium apple diced very thin, 2 small bay leaves, 12 to 18 juniper berries (depending on size) and 1 1/2 pounds of sourkraut, drained; keep at a slow boil until reduced by 2/3. Reserve, then prepare the meats while steaming the red potatoes, (1 large per person).
- Strasbourg Sausages: (1 per person) If not available, use a good quality weiner.
- Pork: Sliced loin, sauteed in duck fat, seasoned with salt, pepper and garlic.
- Garlic Sausage: (3 slices per person) available at Marche Gourmet.
- To Serve Place the "Choucroute" in the bottom of a shallow dish, arrange the meats tastefully on top; Add steamed potatoes, cut into wedges; SprinKle chopped parsley on the potatoes, serve with Dijon Mustard.
- Serve with a fruity white wine, preferably from Alsace Lorraine.

"Choucroute" is availabie on our dinner menu at Marche Gourmet.

Mary Elaine's

Tenderloin of Veal with Garlic-Rosemary Jus Tartelette of White Been Puree and Glazed Spring Vegetable

Chef Alessandro Stratta, Executive Chef
(Serves 4)

- 1/2 cup Extra virgin olive oil
- 1 1/2 quarts Chicken stock
- 4 Eight ounce veal tenderloin

For the sauce
- 4 Sliced shallots
- 5 Peppercorns
- 1 Bay leaf
- 1 Large (3") sprig fesh rosemary
- 1 1/2 cups Veal demiglace

For the garlic
- 2 Heads garlic
- Sprigs of fresh herbs
- 1 Each bay leaf

For the beans
- 2 cups Dry cannelonni beans
- 1/2 cup Carrot
- 1/2 cup Onion
- Salt to taste
- 2 tbsp. Sherry vinegar
- 2 cups Leeks, cut in 1/4" rounds

For the vegetables
- 8 Pencil asparagus tips
- 16 Haricots verts
- 4 Baby carrots
- 4 Red radishes
- 4 Baby turnips
- 4 Scallions
- 2 tbsp. finely chopped chives

For the olive oil dough
- 14 oz. All purpose flour
- 1/2 cup Olive oil
- 1 Egg
- Salt to taste
- 1/2 cup Water

To prepare the veal:
- Season and sear each piece in very hot oil to finish in the oven on pick up.

To prepare the sauce:
- Sweat the shallots and peppercorns and one bay leaf with: the sprig of rosemary.

Continued On Next Page ▶

Recipes

- Deglaze with demi-glaze and reduce by 3/4.
- Strain and reserve warm

To prepare the garlic
- With one slice, cut the tips off the heads of garlic then coat with good olive oil.
- Lay the garlic out on a well-oiled sizzle platter with sprigs of fresh herbs.
- Roast slowly at 300 F until soft, about 2 hours.
- Squeeze the pearls out of the garlic, reserving half of them as garnish.
- Purée the other half into the sauce and reserve.

To prepare the cannellini beans
- Soak the beans overnight in clear water.
- Drain them and recover them with half chicken stock and half water.
- Add the carrot and onion, then bring up to a simmer until 3/4 cooked, keeping the level of the liquid just above the beans.
- Add salt to taste and let cooking finish and liquid reduce.
- Purée half of the beans with sherry vinegar; olive oil and seasonings to medium consistency and keep warm
- Reserve the remaining whole beans in the cooking liquid.

To prepare the leeks:
- Steam the leek rounds.
- Cool in the walk-in and reserve.

To prepare the vegetables:
- Cook the asparagus and haricots verts barely underdone; shock and reserve.
- Braise the remaining vegetables separately in 1/2 tbsp. olive oil at high heat to light color, then adding just enough chicken stock to cook through (covered).
- Lay out and cool.

For the tartlette shells:
- In an electric mixer, turn all the ingredients with the hook, except the water.
- Add just enough water so that the dough balls, and cleans the sides of the bowl.
- Rest 1 hour
- Roll to 1/16", line tart molds and bake golden. Reserve.

Presentation
- Reheat the veal until just faintly pink at the center
- Warm a ragout of whole white beans leeks and the chives with some of the beans' cooking liquid and a splash of sherry vinegar.
- Warm all of the vegetables together with a tbsp. or so of stock and a dash of olive oil.
- Smooth 1 1/2 tbsp. of puree into the tartlette shell and arrange the vegetables atop.
- Plate the tartlette opposite a small pile of white bean-leek ragout.
- Slice the veal to place atop the ragout then nap with the sauce and whole roast garlic pearls.

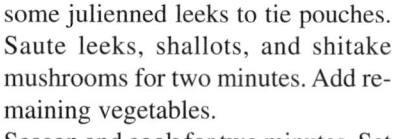

Palm Court
Scottsdale Conference Resort

Grilled Quail Breast in Phyllo with Caper Herb Lemon Butter
Serves 4

8	Quail breasts, skin on
2	Leeks
1	Large carrot
1	Large zucchini
1	Large squash
1	Bunch green onions
10	Shitake mushroom caps
2 cups	Clarified butter
1	Box phyllo dough
	Salt and pepper to taste

Sauce:

1 TB.	Shallot, chopped
2 cups	White wine
1 TB.	Capers
1/2 lb.	Whole unsalted butter, melted
1 TB.	Fresh parsley
1 TB.	Fresh basil, chopped

- Julienne all vegetables. Set aside some julienned leeks to tie pouches. Saute leeks, shallots, and shitake mushrooms for two minutes. Add remaining vegetables.
- Season and cook for two minutes. Set aside at room temperature.
- Grill seasoned quail breasts until done, approximately three-four minutes. Set aside at room temperature.
- Butter phyllo dough sheets one at a time, layering them one on top of the other until there are seven layers. Prepare a total of four stacks.
- Place one quail breast on one stack of phyllo. Place vegetable mixture on top of quail. Shape into a pouch, trimming edges if necessary. Tie with a blanched leek. Bake for twenty minutes in a 350 degree oven.

Sauce:
- Reduce wine with shallots until only 1 TB. remains. Add herbs and capers.
- Whisk in butter until thickened to a syrup consistency.
- To serve, place sauce in serving plate and place phyllo pouch onto sauce.

Royal Barge
Thai Cuisine

Pad Prig Pao Beef
(Serves 4-6)

4 oz	Beef bone soup
1 tsp	Roasted chili paste
1 tsp	Chopped garlic
1 tsp	Chopped bell pepper
1 1/2 tsp	Fish stock
1/2 tbspf	Oyster stock
1 tsp	Sugar

- Vegetable: bamboo shoot, baby corn, green bean, white onion, carrot, mushroom, bell pepper.
- Put canola oil in wok. Add beef, chicken or pork. Add chopped bell pepper and chopped garlic and mix together with meat. Then add balance of ingredients in wok. Put soup (4 oz) into wok and turn heat to high and mix.

Recipes

Drunken Formula Chicken

(Serves 4-6)

4 oz	Chicken bone soup
1 tsp	Fresh chili paste
1 tsp	Chopped garlic
1 tsp	Chopped bell pepper
1 1/2 tbsp	Fish stock
1/2 tbsp	Oyster stock
1 tsp	Sugar

- Vegetable: bamboo shoot, baby corn, green bean, white onion, carrot, mushroom, bell pepper.
- Put canola oil in wok add beef, chicken or pork. Add chopped garlic and mix together with meat. Then add balance of ingredients in wok. Put soup (4 oz) into wok and turn heat to high and mix.

Radicchio Risotto with Roasted Quail, Pancetta and Wild Mushrooms

Chef Alessandro Stratta, Executive Chef

Serves 4

- Arborio rice
- Radicchio &(julienne)
- Pancetta
- Onion
- Butter
- Chicken stock
- White wine
- Parmegiano
- 4 each Quail, de-boned
- Bosc or Bartlett pears

- Start risotto with julienne of radicchio, pancetta and onions. Continue like regular risotto and finish with fresh Juliennie of radicchio and parmegiano. Roast quail and serve on rice with shavings of Bosc or Bartlett pears and parmegiano cheese.

Pepper Encrusted Rack of Lamb with Prickly Pear Dusting

Chef Steven Munichbach

2	Racks of Lamb frenched
1/4 cup	Crushed black peppercorns
2 t	Kosher salt
2	Jalapeno peppers minced
1	Red bell pepper minced
2	Tomatoes (diced)
1 b.	Scallion(white only sliced oriental style)
1 cup	Rasberry vinegar
3	Prickly Pears
1 cup	Tomato juice
2 cups	Sugar

- Season meat with peppercorns and salt. Set aside. Light charcoal, mesquite is preferred.
- Peel Prickly pear, simmer in tomato juice for 5 minutes, puree in blender, run through a fine mesh strainer. Add vinegar and sugar, reduce by 1/2 add diced vegetables and hold.
- Meanwhile grill lamb until desired doneness, approximately 5 minutes a side for medium rare. To serve cut rack between bones and arrange on platter, spoon sauce over.

Veal Black Forestier

(Makes 8 Servings)

1 1/2 lbs	Veal tenderloin
1 lb	Fresh zucchini
1 lb	Fresh mushrooms
2	Lemons
4 Oz	Parmesan cheese
8	Beaten eggs
1 lb	Butter
	Salt and pepper
	Parsley

- Cut veal in 24 slices (3 per serving) and pound very thin (about 1/8 inch). Slice the zucchini about 1/4 inch thick (3 slices per serving). Season veal and zucchini with salt and pepper. Then flour lightly, dip in beaten eggs and sautee in hot butter.
- Slice mushrooms and sautee in butter. Alternate veal and zucchini on warmed platter and cover with sauteed mushrooms. Squeeze the lemon over the preparation, sprinkle with Parmesan cheese and gratine under the broiler.
- Before serving add butter Meuniere and chopped parsley.

Windows on the Green

Chef Robert McGrath

Tenderloin of Beef on a Blueberry Barbecue Sauce Roasted Garlic-Green Chile Mashed Potatoes

serves 4

- 4 7 OZ. beef tenderloin filets kosher salt and fresh cracked black pepper to taste

Continued On Next Page ▶

Recipes

Garnish

- 3 Large russet potatoes cut in cubes
- 2 tbsp. Chopped, roasted garlic
- 2 tbsp. Roasted green chile puree
- 1/2 cup Milk
- 1/4 cup Butter
- Kosher salt and fresh cracked black pepper to taste
- 1/4 cup Blanched haricot vert (tiny green beans)
- 1/4 cup Sweet corn kernels
- 1/4 cup Blanched fava beans
- 1 tbs. Diced red bell pepper
- 2 tbs. Diced red onion
- 1 tbs Butter
- 1/4 cup Fresh blueberries for garnish

Sauce: 1 pint

- 1 pint Fresh blueberries
- 1/4 cup Finely chopped onions
- 1 tbsp. Chopped jalapeno
- 3 tbsp. Brown sugar
- 1/4 cup Rice vinegar
- 1/4 cup Tomato ketchup
- 3 tbsp. Dijon mustard
- 1 tsp. Tobasco sauce
- 1/4 cup Whole butter

- For the sauce, saute the onions and jalapenos. Add the blueberries with the rest of the ingredients and cook at a low boil for 15 minutes stirring frequently. Puree the sauce and run through a strainer. Finish with the whole butter, season to taste.
- For the mashed potatoes, boil the potatoes in salted water until they are tender. Roast the potatoes in a 400 degree oven for 8 to 12 minutes. In a mixer combine the potatoes and the other ingredients then mix slowly. Season to taste.
- For the garnish, heat the tablespoon of butter in a hot skillet then saute the red bell pepper and red onion until just soft. Add the green beans, fava beans and sweet corn. Toss quickly and season to taste.
- Season the filets, grill to the desired temperature. Sauce the plate, place the mashed potatoes off-center and rest the filet against them. Place the succotash in the vortex between the filet and the potatoes.

Main Seafood

Aunt Chilada's
A Beanery Refried

Chili Seared Giant Sea Scallops

- 12 Giant sea scallops (fresh)

Seasoning

- 2 TB. Lawrey's season pepper
- 1 tsp Chili powder
- 1/2 tsp Paprika
- 1/2 tsp crushed red chilies
- 1/2 tsp salt

- Dry scallops on a paper towel.
- Sprinkle scallops on each side with season mixture, wrap in plastic wrap and refrigerate 15 minutes.

Chances Are!! Restaurant-Lounge

Shrimp Gabrielle

(Serves 4)

- 16 Jumbo shrimp
- 1 Large diced tomato
- 4 oz Sliced mushrooms
- 4 Green onions
- 4 Minced garlic cloves
- 3 oz Butter
- 3 oz White wine
- 1 tbsp Cajun seasoning

- Saute shrimp in garlic butter for about 2 minutes, then add rest of ingredients and cook for five more minutes, add wine, last minute. Served with rice Pilaf.

Gianni
CUCINA ITALIANA

Salmone

Farfelle Salmone Affumicato
(Bowties with smoked salmon)

- 1 pack Farfelle pita
- 4 slices Smoked salmon
- 4 Tomatoes
- Heavy Cream
- Fresh parsley

- Boil pasta (al dente). Add heavy cream. Add a pinch of salt and pepper, add tomatoes. When cream starts to boil, add the shredded salmon strips. Then add the pasta. Bon Appetito!

Golden Swan

Orange Honey Barbecued Salmon with Baby Greens in Painted Cilantro Dressing

SERVES: 6

- 6 3oz. Salmon Filets
- 1 Cup Orange Honey Barbeque Sauce
- 5 oz. Cilantro Dressing
- Baby greens of choice

- dip salmon in barbeque sauce and sauté or grill for approximately 3 minutes on each side. Place washed greens on plate and add salmon. Sprinkle with dressing

Cilantro Dressing

- 1/2 Cup olive oil
- 1/8 Cup Malted vinegar
- 2 Tbsp. Cilantro, chopped
- 1 Tbsp. Shallots, chopped
- 1 tsp. Honey
- Salt & Pepper, to taste

- Mix all ingredients and chill

Recipes

Hops! Bistro and Brewery

Soy Ginger Shrimp

- 1 lb Rock shrimp
- 8-10 medium Shiitake mushrooms
- 4 oz Sliced scallions
- 2 tbsp Sesame oil
- 1 tsp Minced ginger
- 3 oz Hoisin sauce
- 2 oz Teriyaki sauce
- 2 oz Soy sauce
- 3 Oz heavy cream

- Black and White sesame seeds, Pasta or rice Heat oil, add garlic, ginger and mushrooms, saute until soft. Add shrimp. Deglaze with Teriyaki and Soy. Add Hoisin, reduce. Finish with heavy cream. Serve over rice or toss with pasta. Garnish with sesame seeds.

Il Forno Ristorante

Pescatore Linguine
Chef Mario

- 1 lb Sword Fish
- 1/2 lb Mussels
- 1/2 lb Clams
- 1/2 lb Calamari
- 1/4 lb Shrimp

Marinara Sauce
- 1 cup WhiteWine
- 2 cups Clam juice
- Salt
- Black Pepper
- Garlic
- Olive oil
- Basil
- Red Pepper
- Parsley

- In a pan, put oil, garlic salt and pepper flakes. Cook until garlic is brown, add white wine and clam juice and stir. Put in fish, calamari, shrimp. Cook for 5 or 6 minutes, add marinara sauces. In a different pan, cook mussels with garlic, clam juice, add olive oil. Add a touch of basil to each pan and cook for 5 minutes. Put pasta in plate with parsley on top.

Pan:
- Oil, garlic, salt and pepper, olive oil. Cuedo esta cafe doido el garlic. Wine white, pone pescado calamari, shrimp. Marinara, clams juice, clams-mussel, basil, pinch. Cook 5 minutes. Add: Pasta put in plate. Parsley on the top.

Mary Elaine's

Sautée of Daurade with Garden Pea Coconut Rice Sweet lobster Sauce
Chef Alessandrn Stratta, Executive Chef

Serves 4
- 1 1/2 lbs. Daurade filets (sea brim) skin oil, 6 oz. each
- 3 tbsp. Sugar snap peas
- 3 tbsp. English peas
- 3 tbsp. Chinese pea pods
- 2 tsp. Cilantro

Coconut Rice
- 1 cup Basmati rice
- 1 1/4 cup Unsweetened coconut milk
- 2 Kafir lime leaves
- 1 tsp. Orange zest
- 1 tbsp. Toasted unsweetened coconut
- 1 tbsp. Butter

- Put all ingredients in a pot, bring to a boil, cover and cook at 500 for 15-20 minutes. Rice should be ligth and fluffy.

Sauce
- 4 Lobster bodies, cut in to fourths, "tamale" removed
- 2 tbsp. Garlic cloves
- 2 tbsp. Diced carrots
- 2 tbsp. Diced fennel
- 2 tbsp. Diced leeks
- 1 tbsp. Ginger root
- 2 Kafir lime leaves
- 1 tbsp. Lemon grass
- 1 tsp. Tomato paste
- 1 tsp. Thyme
- 1/2 cup White wine
- 2 cups Chicken stock
- 2 cups Coconut milk
- 2 tbsp. Butter
- 1 tbsp. Extra virgin olive oil

- Cook like lobster stock; reduce and finish with coconut milk, butter and oil.

Oaxaca at Pinnacle Peak

Broiled Ahi Tuna & Mango Kiwi Compote
by Executive Chef Travis Vierthaler

- 2 7 Oz. filets of Ahi Tuna
- 2 very ripe Mangos, peeled & diced
- 3 Very ripe Kiwi, peeled & diced 7 mint leaves, finely diced
- Juice of one Lemon
- 1/2 cup Honey

- Grill Tuna Steaks to medium rare. Place Mango, Kiwi, Mint, Lemon & Honey in bowl & mix. Place compote on Tuna Steak and enjoy. Exceptional with rice or pasta.

Recipes

Palm Court
Scottsdale Conference Resort

Lobster Mousse and Spinach Roulade With Holland Pepper Chive coulis

Serves 4

- 3 Lobster tails, shelled
- 2 tbsp. Fresh basil, chopped
- 2 lbs. Fresh cleaned spinach leaves
- 1 tbsp. Fresh parsley, chopped
- 1 pint Heavy cream
- Salt and white pepper to taste

Sauce:

- 2 Large golden Holland peppers, peppers, seeded, and cut into 1" pieces
- 1/2 cup White wine salt and white pepper to taste
- 6 cups Light fish or chicken stock
- 2 tbsp. Fresh chives, chopped

• Blanch spinach in boiling water until limp (about one minute) Immediately place into bowl of ice water.

• Remove and place on towel and dry well, Spread out spinach in a large thin layer in a square shape on a large piece of foil or plastic wrap.

Mousse

• Puree lobster tail meat in food processor or blender. Add cream slowly until well blended.

• Mix in chopped herbs, Season to taste, Using a thin spatula, spread mixture in an even layer over the spinach. Roll spinach so that when cut it will have a spiral look.

• Secure in the plastic wrap or foil. Poach or steam in a shallow water bath, covered, for 15-20 minutes in a 375 degree oven. Cut to serve.

Sauce

• Boil all sauce ingredients except chives until reduced to 2 cups. Puree in blender or processor.

• Strain and add chives.

• To serve, place sauce on serving plate and lay slices of spinach roll onto sauce, allowing 2-3 slices per serving.

Pepin
restaurante español

Paella

Executive Chef, Ravel Souto

(Serves 2)

- 2 oz Chistora
- 1/2 cup Onions
- 2 tbsp Garlic
- 1/2 cup Peppers, red and green mixed
- 1/2 cup Tomatoes
- 1/2 cup Olive oil
- 1 1/2 cup Rice
- 3 1/2 cup Chicken stock
- Pinch Saffron
- 4 oz Pork
- 4 oz Chicken
- 2 Lobster slippers
- 4 Shrimp (U16-20)
- 6 Mussels
- 4 Cockle clams
- 1/2 cup White wine
- 2 tbsp Parsley

Method:

• Saute onions, chistora, garlic, pork and chicken. Add tomatoes and parsley. Add rice and stir. Add stock and chaffron. When rice begins to form, add mussels, shrimp, lobster and clams. When "eyes" begin to form, add pepper, white wine, and peas. Cook open face in a 10-12 inch casuela.

Presentation:

• At the table, serve directly from casuela onto oval plates. Each guest receives one lobster slipper, one shrimp, 2 oz. chicken, 2 oz pork, 2 clams, 2 mussels, and one half the rice.

Pepin
restaurante español

Salmon En Salsa Verde

YIELD: 6 portions

- 6 8oz. salmon filets
- 2 Little neck clams
- 3 Oz. White wine
- 2 Oz Clam juice
- 1/4 Lemon, juiced
- pinch Garlic
- 2 1/2 oz. Heavy cream
- pinch Chopped cilantro
- 15 Green peas

METHOD:

• Heat small paellera (no oil) until very hot. Add one salmon filet and sear both sides. Add next five ingredients and cook until reduced by 3/4. Add cream. When it begins to boil add cilantro and continue to cook until reduced by 1/2. Remove salmon. Add peas and taste for seasoning.

PRESENTATION:

• Place rice and vegetables at 2:00 and 10:00 on round dinner plate. Place salmon at 6:00 and put a clam on each side. Pour sauce from pan over top

Marinade:

- 1/2 cup chopped cilantro
- 1T. garlic, chopped
- 4 cup olive oil

The Terrace Dining Room
Chef Alessandro Stratta, Executive Chef

Roasted Swordfish with Warm Tomato and Arugala Salad and Basil Orzo

Serves 4

Orzo pasta:

- 1 cups Orzo pasta
- 2 tbsp. Basil
- 1 tbsp. Pinenuts, toasted
- 1 tsp. Garlic puiee
- 1 tsp. Lemon juice
- 1 tsp. Olive oil

Continued On Next Page ▶

Recipes

4 each	Filet of swordfish (6 oz. each)
2 cups	Tomatoes, peeled and seeded
2 cups	Arugula leaves, juhenne
1 tbsp.	Balsamic viilegar
1 tbsp.	Extra virgin olive oil
	Salt and pepper

To prepare the pasta:

- Cook orzo pasta in salted boiling water until cooked. Rinse, cool and reserve. Chop basil, pinenuts and garlic, mix together and reserve. Heat a sauté pan with a small amount of olive oil; add cooked orzo and basil-garlic mixture and warm thoroughly. Add seasonings and Lemon juice.
- Dice tomatoes and place in a bowl. Mix in julienne of arugula, balsamic vinegar and olive oil. Season well and marinade a few minutes. In a nonstick teflon pan, sear swordfish over high heat until golden brown on both sides. Cook 3 to 4 minutes and keep warm.

Presentation:

- Serve warm pasta under fish with tomato-arugula mixture on top of fish.

Lobster in a Cracked Corn Custard with Wild' Mushrooms Dried Monterey Jack Cheese

Chef Robert McCrath

serves 4

Custard

10 oz.	Cubed lobster meat
1/2 cup	Yellow gristmill (grits)
1/2 cup	White gristmill (grits)
1/2 cup	Water
1/2 cup	Lobster stock
1/4 cup	Heavy cream
1/4 cup	Sliced shiitake mushrooms
1/4 cup	Sliced chanterelle mushrooms
1 tbsp.	Chopped garlic
1 level tbsp.	Finely chopped New Mexico chiles
1 tbsp.	Extra virgin olive oil
	Kosher salt and fresh cracked black pepper to taste

Garnish

2 oz.	Shaved dried Monterey jack cheese
16	Chervil sprigs

- For the custard, bring the water and the lobster stock to a boil then add the grits. Cook until creamy in texture.
- Heat the olive oil in a skillet, add the chiles, garlic and mushrooms. Saute until just tender. Add the cooked grits and the cream. Season to taste.
- Garnish with the shaved jack cheese and the chervil.

Pan-Roasted Black Grouper in Gumbo, Shrimp Remoulade Parsley Potatoes, Onion Shoots and Celery Leaves

Chef Robert McGrath

serves 4

4	6 to 7 oz. Black Grouper filets
2	Limes, halved
1 tbsp.	Olive oil
	Kosher salt and fresh cracked black pepper to taste

Gumbo: yield 1 Gal.

1/2 cup	Clarified butter
1/2 cup	All-purpose
4	Chopped green bell peppers
4	Chopped red bell peppers
2	Chopped poblano chiles
2	Chopped yellow onions
1/4 cup	Chopped garlic
1 gal.	Shrimp stock
1 cup	Tomato paste
2 tbsp.	Granulated garlic
2 tbsp.	Granulated onion
	Kosher salt and fresh cracked black pepper

Remoulade:

1/3 cup	Mayonnaise
1/3 cup	Grilled and chopped rock shrimp
1/4 cup	Tomato ketchup
1	Lemon, juiced
2 tbsp.	Very finely chopped carrots
2 tbsp.	Very finely chopped onion
1 tbsp.	Very finely chopped chives
1 tbsp.	Very finely chopped parsley
1 tbsp.	Very finely chopped jalapeno
1 tsp.	Tobasco sauce
1 tsp.	Chile paste with garlic

Garnish:

1/4 cup	Celery leaves
1/4 cup	Bias-cut onion shoots (or scallions)
8	New potatoes cut in wedges
1 tbsp.	Olive oil
1 tbsp.	Chopped parsley

- For the roux, in a heavy skillet stir the flour into the butter and bake in a moderately hot oven for 2 to 3 hours (stirring frequently) until black in color. Set aside. In a pot, saute the peppers, chiles, onions and garlic until tender. Add the roux and simmer. Add the gallon of shrimp stock, tomato paste and simmer. Season to taste.
- For the remoulade, mix all of the ingredients together in a bowl and refrigerate.
- For the potatoes, fry the wedges in a skillet in hot olive oil. Season them and place in a hot oven for 10 minutes. Finish by sprinkling the chopped parsley over them and tossing.
- Season the grouper to taste. Sear the fish in a hot skillet in the olive oil for approximately 3 minutes. Turn the fish over in the skillet and roast in a hot oven for approximately 3 to 4 minutes. Squeeze the limes over the fish.
- Place a small mound of the potatoes in the center of a wide-rimmed soup bowl. Place the grouper on top of the potatoes and ladle 4 oz. of gumbo around the potatoes/fish. Spoon the remoulade over the grouper. Garnish with the celery leaves and onion shoots.

Continued On Next Page ▶

Recipes

Bread

Pepper Jack Polenta Sticks

1 cup	Oil for frying
2 cups	Chicken stock
1/2 cup	Instant polenta
1/2 tsp.	Course ground black pepper
1/2 cup	Grated pepper jack cheese
1/2 cup	Flour

- Oil a loaf pan. In a medium sauce pan bring stock to a boil. Whisk in polenta. Reduce heat to very low and cook, stirring until polenta pulls away from pan, 4 to 5 minutes. Stir in pepper and pepper jack cheese. Pour into prepared loaf pan and let cool.
- Remove polenta from pan and cut into sticks. Dredge sticks in flour and fry. Serve warm

Taco Shells (makes 6 shells)

served with Chili seared sea scallops on page ???

1 cup	Fresh grated parmesan
1 tsp.	Flour

- Mix flour and parmesan
- Line a sheet pan with parchment paper. On the paper make 6-4 inch circles of parmesan flour mixture. Bake in a 300 degree oven 10 minutes or until cheese just starts to brown.
- To make taco mold take 3 six inch by ten inch pieces of cardboard and fold in half the long way to form a "V". Turn over to form an upside down "V". Drape that with a piece of plastic wrap.
- Remove parmesan circles from oven. While still warm take them off the parchment paper with a spatula and drape over the molds pressing to form a shell. Let sit until shell hardens about 10 minutes.

Dessert

Black Irish Pie

1 1/2 cups	Brown sugar, lightly packed
1/4 cups	Flour
1/3 cup	Cornmeal
6 extra	Eggs
1 1/2 cups	Granulated sugar
2 tsp	Vanilla
3/4 cups	Stout
1/3 cup	Jack Daniels
1 cup	Quality semi-sweet chocolate chips
1	10" Pie crust

- Stir together the brown sugar, flour and cornmeal. Beat the eggs with the granulated sugar until very thick and light in color. Add the vanilla, stout & bourbon to the brown sugar mixture. Put chocolate chips in bottom of prepared pie crust. Pour mature in pie crust and bake in a preheated 1500 oven for 40-45 minutes or until the center is set. Allow to cool until just warm and serve with a dollop of whipped cream.

Bourbon Fruit

Chef Baby Kay

Great with ham, pork chops, turkey, etc. also on vanilla ice cream.

2 cans	Drained fruit cocktail
1 cup	Brown sugar
10 tbsp	Butter
1 tsp	Curry
1/4 cup	Whiskey

- Melt butter over low heat–add fruit. MIx whisky brown sugar and curry into butter, when incorporated slowly pour in whiskey use caution-will flame. Cook over low heat for 5 minutes.

Apple Tart

Chef Christopher Gross

Servings: 20

24	Green apples, peeled cored and sliced thin
8 oz.	Butter, melted
8 oz.	Sugar
18 oz.	Pastry flour or cake flour
9 oz.	Butter, unsalted in small pieces
2	Eggs
4 oz.	cold water
pinch	Salt

Preparations:

- Combine flour, salt, butter and eggs in the processor and turn on. Add water and stop machine. (don't over mix) If needed, finish mixing by hand. refrigerate the dough for 1 hour before using. Roll very thin; cut out a circle with a salad plate for the diameter. Arrange sliced apples, fanned out, around the tart dough. Top with

Continued On Next Page ▶

Recipes

1 ounce sugar. Bake in 350 degree oven on parchment paper for about ten minutes, or until brown. Garnish with strawberry flower and mint leaves. Served with slightly whipped cream on the side

Caramel Sauce

- 2 lb. Sugar
- 12 oz. water
- 2 pt. Cream

Preparations

- Bring sugar and water to a boil and cook until it caramelizes. Stop cooking by adding the cream and cook slowly until all the sugar dissolves.

Christopher's Bistro

Parnassienne De Mousse Au Chocolat (Chocolate Tower)

Chef Christopher Gross
(For sauce see page 118 in "Sauces")
(Makes 8 Towers)

For Chocolate Mousse:

- 5 1/2 oz Dark chocolate
- 3 tbsp Butter, unsalted
- 1/4 cup Whipping crearn
- 10 Egg whites, whipped sriff
- 4 tbsp Superfine sugar
- 1 Large sheet Parchment paper
- 2 oz Dark chocolate, melted
- 5 oz White chocolate, melted

- Place 5 1/2 oz of the dark chocolate and 3 tbsp butter in a medium bowl and place on top of the stove in a water bath. The water should just simmer. While the chocolate and the butter are melting, stir with a wooden spoon occasionally to mix. This should take about 5 minutes. At the same time with a hand held mixer or whip, in a medium bowl beat the heavy cream until stiff. Set aside. To finish mousse, fold the chocolate and egg whites together, then fold the cream in with a spatula.

- You will need one large sheet of parchment paper, tape and a pastry bag. Cut parchment paper in strips of 3 1/2 inches by 5 inches. Cut out 8 of these shapes. Roll out strips into the shape of a tube and tape. Stand them up and fill with the chocolate mousse using a pastry bag. They are to be placed in the freezer until frozen.

- Take 8 pieces of the paper, melt 2 oz of dark chocolate in a water bath. Stripe the paper using a pastry bag. Make diagonal lines in a grid. Place these sheets of paper into the freezer.

- When frozen, unwrap mousse tubes. Coat the stripped frozen sheets with the 5 oz white chocolate that has been melted in a water bath. Wrap coated parchment around frozen mousse ajZ–refrigerate. After 5 minutes you may peel the paper off. The chocolate will remain around the mousse. (For sauce see page 118 in "Sauces")

Oaxaca at Pinnacle Peak

While & Dark Chocolate Amaretto Pate

by Executive Chef Travis Vierthaler

- 6 oz. Unsalted butter
- 2 1/4 cups Heavy cream
- 1 1/2 lb. Dark bittersweet chocolate
- 3 tsp Vanilla

- Melt the above and place in deep bread pan that has been oiled. Chill for one hour.

- 6 oz. Unsalted butter
- 1 cup Heavy cream
- 1 1/2 lb. White chocolate
- 3/4 cup Amaretto, cooked down to 3 tsp.
- 1/4 cup Vanilla

- Melt the above and pour on top of chilled dark chocolate layer. Chill until firm. Pop out of bread pan and slice as needed. Garnish with fresh raspberries.

GLOSSARY

PHOENIX CUISINE '96

5th Anniversary Issue

Glossary

A

aceto
Vinegar (Italian) Balsamic is a very fine vinegar made in Modena, Italy aged in special oak casks.

achiote
Paste made from ground annato seed, vinegar, salt and spices.

"Ahi" tuna
this is a grade of tuna. It refers to the fish being sushi quality, or the best available. Most Ahi is from Bluefin tunas. It is very deep red in color, firm fish. There will not be a fishy taste to this type of tuna. The stuff used for canning is generally albacore. It is lighter in color, (white tinged with pink).

à la carte
each course individually priced.

à là king
Meat, fish or poultry prepared delicately in a cream seasoned sauce.

antipasto
Italian hors d 'oeuvres, served before pasta dish consisting of fish, vegetables and/or cold meat.

annatto
a pod used in making achiote.

apèritif
alcoholic beverage served as an appetizer.

Arborio rice
short, fat-grained Italian rice that is high in starch and used in risotto and other moist rice dishes.

artichoke purée
artichoke hearts, ginger, shallots, rice vinegar, eggs, chipotle peppers and olive oil.

arugula
a scalded curd cheese usually made from skimmed milk and aged for up to two years.

aspic
a gelatin made from meat or vegetable stock or from fruit used to coat meat, poultry fish or to form a moulded salad.

asiago
a scalded curd cheese usually made from skimmed milk and aged for up to two years.

au gratin
sauced food topped with buttered bread crumbs or grated cheese and baked or broiled until brown.

a jus
meat served with only natural, unthickened cooking juices.

B

baklava
Greek pastry dessert.

bard
fowl or roast covered in strips of fat for automatic basting.

bernaise
a type of Hollandaise, flavored with shallots, wine, vinegar and tarragon usually served with meat, fish and egg dishes.

bechamel
a basic white sauce of flour and butter to which milk is added.

Belgian endive
a specially cultivated chicory whose leaves are cut off and shielded from light, so the new pale yellow leaves grow back in their characteristic cigar shape.

beluga caviar
premier caviar (fish eggs) obtained from Black Sea.

benedict
salt cod prepared with eggs in a creamy sauce; also, English muffin with eggs and ham served with Hollandaise sauce.

bisque
a thick cream soup usually made from fish or vegetable purées; also made from fruit or nuts served as a frozen dessert.

bitters
a liquid steeped with aromatic herbs and roots.

blini
Russian for Pancake, usually made from buckwheat flour and served with sour cream and caviar.

bok choy
This is an oriental vegetable similar to nothing. It is dark green and leafy (very healthy) at the top and very white, crunchy and like a thick stem at the bottom. The flavor is very mild.

bonne femme
home style; a simply prepared entrée served with different vegetables.

bouillabaisse
fish cooked with various herbs and spices in white wine or water, served as a soup.

bouquet garni
small bundle of herbs, wrapped in cheese cloth and added during cooking to add flavor, removed before serving.

bourguignon
cuts of red meat prepared with red wine sauce, mushrooms onions.

braise
to cook with small amount of liquid in a tightly covered pan at a low temperature.

bratwurst
a German pork sausage seasoned with herbs and spices, enjoyed served hot with vegetables.

brioche
a cake or roll made of yeast dough in a cylindrical shape.

brochette
a skewer used for broiling small pieces of meat or vegetables.

brushetta
angle cut baguette toasted with garlic

beurre noir
a butter based sauce cooked until brown, served hot.

C

cajun spice
a mixture of spices; garlic powder, onion powder, paprika, dry leaf thyme, salt, black pepper, cayenne pepper. It is zesty and slightly spicy. Also referred to as blackening spice.

canapé
an appetizer, small opened faced sandwich or crust- less slice of bread sauteed in butter on which asparagus and mushrooms may be served.

cannelloni
boiled pasta squares, stuffed, rolled and browned.

cannoli
pastry tubes filled with cheese chocolate and candied fruit.

cantonese
southern China cooking style; examples include egg rolls and egg foo young.

caper
the bud of young fruit of a climbing plant, native to Africa and the Mediterranean, which is picked to make a condiment. Nasturtium buds or seeds are sometimes used.

Glossary

capon
castrated male chicken grown plump and tender.

carambola
(starfruit) thick-skinned, glossy fruit that forms golden star shapes when sliced. The flavor is complex, bitter sweet with hints of artichoke heart.

claret
term referring to the red wines of the Bordeaux region.

clarified butter
butter which has been heated to separate the fat solids from the milk solids.

croquette
a thick creamy mixture containing various meat and vegetables shaped and coated with egg and crumbs then fried.

croûte
hard, toasted slices of bread used as a garnish for soup and salad or filled and served as hors d'oevures.

crêpe
thin egg and flour pancake served as main course or dessert usually filled and covered with sauce.

croissant
light flaky pastry made of dough with butter in crescent shape prior to baking.

confit
a meat item cooked in it's own fat and preserved in that same fat.

consommé
meat stock that has been fortified and clarified.

court bouillon
well seasoned liquid flavored with stock vegetables, used for cooking fish vegetables and a variety of meals.

crime anglaise
a light egg yolk, sugar and milk custard sauce used in fruit or pastry desserts.

Chateaubriand
a grilled beef fillet in Bernaise sauce served with potatoes, and vegetables.

cherries jubilee
black cherries and vanilla ice cream flamed with Cognac; a dessert.

contorni
Italian for vegetables or garnishes accompanying main course.

ciotto
leg of lamb.

cilantro
fresh coriander.

crustacean
shellfish such as lobster, crab.

D

daub
braised meat and vegetable stew.

deglacer
adding wine, stock or cream to dilute pan juices for gravy.

demitasse
half cup of black coffee served after dinner.

Dijon mustard
mustard of French origin varying from mild to highly seasoned.

drawn butter
also known as clarified butter, butter cleared of water and impurities by slow melting and filtering.

dumpling
used to garnish stews, small balls of dough containing meat or potato mixture which are steamed or poached.

dusting
sugar, spice or seasoning sprinkled lightly.

E

eclair
light, oblong shape made of choux pastry split, filled with cream and topped with chocolate.

egg foo young
pancake made of bean sprouts mushrooms and eggs with shellfish, chicken or meat, served with stock sauce.

en croûte
pastry encased food.

entrée
1. main dish served with sauce and garnish 2. in formal meal is third course following fish course

escargot
edible snail served in shell.

F

farina
flour of wheat, nuts and potatoes, very fine.

feta
Greek cheese made from goat's milk, salty.

fettuccini
pasta, 1/4 inch ribbon.

filet
piece of meat, fish or poultry which is boneless.

flambé
brandy or liquor added to food and then set alight.

flan
fruit or custard filled pastry shell.

florentine
dishes presented on a bed of spinach or spinach used as a ring or topping.

flute
decorative indentations.

foie gras
preserved liver of specially fattened goose served as a paté.

fondue
melted cheese into which cubes of bread are dunked.

fricadelles
meat balls of pork and veal spices and bread-crumbs poached or shallow-fried.

friccassee
stew made of pieces of chicken or veal, cooked in a gravy.

fritter
small quantity of batter mixture fried in deep fat until crisp.

fruits de mer
combination of seafood served in salads, cold.

fumet
concentrated broth or stock made from fish, meat, or vegetables.

G

galantine
cold dish of boned and stuffed poultry glazed with aspic.

galette
flat cake of mashed or sliced potato.

gazpacho
cold soup ~ Spanish, made with tomatoes and other fresh vegetables.

genoise
rich sponge cake baked in a flat tin.

giblets
edible internal organs and trimmings of poultry and game.

glace
frozen or iced, also ice or ice cream.

Glossary

gluten
the protein strands that are formed when making doughs. These are what give the dough it's elasticity.

gnocchi
dumplings made from semolina, potatoes or choux pastry, small.

goulash
beef and onion stew seasoned with paprika and tomato.

grenadine
pomegranate-flavored syrup used as flavoring and sauce.

gumbo
thick soup or stew made with meat, poultry, fish or vegetables.

H

haggis
Scottish pudding, made from sweet onions, oatmeal which is boiled in the stomach lining of a sheep.

hard sauce
hard, sweet butter sauce flavored with brandy melts when served on hot pudding.

hollandaise
egg yolks, butter, lemon juice made into creamy sauce, served with fish or vegetables.

hors d' oevures
foods served as appetizers, first course, hot or cold.

I

indienne
dish cooked Indian style, usually with curry, rice etc.

Italian dressing
dressing of oil and vinegar with various spices.

Irish coffee
Irish whiskey added to coffee and topped with thick cream, enjoyed after dinner.

J

jardiniere
French term meaning garnished with fresh vegetables, diced and cooked arranged in separate groups.

jubilee
cherries: dessert of black cherries, ice cream flamed with cognac.

julienne
vegetables or meat cut into thin strips.

jus
juices created from roasting meat, usually used as gravy.

K

kebob
marinated meat cubes put on a skewer and grilled, served on skewer.

kedgree
dish of cooked fish or meat, rice and eggs served at breakfast or lunch.

kosher
food ritually fit for eating according to Orthodox Jewish law.

kumquats
citrus fruit, yellow-orange in color and has a tart orange flavor.

L

lagouste
crawfish.

langue de chat
flat, crisp biscuit, finger shaped, served with cold desserts.

lasagna
ribbon-like noodles about 2" wide, sometimes green.

leaven
yeast-like substance which causes dough to rise.

legumes
vegetables with seed pods peas or beans.

lentils
seeds of legume soaked and used in soups and stews.

loquat
yellow-orange pitted fruit, juicy small and sour.

lyonnaise
usually served with onions, Lyons style.

M

macaroni
pasta shaped like tubes and cut into various lengths and sizes.

macedoine
raw fruit and vegetables mixture.

macerate
food softened by soaking in a liquid.

marinade
mixture of oil wine or vinegar and spices used to tenderize meat, poultry or fish.

mannite
stock pot made of earthenware.

marsala
sweet wine occasionally used in cooking.

medallions
small circular cuts of meat, fish or paté.

melba
usually peaches served with ice cream.

meringue
whisked egg while blended with sugar used on top of desserts or baked alone in small shapes at a low temperature until crisp.

meuniere
fish cooked in butter, lemon juice and parsley.

milanese
Milan style breadcrumbs with seasonings.

mirabelle
liquor made from the mirabelle fruit, small yellow plum.

mirepox
base for brown sauces and stews made of a mixture of finely diced vegetables and ham, fried in butter.

mocca
coffee served after dinner very high quality

mollusk
shellfish such as clams and oysters.

mornay sauce
Bechamel sauce with cream and grated cheese, used on vegetables and fish.

Glossary

mauler
to grind dry food into a powder or soft food into a purée.

moussaka
Eastern dish made of minced meat aubegines and tomatoes, topped with cheese sauce, baked.

mousse
cold dessert made with whipped cream/ egg whites very light and sweet.

mozzarella
cheese, mild usually served melted.

N

napoléon
pastry layer cake with alternating layers of cream.

navarin
lamb stew with vegetables.

neopolitian
different colored and flavored ice creams and sweet cakes in layers.

newburg
served with a cream and sherry sauce usually over lobster.

nopales
cactus paddles which can be cooked like a vegetables and used as is, or in salsas. It is soft but, crunchy with a flavor similar to bell pepper and asparagus combined.

nicoise
cooked with tomatoes, garlic, onions and black olives, in the Nice style.

O

offal
edible internal organs of meat, poultry and game.

omelette
pancake made of beaten eggs.

osso buco
dish of braised marrow bones, usually prepared with tomatoes and wine.

P

paella
rice dish with chicken vegetables and shellfish, named for the large shallow pan in which it is traditionally cooked.

palm hearts
the new buds or shoots of the palm tree, which are cooked and brined.

panetone
Christmas bread with raisins.

paprika
strong, ground red pepper, ground.

parfait
dessert, made of whipped cream and fruit purée frozen.

parmesan
cheese yellow and hard usually served or used in cooking when grated.

pasilla chile
also known as Poblano, six inches in length with a wide top end. Very spicy.

pasta
flour paste used to make macaroni, spaghetti, etc.

paté
spread of ground seasoned meat, or vegetables served hot or cold.

paupiette
slice of meat thin, rolled around filling.

pavé
sponge cake, square, filled with butter cream and coated with icing.

peas pudding
dried peas cooked and puréed, made into puddings and served with pork.

pinenuts
seeds from the pine cones of pine trees

petit four
small decoratively iced cake.

pilaf
Eastern dish of spiced cooked rice mixed with meat chicken or fish.

piquante
pleasantly sharp and appetizing.

pith
white lining cover the flesh of citrus fruit.

plat du jour
dish of the day.

poaching
food cooked in simmering liquid, just below boiling point.

polenta
thick mushlike dish made from maize which is dried and ground, used in main dishes as an accompaniment.

potage
thick soup.

parline
sweet of unblanced almonds carmalized in boiling sugar.

prawn
large shrimp, term used on the West coast.

prickly pear
also known as cactus fruit. An edible cactus with a spiny exterior and soft interior flesh. The fruit has the shape of a kiwi fruit and melon like flavor.

printanier
garnish of spring vegetables.

prosciutto
raw, flavorful smoked ham, served sliced.

provencale
cooked with garlic and tomatoes, in the Provence style.

purée
1. raw or cooked food sieved 2. thick vegetable soup which is passed through a sieve.

Q

quenelles
light dumplings made of meat or fish, used as a garnish or in a sauce.

quiche
open-faced pastry case filled with a savory mixture, served as a main dish.

Quiche Lorraine
quiche prepared with bacon and cheese.

R

ragout
stew of meat and vegetables, thick.

ratatouille
stew made of aubergines, onions, peppers and tomatoes cooked in olive oil.

ravigote
hot or cold white sauce, highly seasoned.

Glossary

ravioli
small pasta envelopes, filled with meat boiled and served with a tomato sauce.

rice paper
white paper made from the pith of a Chinese tree, edible.

rigatoni
ribbed macaroni.

rissoto
fried rice cooked in stock or tomato juice and garnished with cheese.

rissole
roll or patty of cooked minced meat.

romaine
long-leafed lettuce.

roquefort
cheese made from ewe's milk with bread mold throughout.

roulade
describes roll of meat, vegetable, chocolate cake, etc.

roux
mixture of fat and flour used as a sauce base.

S

saffron
the deep orange dried stigmas of a particular crocus which must be gathered by hand, which dictates a very high price.

saignant
meant underdone.

salsify
plant, root resembles oyster flavor.

salsa base
a puréed, grilled tomato based sauce. It also contains garlic, serrano peppers, cilantro, salt and pepper.

sauté
to fry food in hot fat until evenly browned.

scampi
shrimp or a shrimp dish in garlic sauce.

searing
meat browned rapidly with high heat to seal in juices.

small shrimp
these are termed 31-40s. That means that there are between 31 and 40 to a pound. Cooked these are about the size of a thick quarter.

sorbet
sherbert made from fresh fruit and/or liquor.

soufflé
baked dish made with egg whites beaten and thickened with egg yolk.

sousing
pickling food in brine or vinegar.

spaghetti
pasta made into solid strands of varying thicknesses.

spumoni
flavored and colored ice cream made with whipped cream/egg whites.

strudel
pastry dough made into thin leaves and filled with various mixtures then rolled and baked.

sushi
rice molded and topped with raw fish.

T

table d' hôte
meal at a fixed price usually three or more courses.

tagliatella
ribbons of egg noodles about 1/4" wide, thin and flat.

tamarind
the pod or fruit of a large tropical tree native to India. When fresh, it's pulp is white, crisp and has a sweet/sour flavor. When dried, it turns brown and very sour.

terrine
meat, fowl and or vegetable baked in a dish called a terrine and served cold.

tequila beurre blanc
uses tequila as the base liquid and orange juice, shallots, peppercorns. After the sauce is made add cilantro to the finished product.

timable
hot pie filled with meats or vegetables, decorative, cooked in a timbale dish; cup-shaped earthenware or metal mould.

torte
cake or meringue-type dessert baked in layers filled with various sweet items.

tortilla
Mexican bread very thin and made of cornmeal or flour.

truffles
mushroom like fungus, rare, firm texture black and white in color mainly used or garnishing.

tuile
a crisp cookie, usually made from crushed almonds, sugar and egg whites.

turmeric
a spice obtained from the dried and powdered rhizome of an Indian plant. In the middle ages its color made it a substitute for saffron.

U

unleavened bread
bread which when baked is thin flat and round as rising agent is not added.

V

velouté
white sauce made with chicken veal or fish stock, very creamy.

vermicelli
the finest strands of pasta.

vichyssoise
potato and leek soup, creamy served cold.

vinagrette
mixture of oil, vinegar, salt and pepper and sometimes herbs for flavor.

W

won ton
pockets of dough for stuffing.

Y

yakitori
chicken marinated in soy sauce, Japanese dish skewered and broiled.

Z

zest
coloured outer skin of citrus fruits which is grated and used for flavoring foods and liquids.

Notes

Notes

Notes

The Perfect Special Occasion Gift

- Christmas
- Valentines Day
- Thank You
- Father's Day
- Get Well
- Mother's Day
- Business Gifts
- Anniversary
- Trade Shows & Conventions
- Hostess Gift
- Easter
- Visitors Promotion
- Birthday

It's easy. Simply call or write us. Send us your check or money order and we'll mail you a copy of Phoenix Cuisine. We can also send a copy, together with a gift card bearing your name and personal message, to the person of your choice.

A gift that is used, appreciated and remembered.

Watch for our Cuisine publications in other North American Cities.

Business Opportunity

Ryan Hart Marketing is seeking individuals with successful sales track records to expand our dining publications group to other cities. Minimum investment required with immediate first year return. Please sent your resume to:

Ryan Hart Marketing
16605 Palisades Blvd., Suite 124-271
Fountain Hills, AZ 85268

Please send me my OWN copy of Phoenix Cuisine 96.

Ship to

Name _____

Address _____ Apt# _____

City _____ State _____ Zip _____

Pricing
For large quantities, call R&H Publishing at 837-7857

- ☐   1-6 books.... Save 10% .... $5.35 each x Quantity: _____ books = $_____
- ☐   7-12 books.... Save 15% .... $5.05 each x Quantity: _____ books = $_____
- ☐   13-25 books.... Save 25% .... $4.45 each x Quantity: _____ books = $_____

                                               Shipping and Handling   _____ + $2.25

                                                              Total   _____

Payment   Make checks or money orders payable to R&H Marketing.
R&H Marketing, Inc. • 16605 E Palisades, Suite 124-271 • Fountain Hills, AZ 85268

--- ✂ ---

Please send me my OWN copy of Phoenix Cuisine 96.

Ship to

Name _____

Address _____ Apt# _____

City _____ State _____ Zip _____

Pricing
For large quantities, call R&H Publishing at 837-7857

- ☐   1-6 books.... Save 10% .... $5.35 each x Quantity: _____ books = $_____
- ☐   7-12 books.... Save 15% .... $5.05 each x Quantity: _____ books = $_____
- ☐   13-25 books.... Save 25% .... $4.45 each x Quantity: _____ books = $_____

                                               Shipping and Handling   _____ + $2.25

                                                              Total   _____

Payment   Make checks or money orders payable to R&H Marketing.
R&H Marketing, Inc. • 16605 E Palisades, Suite 124-271 • Fountain Hills, AZ 85268

--- ✂ ---

Please send me my OWN copy of Phoenix Cuisine 96.

Ship to

Name _____

Address _____ Apt# _____

City _____ State _____ Zip _____

Pricing
For large quantities, call R&H Publishing at 837-7857

- ☐   1-6 books.... Save 10% .... $5.35 each x Quantity: _____ books = $_____
- ☐   7-12 books.... Save 15% .... $5.05 each x Quantity: _____ books = $_____
- ☐   13-25 books.... Save 25% .... $4.45 each x Quantity: _____ books = $_____

                                               Shipping and Handling   _____ + $2.25

                                                              Total   _____

Payment   Make checks or money orders payable to R&H Marketing.
R&H Marketing, Inc. • 16605 E Palisades, Suite 124-271 • Fountain Hills, AZ 85268

PHOENIX CUISINE 96

Order Phoenix Cuisine At A Discount. See Pages 158-159